I0793256

IMAGES
of America

MONTICELLO

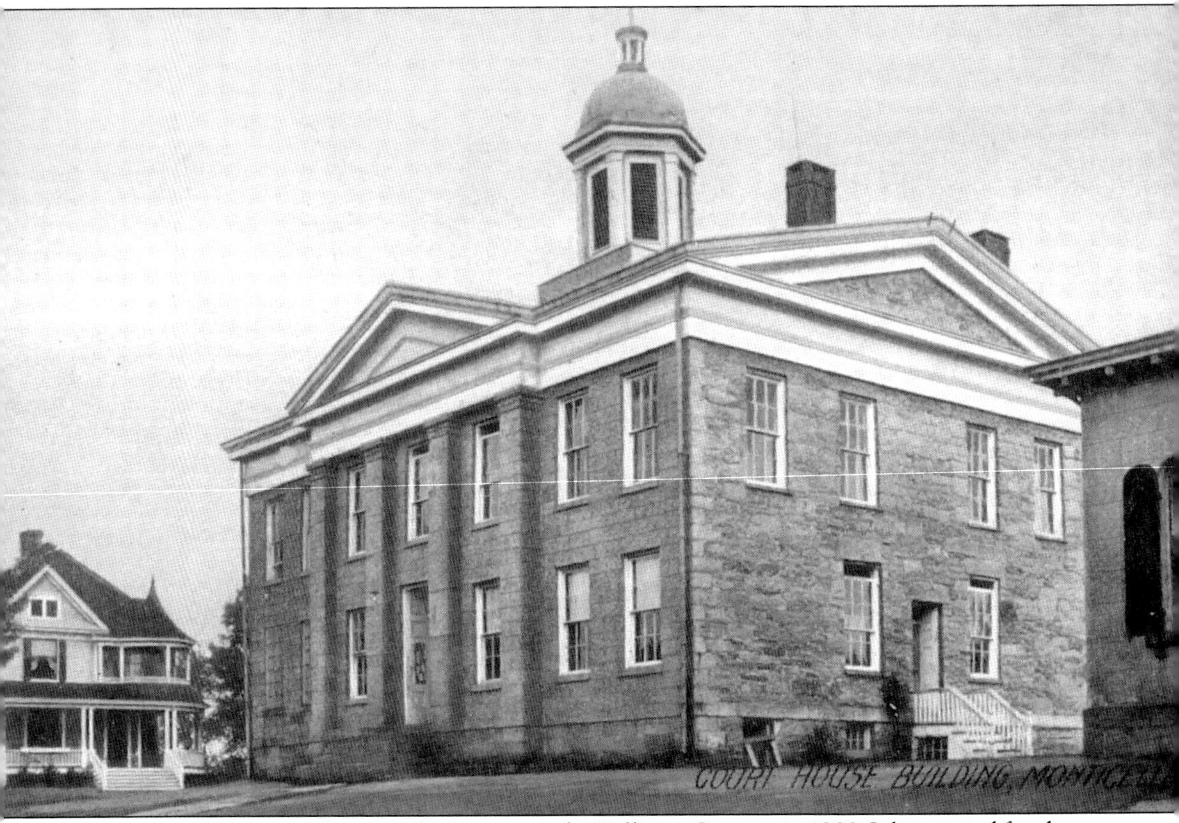

Monticello became the seat of government for Sullivan County in 1809. Liberty vied for the same recognition but lost the contest through the trickery of Samuel F. Jones. The first courthouse burned January 13, 1844, and was replaced by this structure designed by Thornton MacNess Niven of Newburgh, a brother of Archibald Campbell Niven. It was the scene of several hangings and was demolished in 1909 to be replaced by the present, larger courthouse. At right is the old clerk's office (rebuilt between 1845 and 1856, architect unknown), which also burned in 1844. Seen at the corner of Bank and North Streets (left) is what was then the official residence of the sheriff. (Courtesy of Richard Benjamin Sr.)

On the Cover: The third grade class of 1917 in Lillie M. Marshall's room was in the rear of the school on Saint John Street facing the playground. The teacher (not pictured) was 33 years of age when this photograph was taken. She boarded with James Cauthers, M.D. (the president of the Village of Monticello Board of Trustees) and Ralph S. Breakey, M.D., half a block to the north in a spacious Broadway residence. The building was owned by Dr. Cauthers, who apparently rented out rooms or portions of the house. (Courtesy of Daniel K. Niven.)

IMAGES
of America

MONTICELLO

Tom Rue

ARCADIA
PUBLISHING

ISBN 978-0-7385-7328-1

Published by Arcadia Publishing
Charleston, South Carolina

Printed in the United States of America

Library of Congress Control Number: 2010920196

For all general information, please contact Arcadia Publishing:
Telephone 843-853-2070
Fax 843-853-0044
E-mail sales@arcadiapublishing.com
For customer service and orders:
Toll-Free 1-888-313-2665

Visit us on the Internet at www.arcadiapublishing.com

To the generous people of Monticello

Contents

ACKNOWLEDGMENTS

Writing may be a solitary activity, but writing a book like this is not. Too many people have assisted with the creation of this book to list each one here.

But I must thank the Village of Monticello Board of Trustees; as well as village managers Zachary Kelson and Raymond Nargizian and village employees for their support, encouragement, and help in finding photographs and information. Many who lent photographs expressed how valuable their photographs are to them. A few stand out for special thanks: Susan Benton Schock, daughter of the late Alvin Benton, local Masonic historian and former editor of the *Republican Watchman* (much of which is online at www.fultonhistory.com); Dr. Daniel K. Niven, son of Kenneth D. Niven, for providing endless consultations by e-mail; and Sullivan County historian John Conway, who also was generous with time and resources. These three, each of whose knowledge is greater than mine, reviewed the manuscript and patiently provided invaluable aid; any errors that may remain in the text are mine alone.

Dr. Patrick Michel of Monticello Central School District was generous in response to every request. The worshipful master, officers, and members of Monticello Lodge No. 532, F&AM (monticellolodge532.org), loaned antique photographs from their walls. Richard Benjamin Sr. of South Woods allowed unlimited access to his vast private collection. Likewise, Jan Van Etten, president of Van Etten Oil Company (owner of the former Monticello railroad depot); Bill Horton of Forestburgh; George Kelly and Lynn Sullivan, past chiefs of the Monticello Fire Department; and Dr. Nicola J. Davies aided in a search for information on the European travels and activities of the namesake of Monticello's public library, Ethelbert B. Crawford. Vicky Lopez-Terrill of the Morgan Library of Colorado State University shared a photograph and information on the professional life of Maude Sheridan (see page 106). I thank the Sullivan County Historical Society and Dan Hust and Frank Rizzo of the *Sullivan County Democrat* for editorial coverage and for using the newspaper's best cameras to photograph two oil paintings of notable personages from Monticello's past.

Introduction

Like many here, I am a transplant to Monticello. After spending my youth and young adulthood living in such diverse places as New Jersey, Utah, Colorado, Israel, Texas, and Pennsylvania, I came to Monticello in 1988 from Wayne County, across the Delaware at Skinners Falls. Commenting on the interest that I took in learning about and interpreting local history, a former village manager remarked to me years ago that I seemed to have "an unusual sense of place."

Local history is partly a matter of grounding one's self in a location, literally focusing on where one's feet are. It instills respect for the present viewed through the lens of its past. The history of a small area is a microcosm of a nation's history—a method of viewing humanity at a cellular level.

The toil and dedication to loved ones and social and community supports that went into building Monticello explain the motto on the village's corporate seal. *Crescit eundo* ("It goes as it grows") comes from the epic poem *De Rerum Natura* (*On the Nature of Things*) by first-century BCE poet Lucretius, in which he refers to a thunderbolt increasing in strength as it moves across the sky, and it is referenced by the selectors of the motto as a symbol of dynamic progress.

Monticello has been the seat of Sullivan County, New York, since the county was founded in 1809. In the not-so-distant past, Monticello was known as the "Garden Spot of the Mountains." With hope and nurturance, it will flourish again. At 1,512 feet (461 meters) above sea level, Monticello is embedded in the hills of the southern Catskill Mountains. The village was named for the Virginia home of Thomas Jefferson (locals pronounce the village's name as "mon-tah-sell-oh"), a word Jefferson coined meaning "heavenly mountain".

Never in Monticello's two centuries have local economic and social conditions been worse than now. In 1909, the whole downtown district was devastated by a huge fire. But business bounced right back. Reconstruction was immediate. The economy continued to prosper. In short order, Monticello was again a booming village. All through the Great Depression, local shops, newspapers, and tourist establishments thrived. My hope is that allowing readers a visual glimpse of Monticello's past may generate not just nostalgia but hope and new vision for a prosperous future.

Established in 1804 by John Patterson Jones and his brother Samuel Frisbee Jones, Monticello was born by an act of the New York State Legislature. Chapter 313 of the laws of New York passed on April 20, 1830, announced, "The freeholders and inhabitants aforesaid are hereby constituted and declared a body corporate and politic, by the name of the Trustees of the Village of Monticello."

Its municipal boundaries were originally described in 1830 legislation as "a parallelogram half a mile in width and one mile in length" (today it is 4.1 square miles). Had it not been for a slight turn taken by the Newburgh-Cochecton Turnpike, Monticello could not have become the thriving community that it did. The turnpike survey through the town of Thompson was done by Samuel F. Jones and his brother John P. Jones in 1804. They laid plans for a community they truly envisioned as the seat of Sullivan County. This turnpike cut a swath through dense forests and swamps by which, many generations later, we still find our way.

John P. Jones himself built his home on the turnpike section then known as Main Street (Broadway) at Mill (Saint John) Street, opposite the plot he marked out for a stone courthouse. He also built a home for his brother Samuel, which became the residence of Gen. Archibald C. Niven in later years. The structures and personalities have faded. What remains are memories, bits of charred newsprint, faded photographs, and word pictures amplified and interpreted in the mind.

—Tom Rue
Monticello, New York
www.tomrue.net

One

People and Places

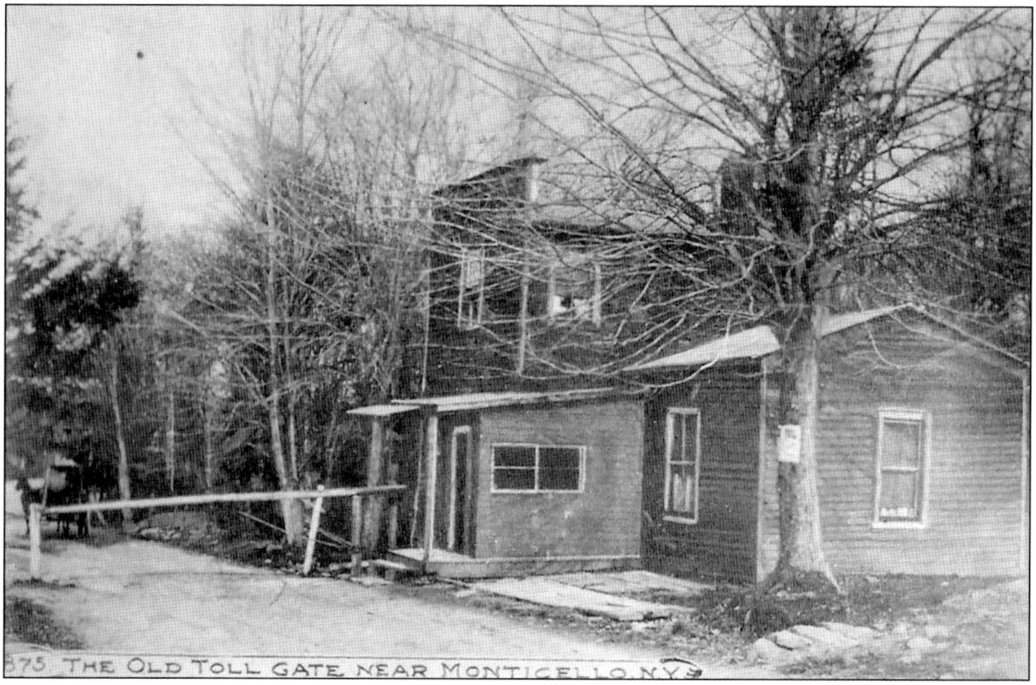

In 1801, the New York State Legislature chartered the Newburgh and Cochecton Turnpike Company to survey and cut a road through Orange and Ulster Counties connecting the Delaware and Hudson. Without this, there would have been no Monticello. The Monticello-Jeffersonville Turnpike tollhouse charged 6¢ to horse and carriage riders, 12¢ for a team, and more for cattle in 1875. (Courtesy of Richard Benjamin Sr.)

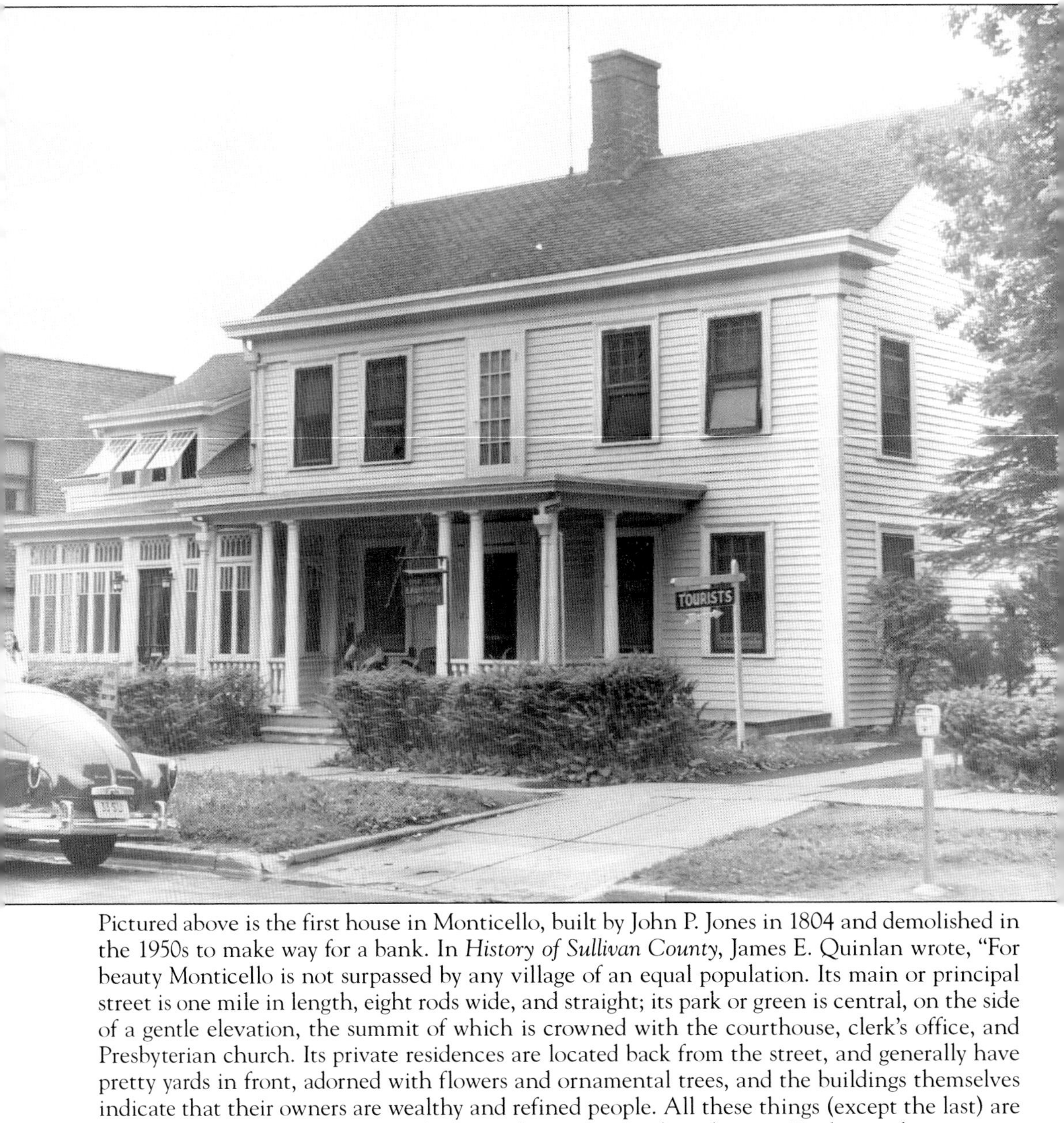

Pictured above is the first house in Monticello, built by John P. Jones in 1804 and demolished in the 1950s to make way for a bank. In *History of Sullivan County*, James E. Quinlan wrote, "For beauty Monticello is not surpassed by any village of an equal population. Its main or principal street is one mile in length, eight rods wide, and straight; its park or green is central, on the side of a gentle elevation, the summit of which is crowned with the courthouse, clerk's office, and Presbyterian church. Its private residences are located back from the street, and generally have pretty yards in front, adorned with flowers and ornamental trees, and the buildings themselves indicate that their owners are wealthy and refined people. All these things (except the last) are the result of a fixed purpose on the part of two apparently utilitarian Yankees, who were not considered remarkable as lovers of the aesthetic, and this purpose was formed when the village-site was literally a cover for wolves and bears!" (Courtesy of Sullivan County Historical Society.)

John Patterson Jones (1779–1858) inscribed the following in his family Bible: "The Family Record of John P. Jones, who with his brother Samuel F. Jones, founded and named, the Village of Monticello, in the then wilderness; the first tree was cut by J. P. Jones, and his present dwelling erected in the month of September in the year of our Lord 1804." (Courtesy of Dan Hust.)

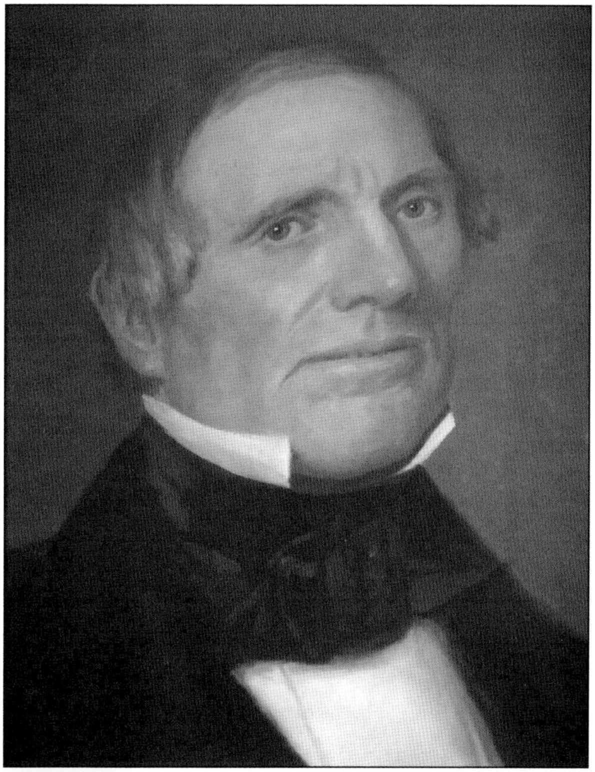

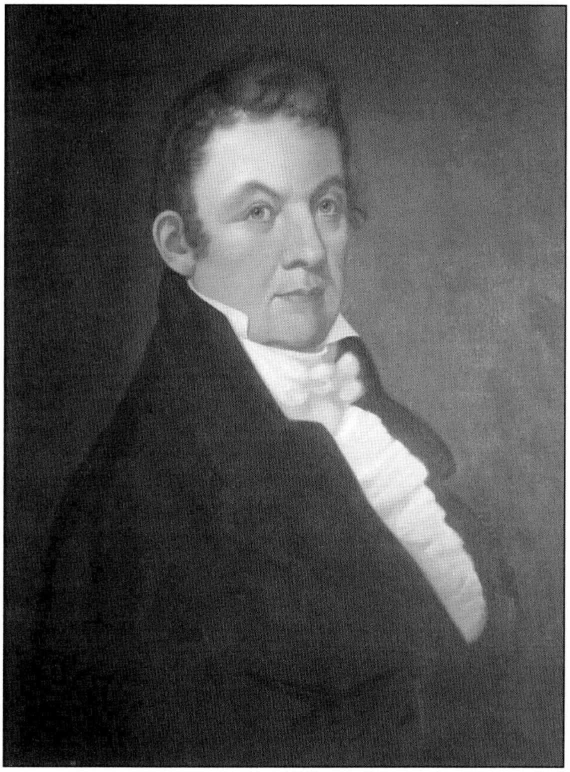

At the start of the 19th century, William A. Thompson (1762–1847), an immigrant from Connecticut, established the first permanent English-speaking settlement in the town of Thompson. The hamlet was later called Thompsonville in his honor. (Courtesy of Dan Hust, *Sullivan County Democrat*.)

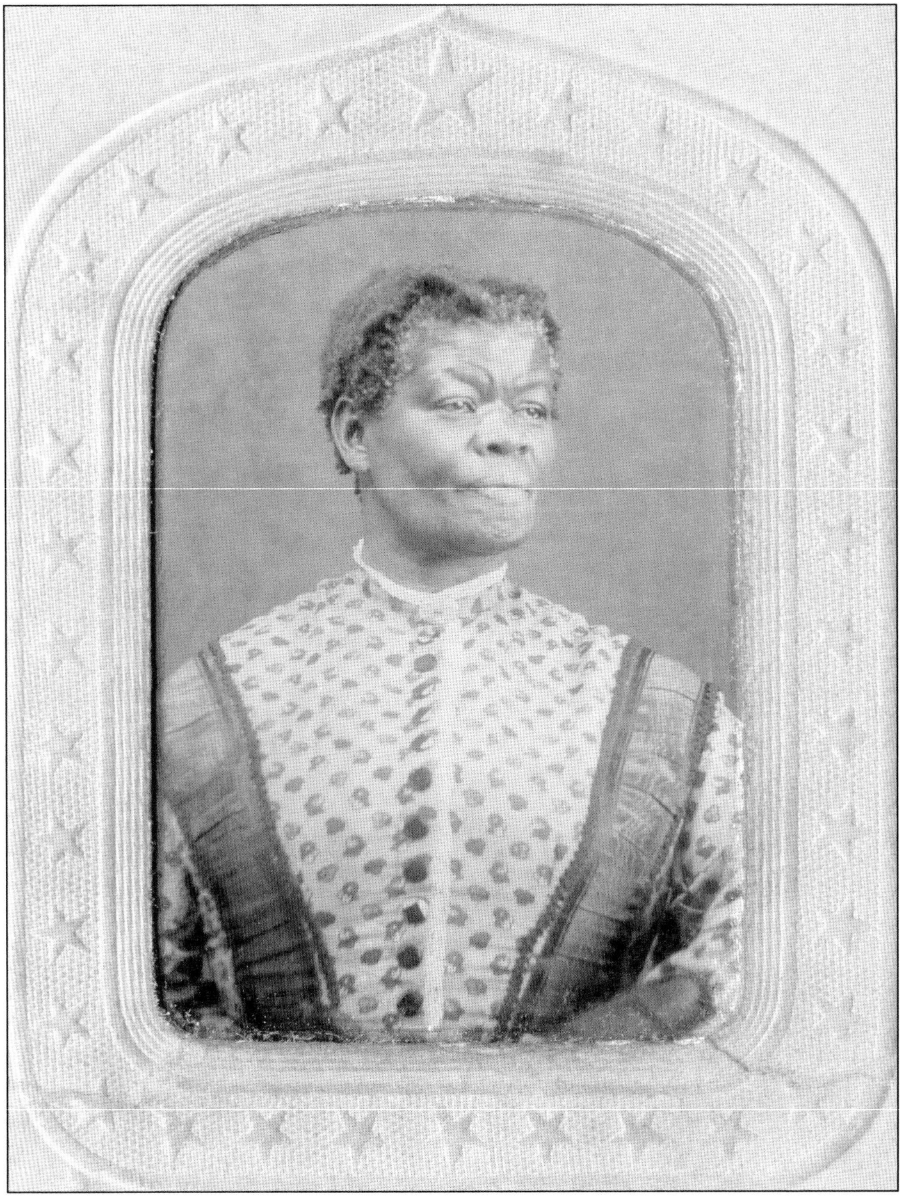

Jennie (or Jane) Thompson was five when she was bought by the first judge of Sullivan and Ulster Counties, William Thompson, for whom the town of Thompson is named. After slavery was abolished in New York in 1826, Judge Thompson's daughter, Helen Allyn, reportedly told Jennie she was free to leave. "Go yourself," was the alleged retort. Jennie married a Methodist preacher named Cobe Gregory. At the age of 50 years, the census listed her as single and a domestic worker on the farm of Squire and Anna Reynolds near Monticello's Frank Leslie Hotel. By 1880, she was listed in the census as a 60-year-old widow, living alone and keeping house. Census records describe her as born in New York, and her parents' birthplace as "Don't know." An 1896 report on the county's poor farm notes, "The oldest female is black Jennie the old Thompson slave who was born in 1810." She died at 87, one year later, and is reportedly buried in the Thompsonville cemetery. In 1810, there were seven slaves in the township, a year after its founding, and nine in 1820. (Courtesy of Daniel K. Niven.)

Archibald C. Niven (1803–1882), below, was born December 8, 1803, to Daniel and Ann Van Riper Niven (pictured at right). A. C. Niven married Jane Thompson in 1832 and had a varied career, serving as Sullivan County judge and surrogate, master in chancery, and district attorney. He was president of the Village of Monticello four times and state senator in 1864. He was appointed by Gov. Samuel Tilden as inspector of state prisons, and Gov. DeWitt Clinton appointed him captain of the 10th Artillery Regiment in 1827, the same year he became major. In 1830, Gov. Enos Throop appointed him colonel. He became brigadier general in 1837 and adjutant general of New York in 1843. General Niven retired from the military upon being elected to Congress in 1845. He was also president of the National Union Bank and a trustee and president of the Monticello Academy. (Both, courtesy of Daniel K. Niven.)

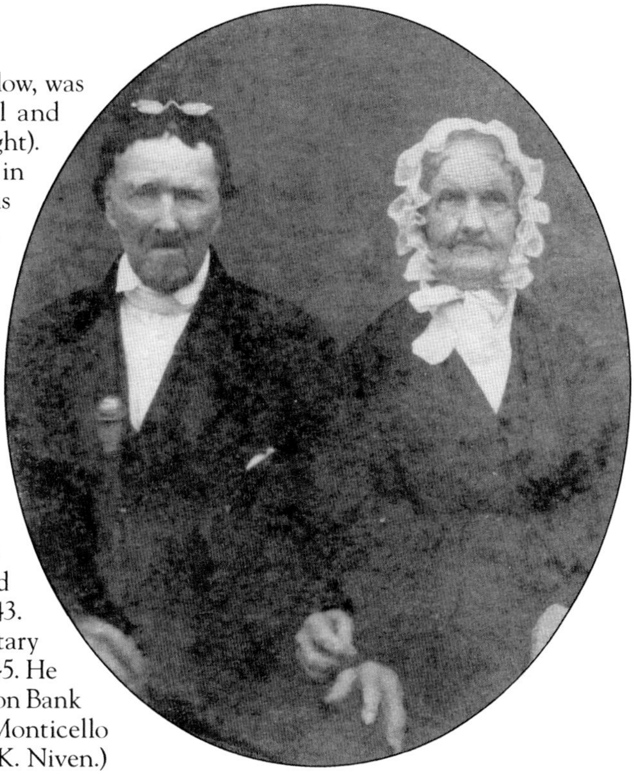

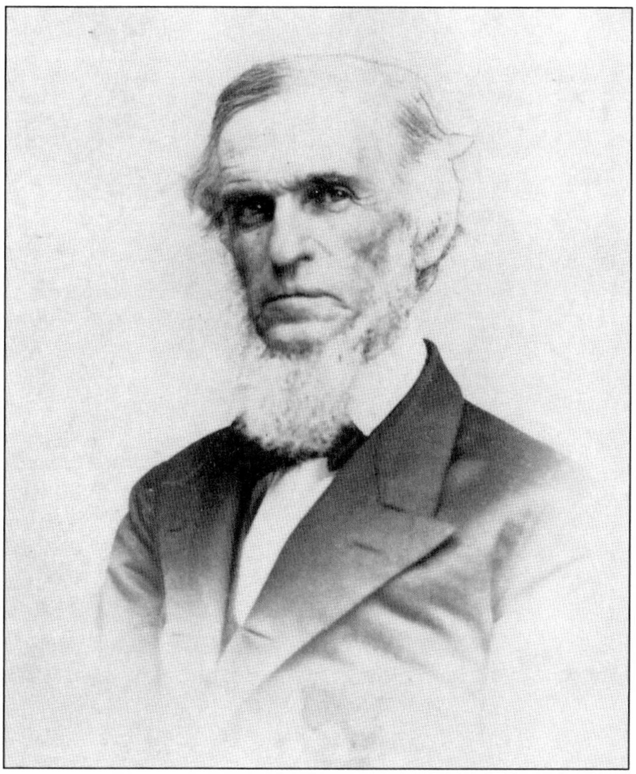

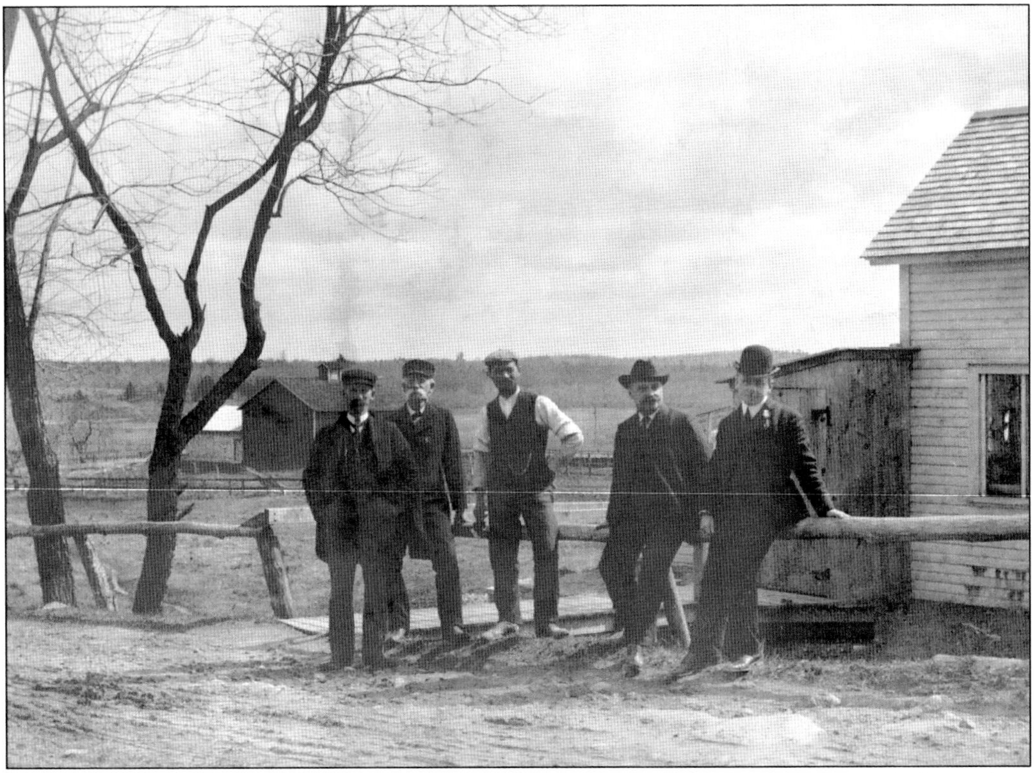

This photograph was taken about 1910 from East Broadway in front of K. D. L. Niven's florist shop just downhill from Waverly Avenue, looking south across the Niven farm towards the current landfill. The original log cabin on this property was built by Revolutionary War veteran Maj. Abraham Brownson. From left to right are K. D. L. Niven, Rev. D. C. Niven, unidentified, A. H. Folger, and Ed Curley, author of *Old Monticello*. (Courtesy of Daniel K. Niven.)

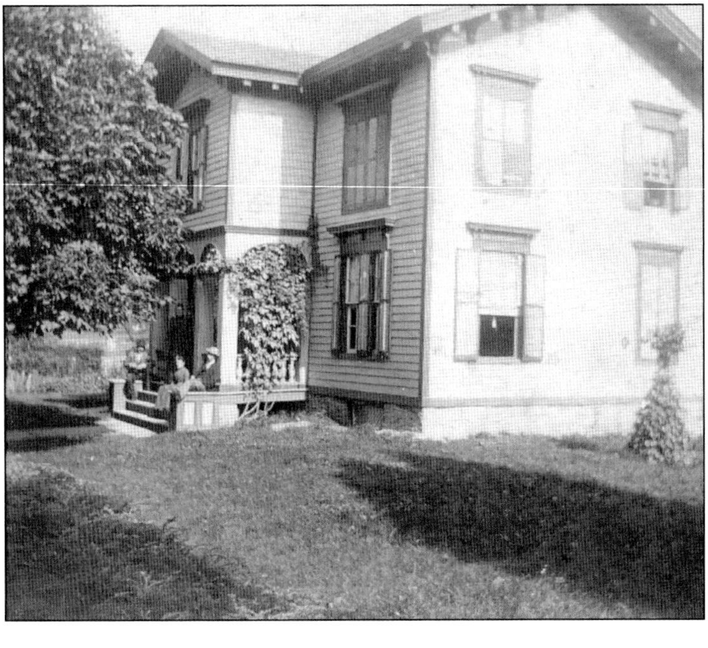

Virginia Thompson and children sit on the front porch of the East Broadway home of her father, John Alexander Thompson (unrelated to the Thompsonville branch of Thompsons.) John came from the Thompson Ridge area of Orange County, New York, to practice law with General Niven, the husband of his older sister, Jane Thompson Niven. He also farmed part of Starr Hill, including the area now subdivided into Hammond Street and Fraser, Fisk, and Thornton Avenues. (Courtesy of Daniel K. Niven.)

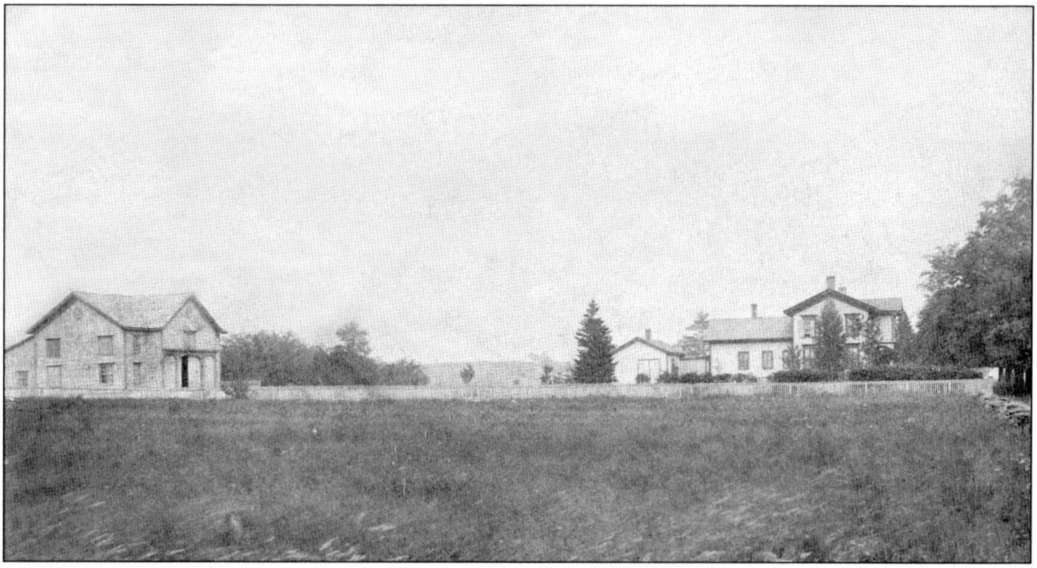

This is the same home as on the preceding page, belonging to John A. Thompson and his wife, Agnes Nancy Dunham, who moved to Monticello to teach at the Monticello Academy. Built in the 1870s on property purchased from the estate of John S. Fraser, it was sold in 1905 to Monticello barber Daniel Buckley. He ran it as a boardinghouse and called it The Buckley. The house, carved into several apartments with an added third story, now stands vacant. (Courtesy of Daniel K. Niven.)

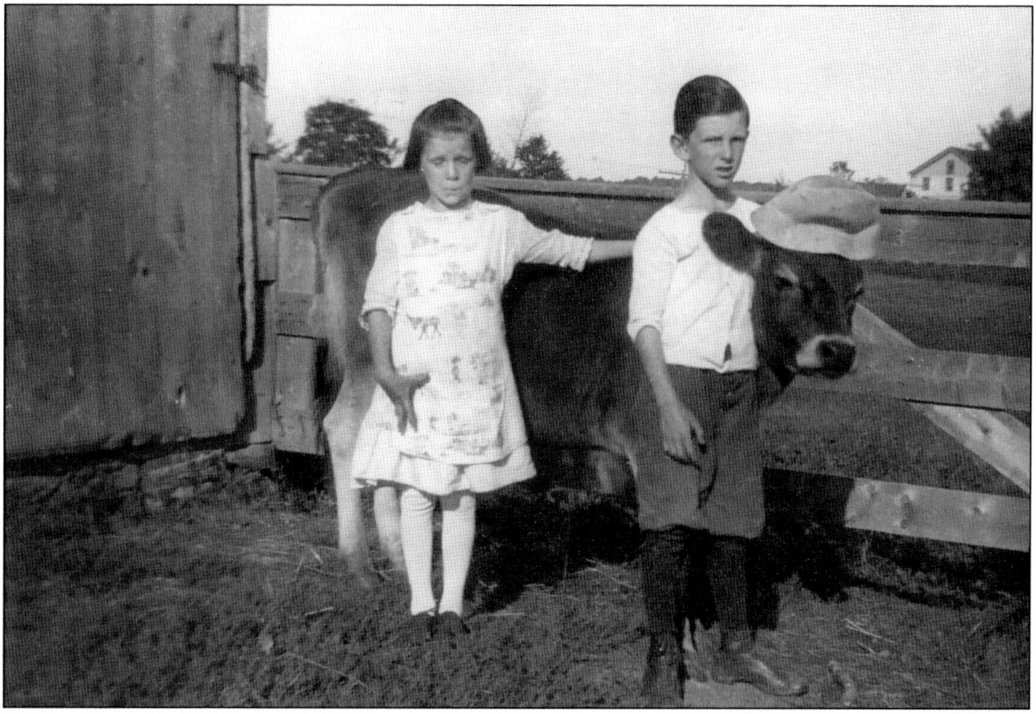

Augusta Niven (later Lyons), born 1910, watches as her brother Kenneth D. Niven, born 1908, tries his hat on the head of one of the family's cows. The parents of these children were Virginia Thompson Niven and Broadway florist, farmer, and postmaster Kenneth D. L. Niven. The Thompson boardinghouse is visible at rear. (Courtesy of Daniel K. Niven.)

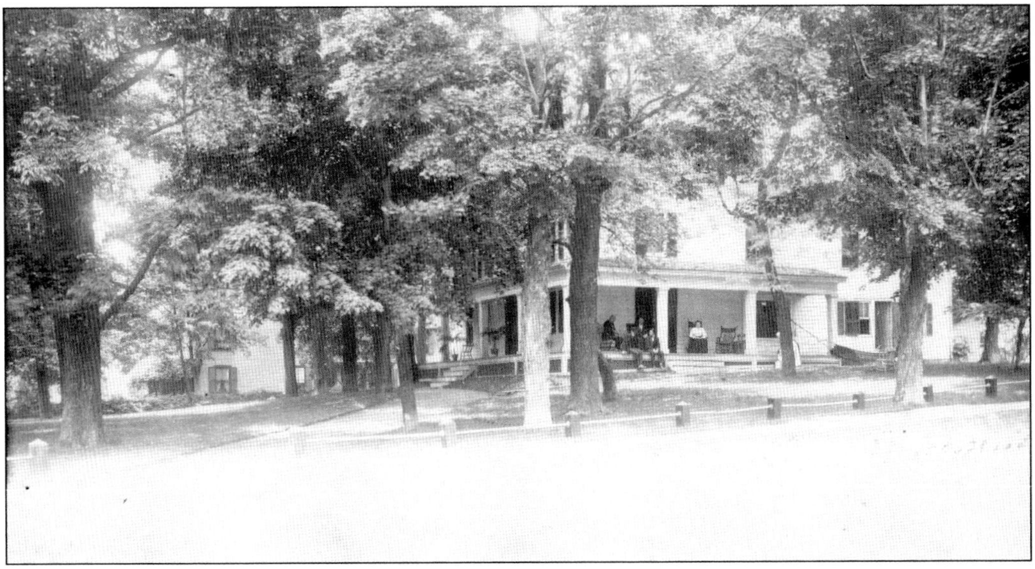

This manse at Liberty and Main Streets was built in 1873 for Rev. James Adams, the longest-serving minister on Monticello's Presbyterian pulpit during the church's first century. From 1862 to 1864, it was home to Rev. Samuel Bayard Dod. When this photograph was taken, the home was the residence of the Barney Lefferts and George Hembt families. The post office has stood here since 1933. (Courtesy of Sullivan County Historical Society.)

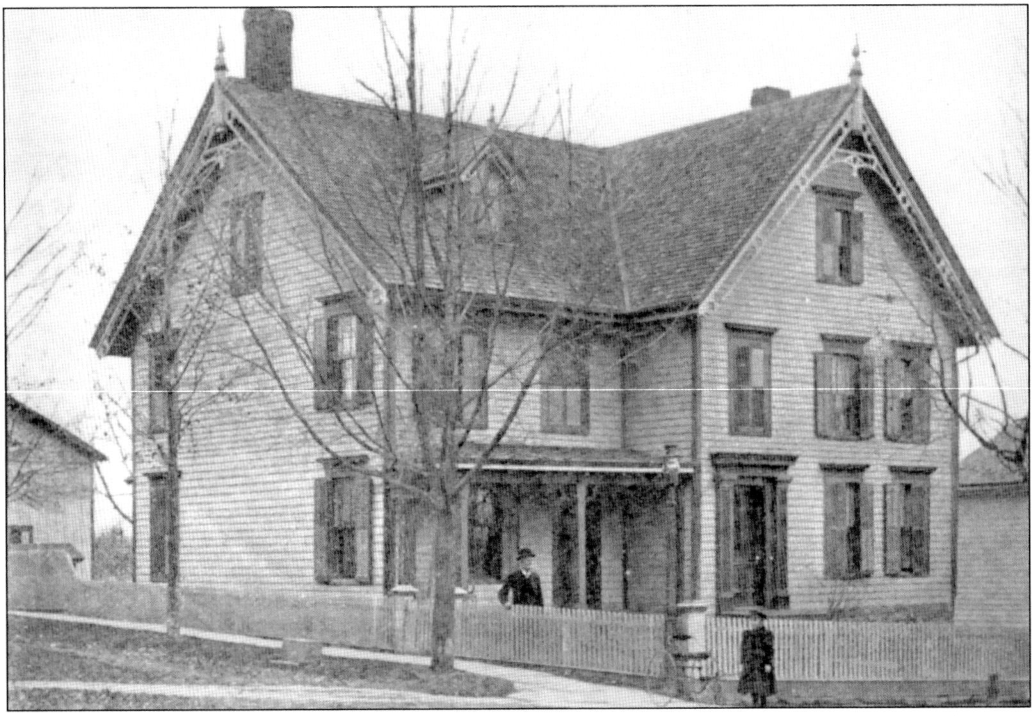

The word manse usually denotes the residence of a Presbyterian minister. This is the second manse of the First Church of Monticello Presbyterian. Rev. A. J. Waugh is shown in the yard. It stood at Broadway and Pleasant Streets, the site of the current village hall. The church purchased it in 1873 and sold it in 1905. (Courtesy of First Church of Monticello Presbyterian.)

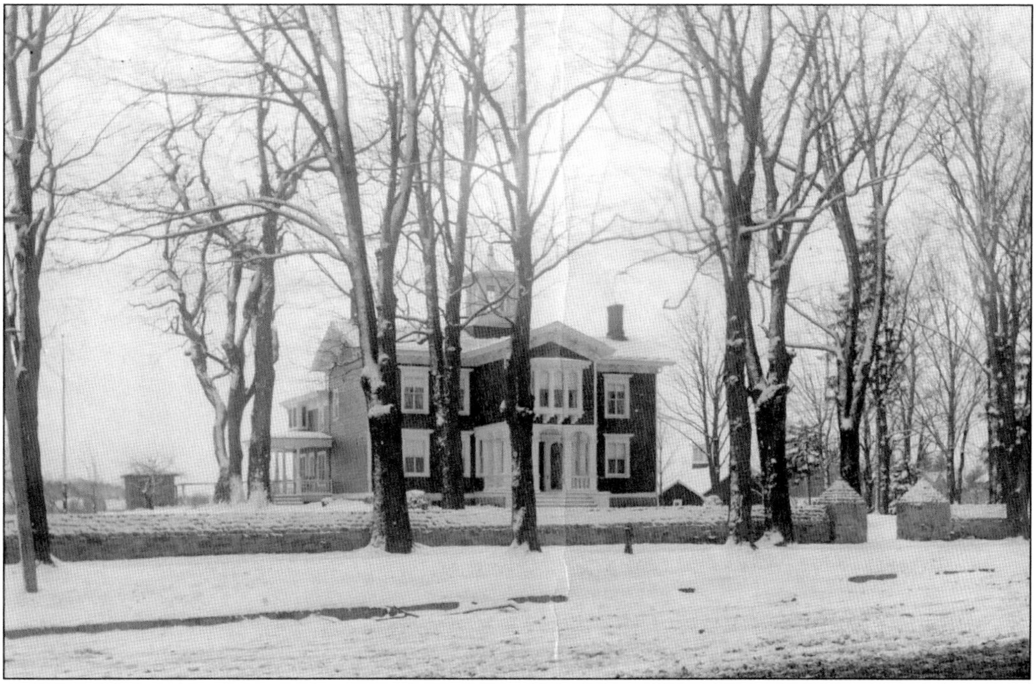

At the center of a 200-foot lot with an immense lawn facing Broadway was the mansion of Gen. Archibald C. Niven (1803–1882). It was originally built by John P. Jones as a home for his brother Samuel while the latter was busy surveying the Newburgh-Cochecton Turnpike. General Niven married Jane Thompson 1832. "Fifty years ago this was the finest property in town," a reporter wrote. "It was the bon ton place of the town." The general's daughter, Mary Niven (Wright) died June 2, 1896, leaving the mansion to her niece, Jennie Lee Niven. The *Republican Watchman* reported in August 1930 that it was "being dismantled board by board and is being carted away to Sackett Lake, by Sam Katzman . . . [to] use the lumber to build several cottages." The photograph above was taken in 1875, the one below in 1910. (Both, courtesy of Daniel K. Niven.)

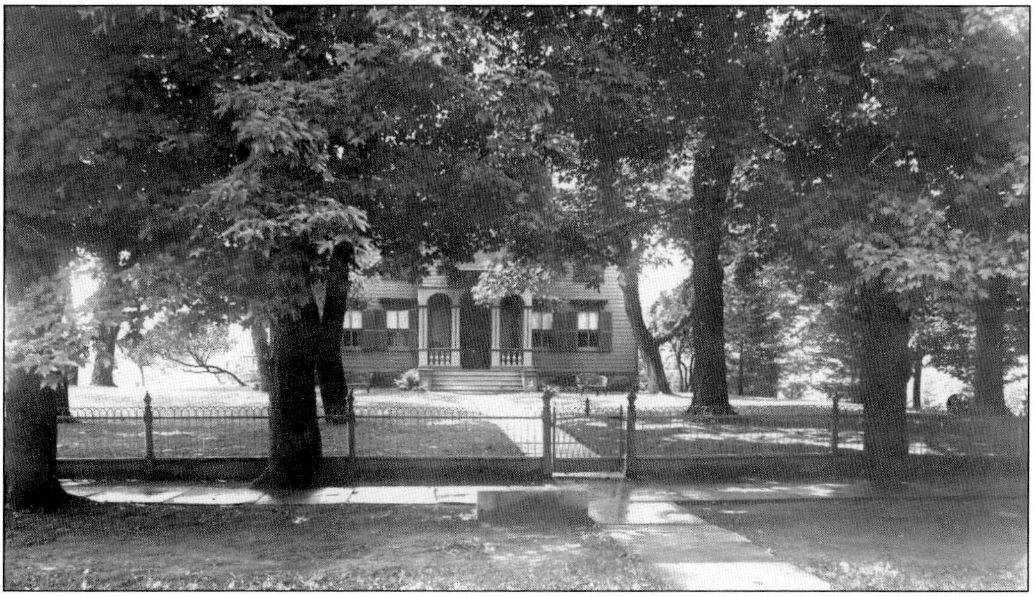

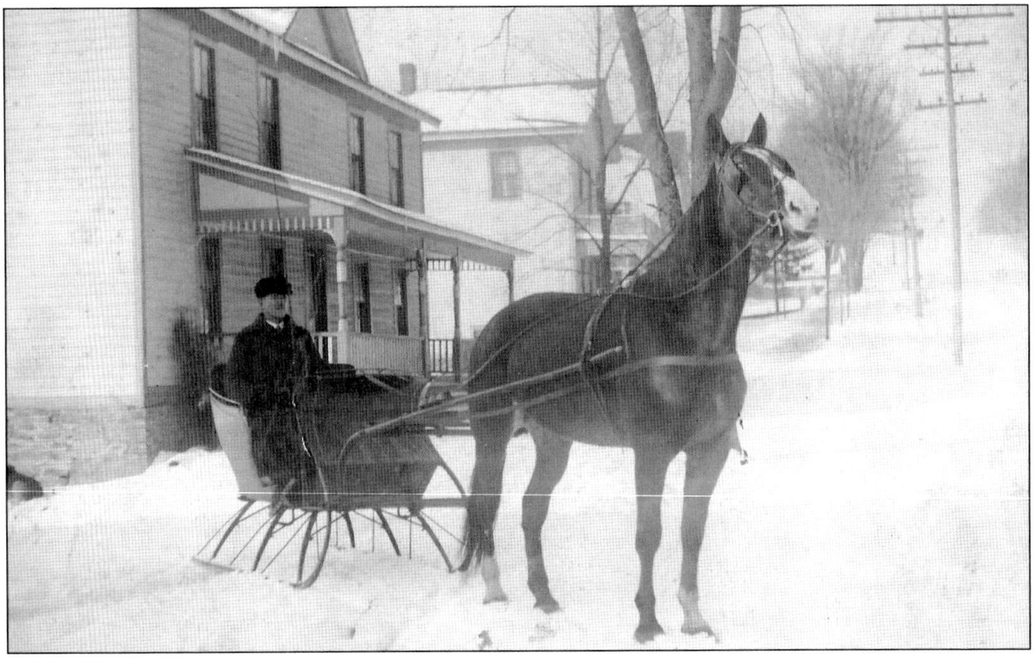

A horse named Jim D stands on East Broadway near Spring Street and the present Kristt Company and J. J. Sommers Company with its unidentified driver. A book containing this picture includes a sign, cut from this print by the photographer: "JIM D—Record 2.30 1/2—Wagon 2.12," likely meaning a record of 2 minutes, 30.5 seconds per mile, probably with a sulky. (Courtesy of William Horton.)

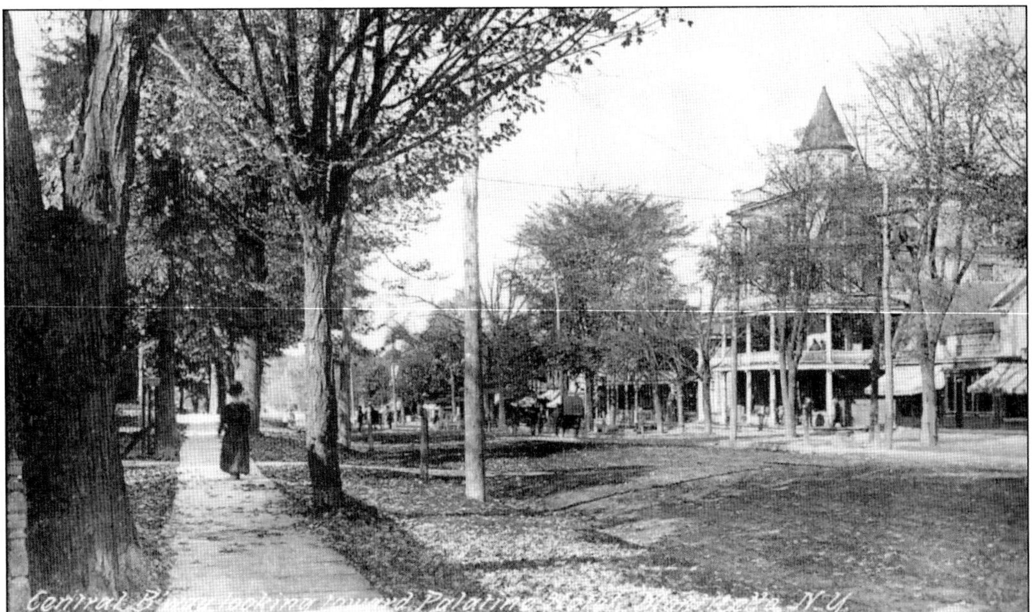

With its coned spire, the Palatine Hotel was a landmark of central Main Street (now Broadway) and Orchard Avenue (now Landfield Avenue) before the fire of August 10, 1909. Behind this hotel to the north was the Murray Electric Light and Power Company, where the catastrophic fire began, wiping out much of the business district of old Monticello. (Courtesy of Richard Benjamin Sr.)

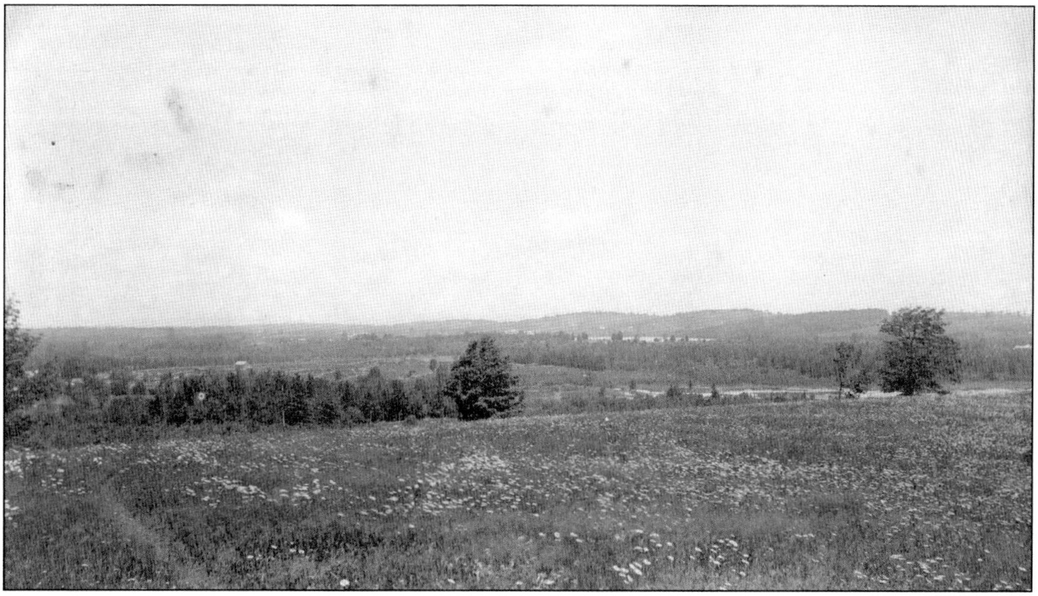

This wide-angle view from Landfield Hill above High Street looks west toward Kiamesha Lake (top) and east toward Monticello (bottom). The image of town is described on the photograph as "a view from the water tower" near the corner of High Street and close to what would soon be the site of Monticello Hospital, later called Monticello Manor adult home. (Courtesy of Daniel K. Niven.)

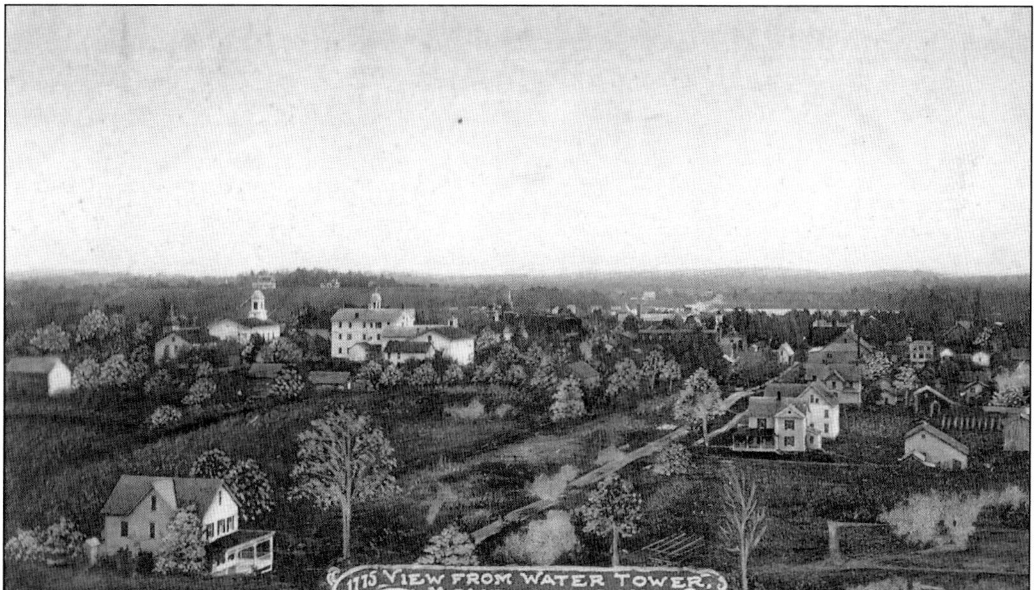

A closer view of Monticello taken from Landfield Hill shows High Street and beyond that Bolsum (now Cottage) Street. Off to the left, the courthouse spire stands beyond the Frank Leslie Hotel. Left of center is the intersection of Liberty and North Streets, with the bell tower of the old firehouse and town hall toward the right. (Courtesy of Richard Benjamin Sr.)

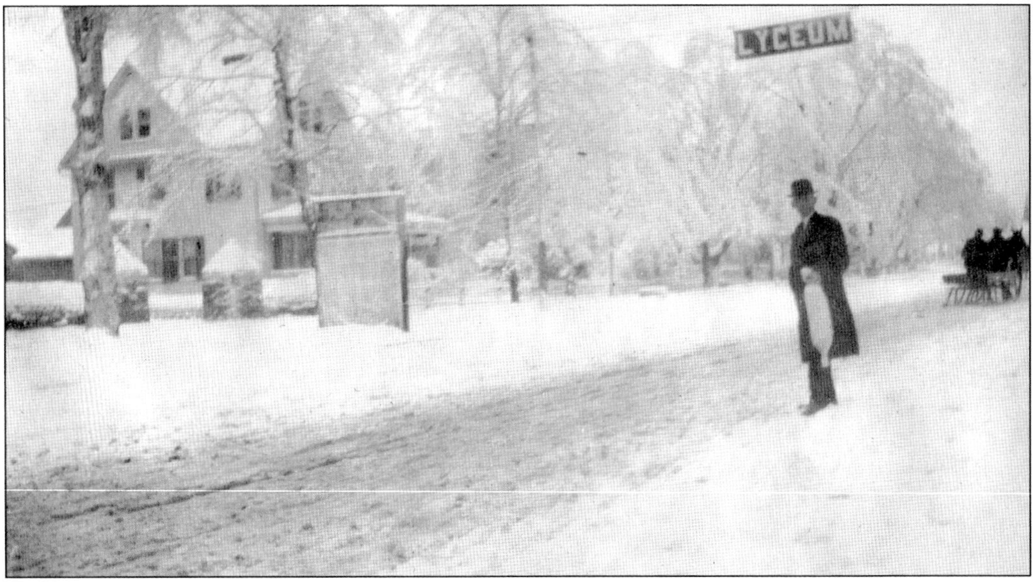

Florist K. D. L. Niven crosses Broadway in a snowstorm, carrying flowers. The Lyceum, owned by Jennie Niven Guimond, was the region's largest theater and amusement hall. In 1921, the village outlawed signs overhanging Broadway like the one shown here. Officials called the sign a public nuisance and removed it. Jennie and Louis Guimond sued the president and trustees of the Village of Monticello in supreme court to keep the sign but lost. In their suit, they implied the owner of their competitor, the newer and flashier Rialto Theater across the street, conspired with village officials to wrongly remove the sign. After more than one instance of arson, the theater business did not end well for the Guimonds. (Both, courtesy of Daniel K. Niven and Sullivan County Historical Society.)

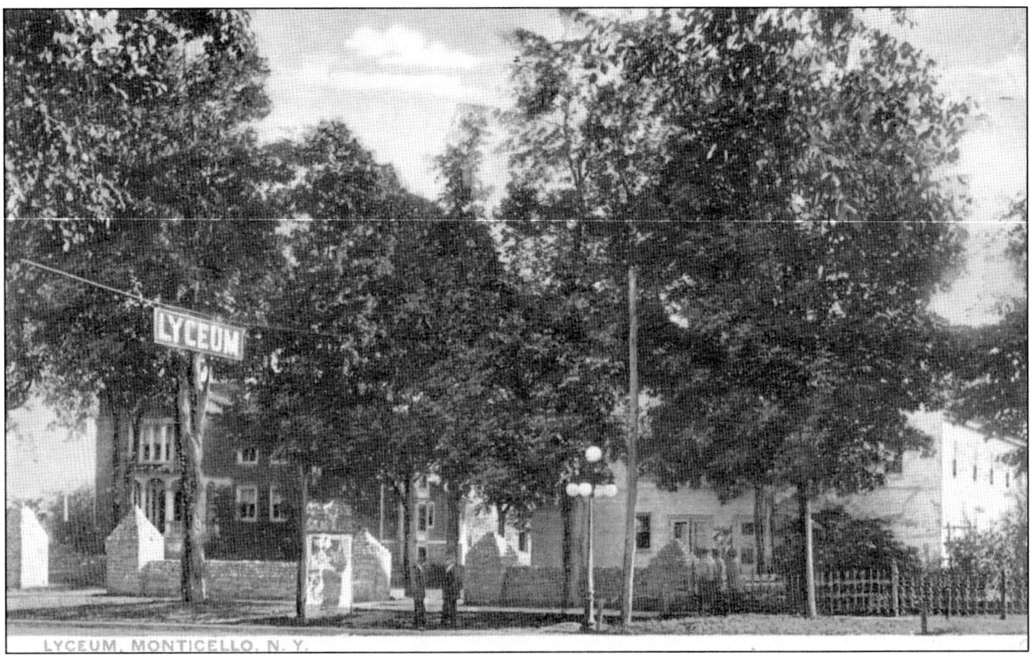

Thornton A. Niven (son of Gen. A. C. Niven) was a Princeton-educated attorney, New York assemblyman from 1877 to 1878, town of Thompson supervisor 1884–1887 and 1889–1899; and chaired the Sullivan County Board of Supervisors 1894–1895. He married Pluma A. Tremain. Their only child was Jennie Lee Niven, whose middle name was for Confederate general Robert E. Lee. (Courtesy of Daniel K. Niven.)

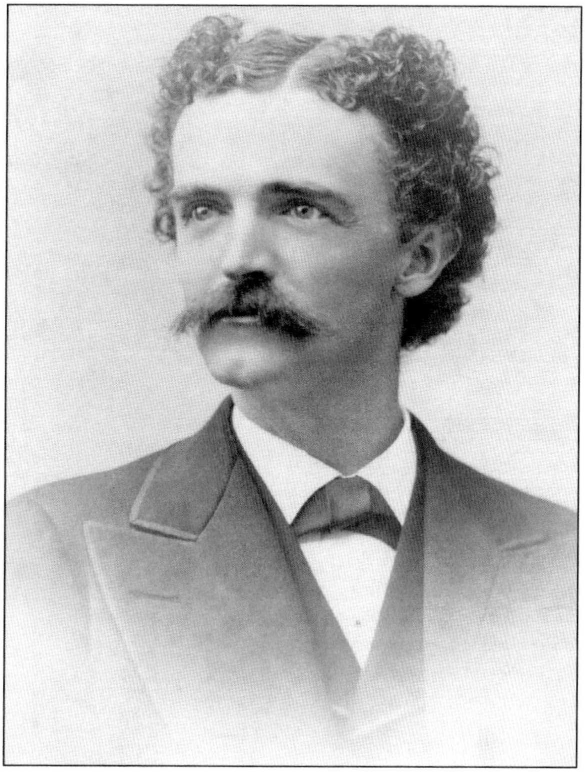

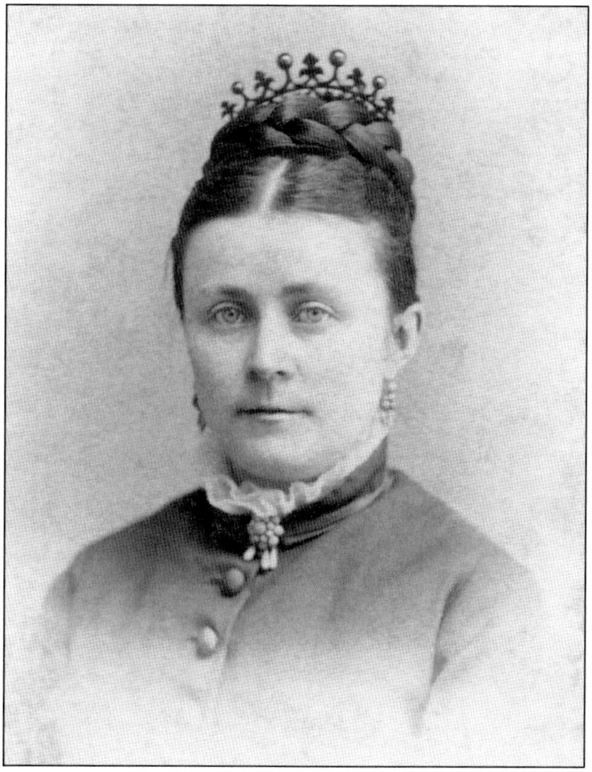

Pluma A. Tremain Niven (1843–1912), seen in this photograph dated May 1888, led a county-wide drive for a veterans' monument on the village green. Controversy erupted, and a split occurred against Niven. Disaffected members incorporated and sued for the donations collected. The Niven side lost the suit but got the prime location. The second monument was erected at the corner of Jefferson Street a block east. (Courtesy of Daniel K. Niven.)

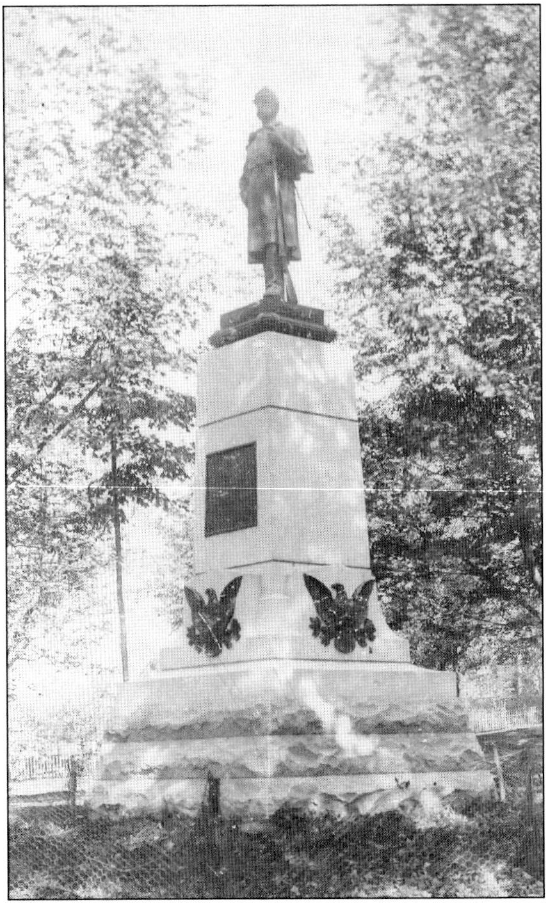

On the back of this photograph is penciled "Mrs. Niven's monument" (probably by Minnie Osborn, who belonged to the incorporated split-off group and owned this photograph). Beneath the soldier's heel is inscribed: "To Sullivan County, in memory of her heroes, from Pluma A. Niven." The original association was led by the wife of town supervisor and chairman of the Sullivan County Board of Supervisors, Thornton A. Niven. (Courtesy of William Horton.)

On the reverse of this image of the war monument at the courthouse, pacifist newspaper publisher A. M. Scriber pointedly wrote, "Heaven is my home but at the present time I abide just across the street from this monument. Choo, choo, look out for the big soldier. I am historic, patriotic, and enthusiastic and then some. Don't reveal my family skeleton to a soul." (Courtesy of Susan Benton Schock.)

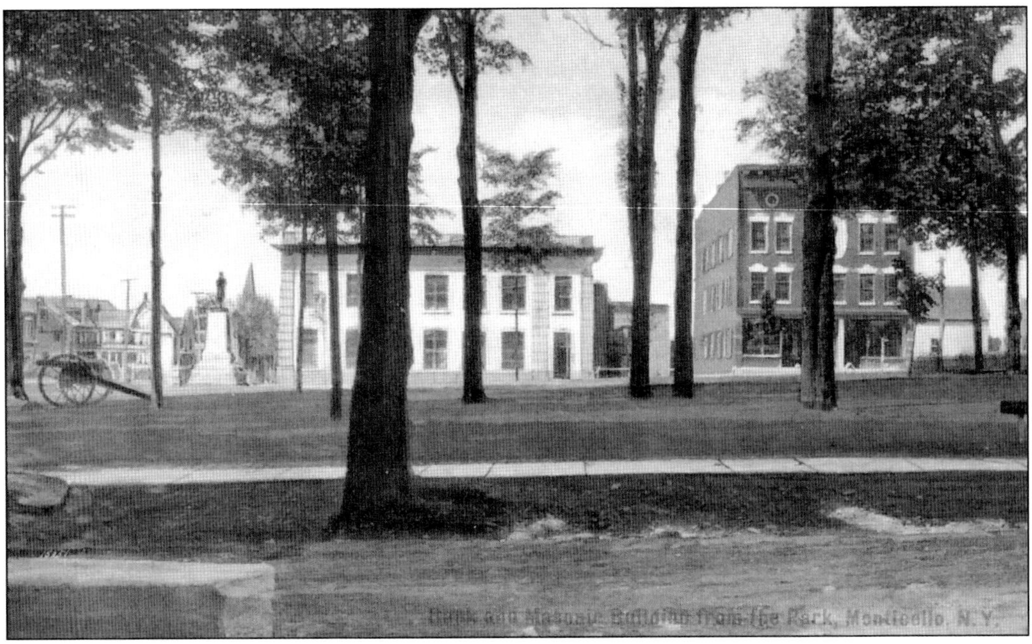

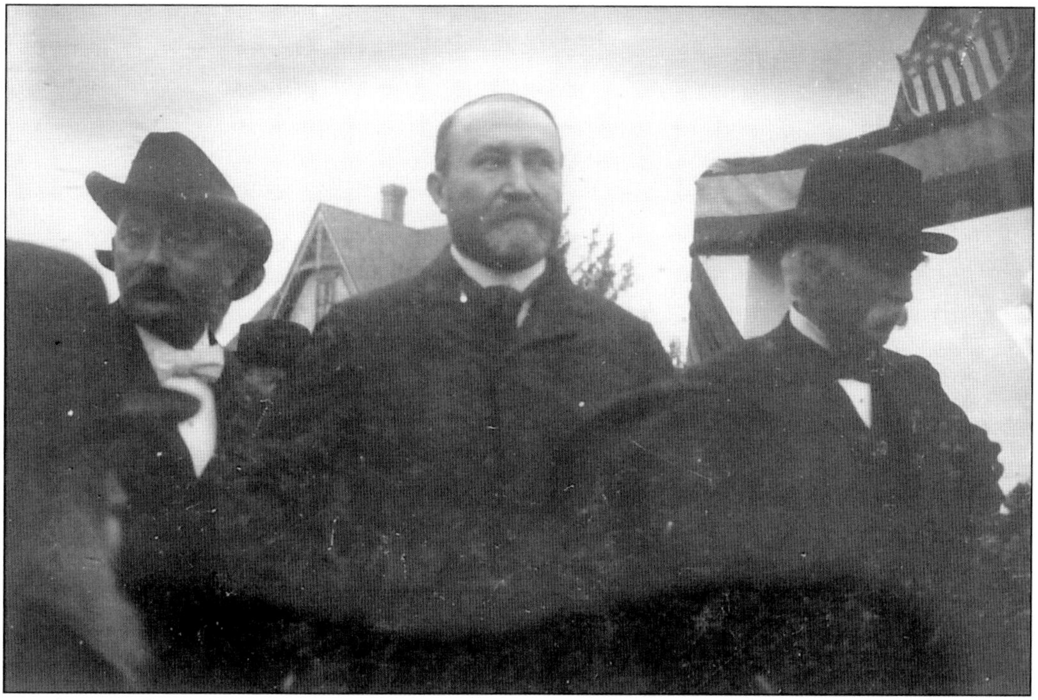

On the grandstand unveiling the monument at Memorial Park on October 6, 1896, from left to right are Capt. J. T. Anderson (lower left), George Fraser (county clerk), Col. Fred Grant (oldest son of Ulysses S. Grant), and retired county court judge Timothy Bush. Fund-raising and construction of Monticello's second such monument were led by Mary Bush, the judge's wife and president of the Sullivan County Ladies Soldiers and Sailors Monument Association, Inc. (Courtesy of Sullivan County Historical Society.)

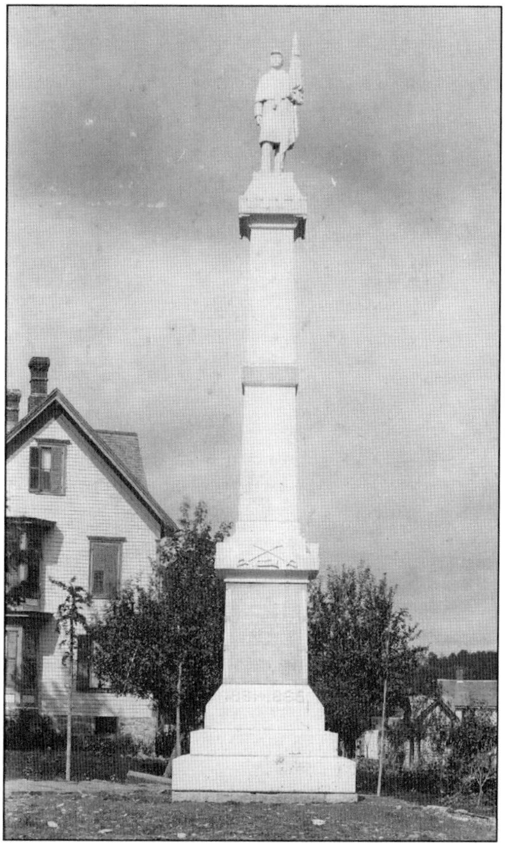

"Erected by the Sullivan County Soldiers and Sailors Monument Association, Incorporated," this granite sentry guarded Memorial Park from 1896 to 1972, when it was moved to a more obscure location by Irv Feinstein's Sullivan County Monument Works for $3,500. The cost of the monument in 1896 was $2,500. Unfortunately, the middle and bottom parts were improperly oriented in 1972 and remain so today. (Courtesy of William Horton.)

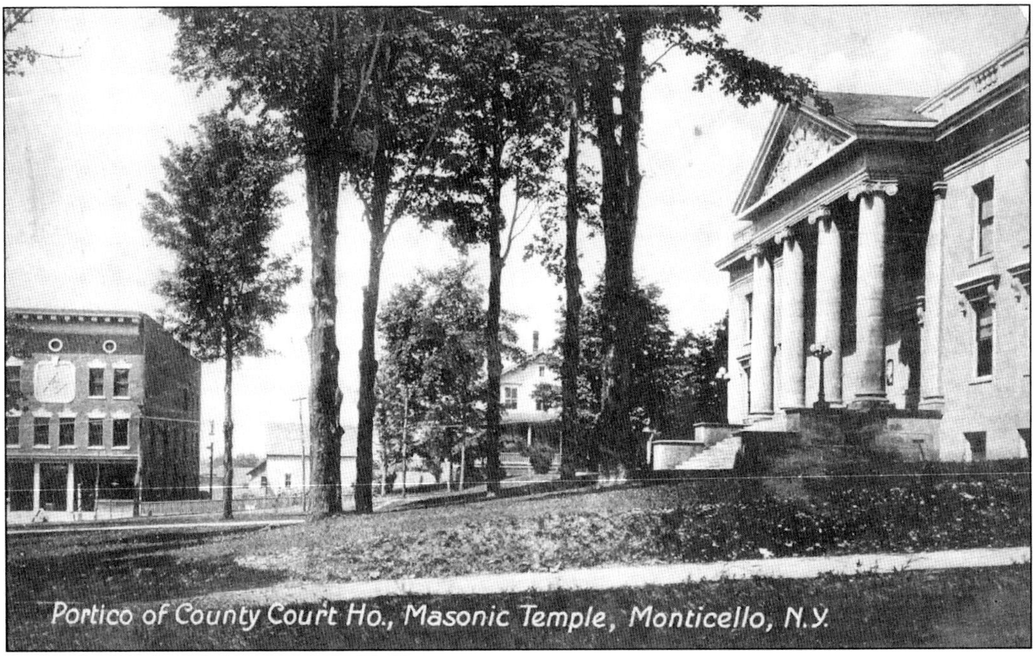

This view of the present Sullivan County Courthouse shows the proximity to the Masonic temple at 5 Bank Street (left) and the home of Capt. John C. Holly of the 143rd Regiment at 9 Bank Street (center). Coincidentally, it also happens to show the northern wall of the Masonic building, the middle of the second floor, which concealed the sanctuary of Adelaide M. Branch in the law offices of Melvin Couch (see page 25). (Courtesy of Richard Benjamin Sr.)

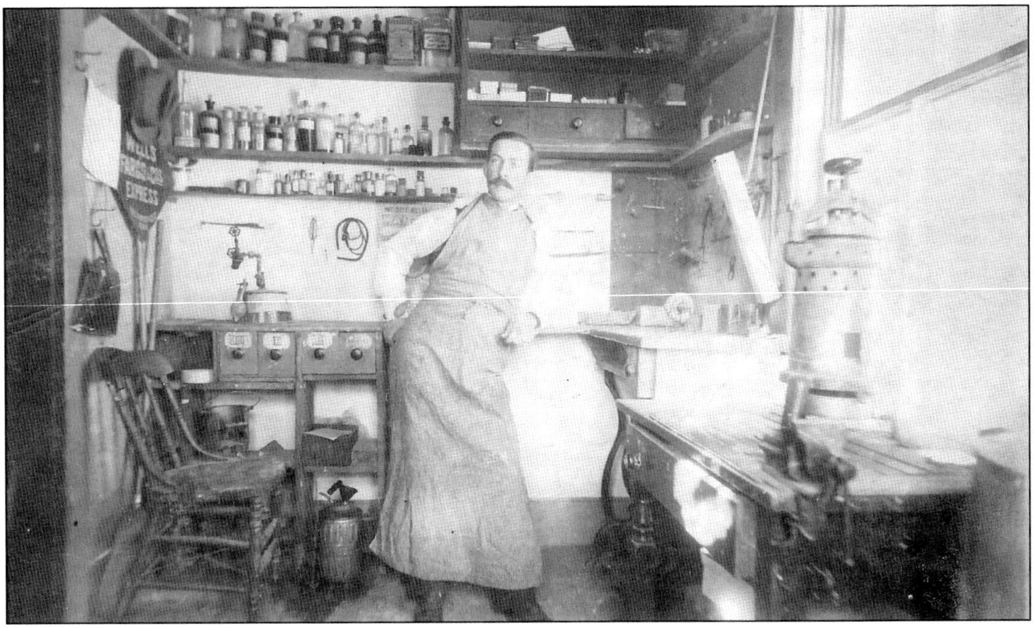

Dr. Seth Osborn is shown in his Monticello orthodontic laboratory, where he made teeth for his dental parlor on the floor below, located in the Masonic building on Bank Street. Dr. Osborn graduated from Philadelphia Dental College in 1895. After Dr. Osborn's death, other dentists maintained practices in the Masonic building. (Courtesy of William Horton.)

A Monticello love story captured the nation's attention in December 1913 when former county prosecutor Melvin Couch (right), another Masonic building tenant, died of a ruptured aorta and his hidden "heart wife" emerged. Adelaide Branch, Couch's lover, remained closeted for much of their 15-year relationship in the lawyer's office on the second floor of the Masonic temple, where Couch was a past master. "We kept our love a secret for years . . . There are 2,000 [people] in Monticello, with 2,000 tongues and 4,000 ears. I was careful," Branch told the *Syracuse Herald*. Pictured below, from left to right, are Adelaide Branch, Susan Ostrom, and her daughters Mary Ostrom and Jenny Ostrom. Branch made a rare journey to attend Mary Ostrom's wedding in Goshen on September 3, 1912. Before becoming Couch's companion, Branch boarded there. (Both, courtesy of Susan Benton Schock and Donald White.)

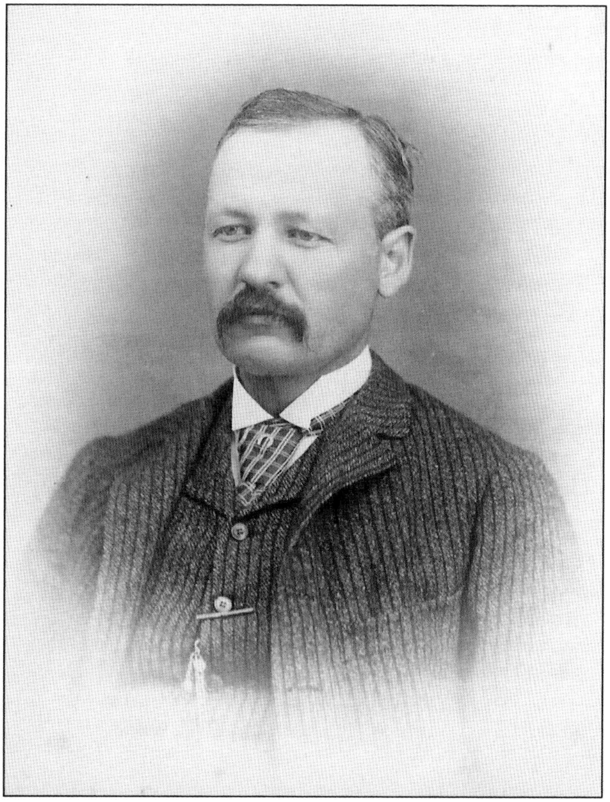

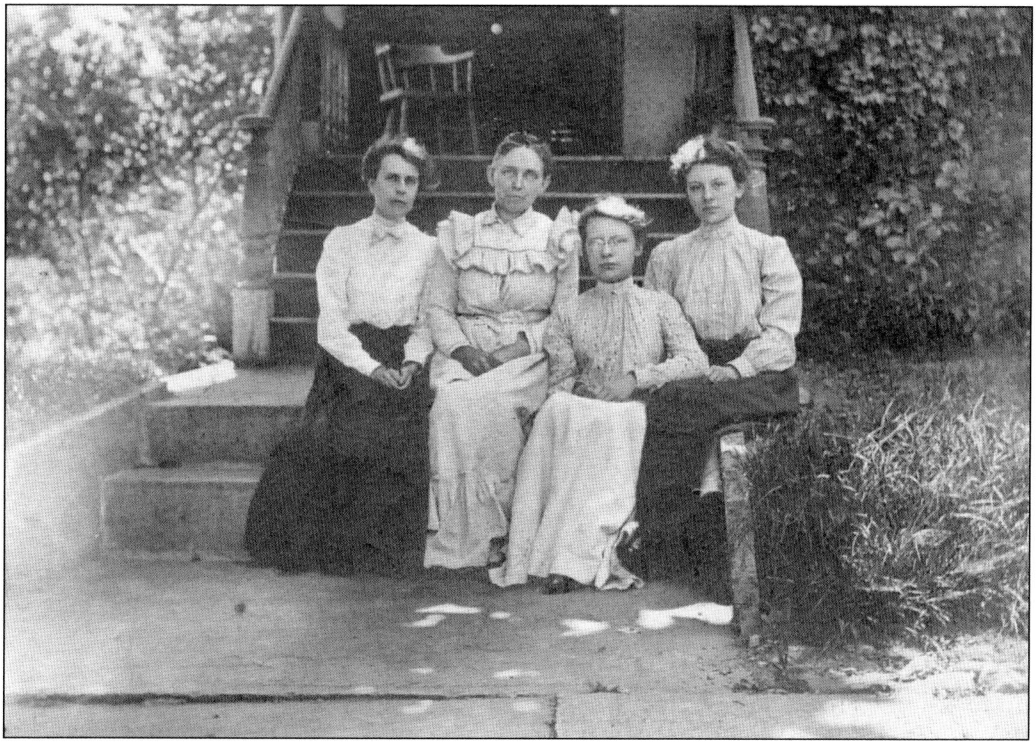

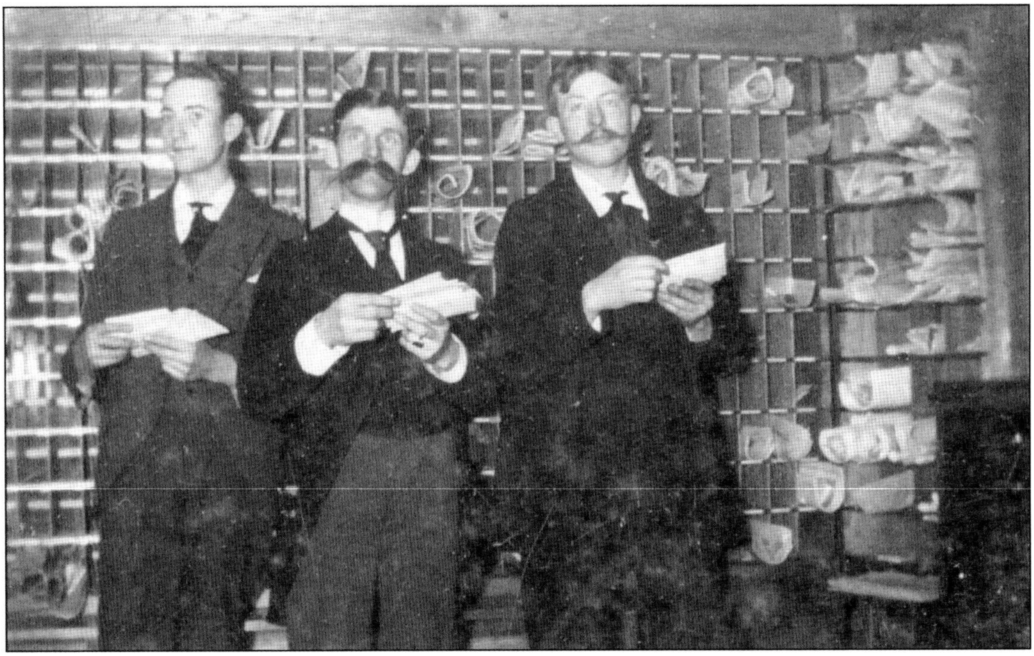

Blake Stratton (left), K. D. L. Niven (center), and Bert Scriber sort mail at the post office in March 1896. Twenty years later, county judge George H. Smith described the structure to Congress as "an old wooden store . . . occupied by the post office on the ground floor, and . . . telegraph and telephone office upstairs." Local requests to locate a new post office opposite the courthouse were rejected by Washington due to cost of land. (Courtesy of Daniel K. Niven.)

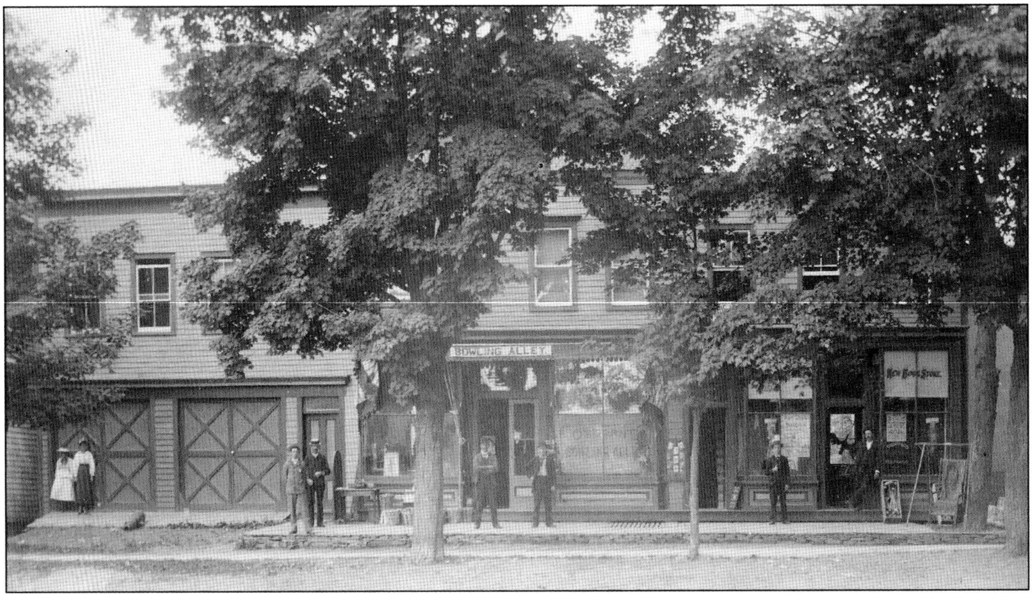

The New Bookstore was located on the south side of Broadway, west of Bank Street, beside a fire station and Osborn's Bowling Alley. Around 1894, the New Bookstore advertised newspapers and books for sale, as well as "Colgate and Sons Toilet Soaps and Perfumery," and "Jolly Tar, Joker, and Climax Plug Tobacco." A broadside on the window announced a meeting at Waller Hall of an association to build a soldier's monument on September 2. (Courtesy of William Horton.)

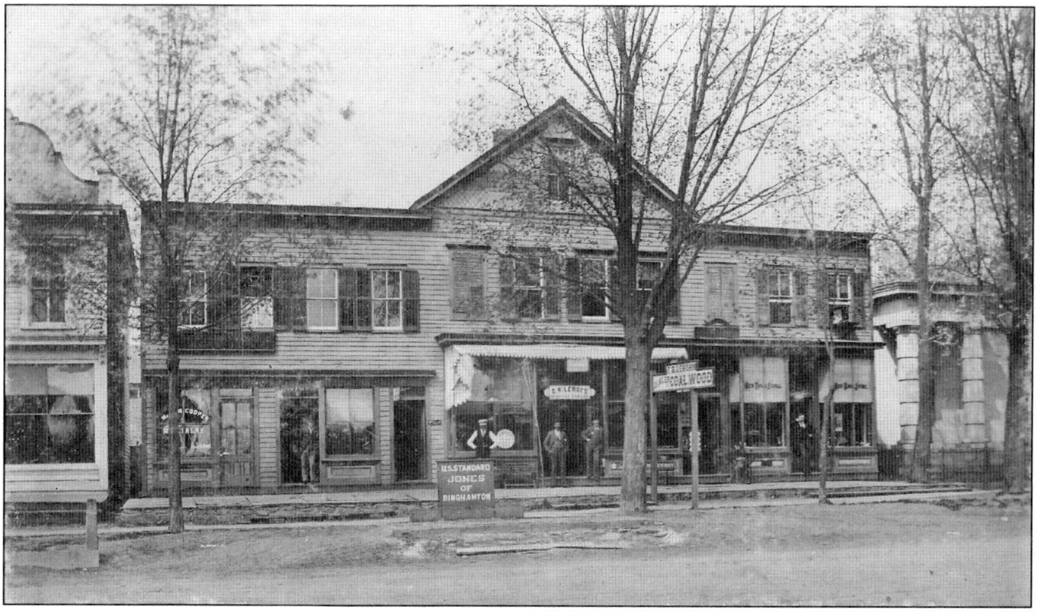

Shown here around 1846 are Frank Osborn's Coal and Wood; G. R. Leroy's Sporting Parlor, which served sweet cider; Cooper's Millinery, where fine hats were sold; and the New Bookstore, where "25 cents a month will allow you to take one book each day from the circulating library of the New Book Store—10,000 volumes to select from." (Courtesy of William Horton.)

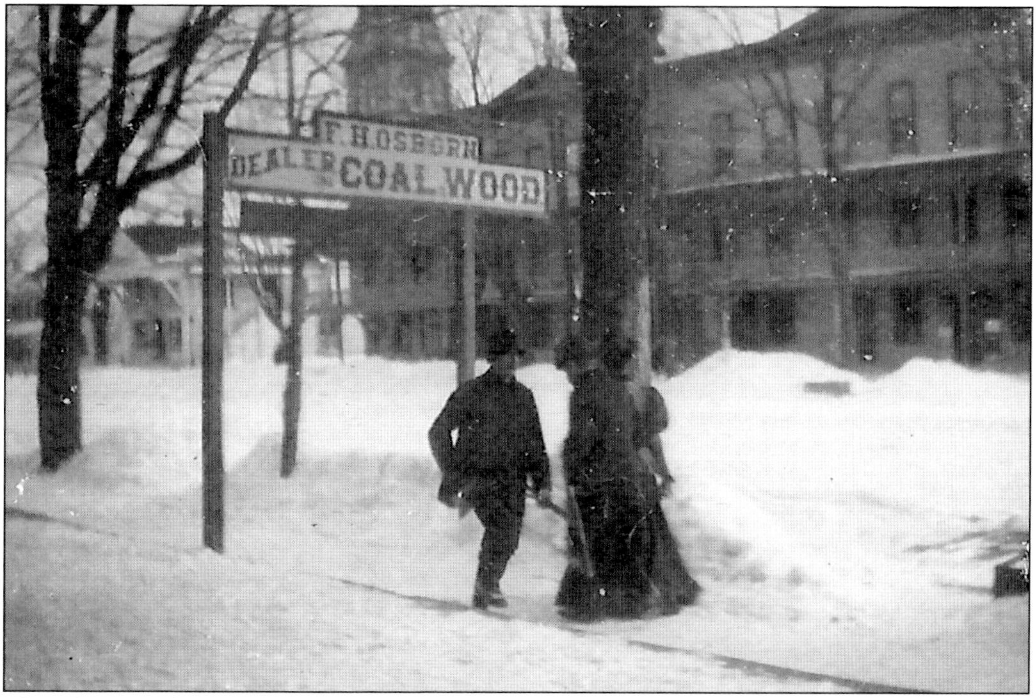

This photograph was taken directly in front of Frank Osborn's Coal and Wood, looking across Broadway toward the Hotel Rockwell and Mill (Saint John) Street. On the far corner is the village post office and telegraph station. The identities of these people, one of whom is carrying a lumber saw, are unknown. (Courtesy of Gary Schmidt.)

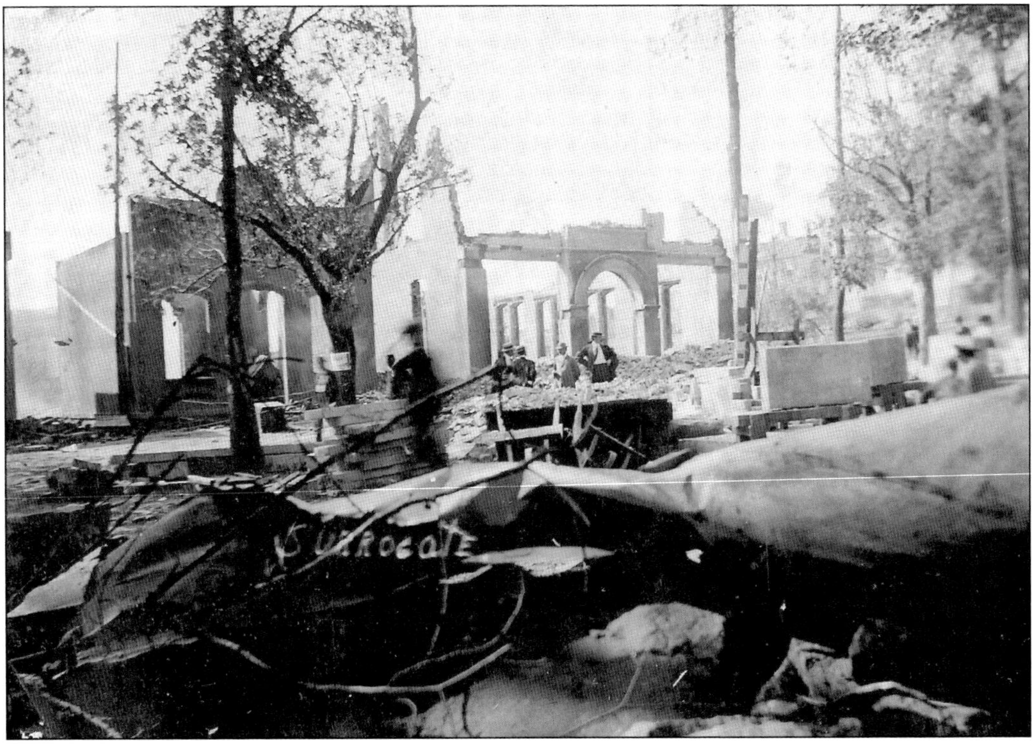

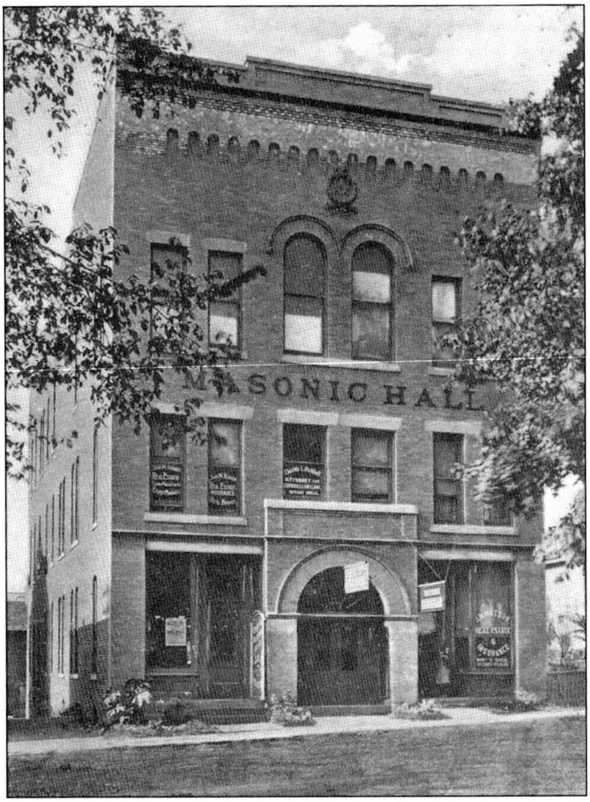

On August 10, 1909, an explosion at the Murray Electric power plant sparked the most damaging fire in Sullivan County's history. Shortly after it began, the fire spread to the adjacent Palatine Hotel, razing it and much of the vicinity. Monticello burned all night and into the next day. By the time the blaze was out, 74 properties were lost at a value of $1 million ($17 million in modern dollars). In the foreground of the above photograph, marked "Surrogate," are the charred remains of the courthouse. Across Bank Street are the dilapidated arches of the 1896 Masonic temple, just 13 years old. Downhill and to the left is the National Union Bank, where all but the vault was destroyed in the holocaust. The new temple (left) was dedicated October 29, 1898. (Both, courtesy of Susan Benton Schock and Monticello Fire Department.)

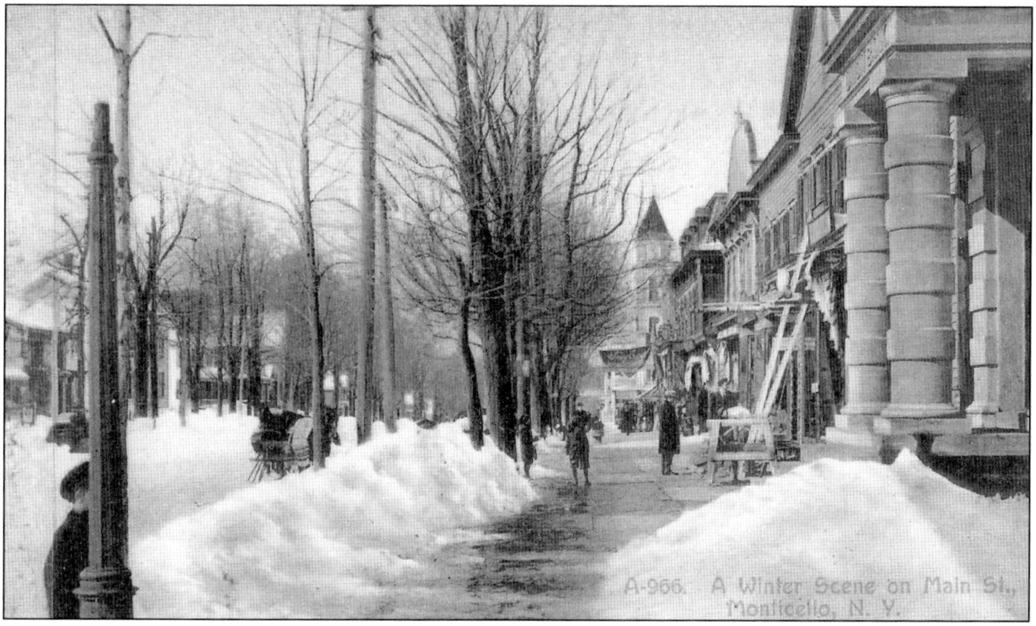

Pictured at right in this pre-1909 image were the National Union Bank, Thornton's Pharmacy, Hammond and Cooke's, and James Kelly's confectionery. Farther down Main Street, with its distinctive conical spire, is the Palatine Hotel owned by Peter Murray and the stationery and book store of William Strong. Beyond the Palatine was the Monticello Telephone Company. At left, obscured by a birch tree, is the Monticello Methodist Church. (Courtesy of Richard Benjamin Sr.)

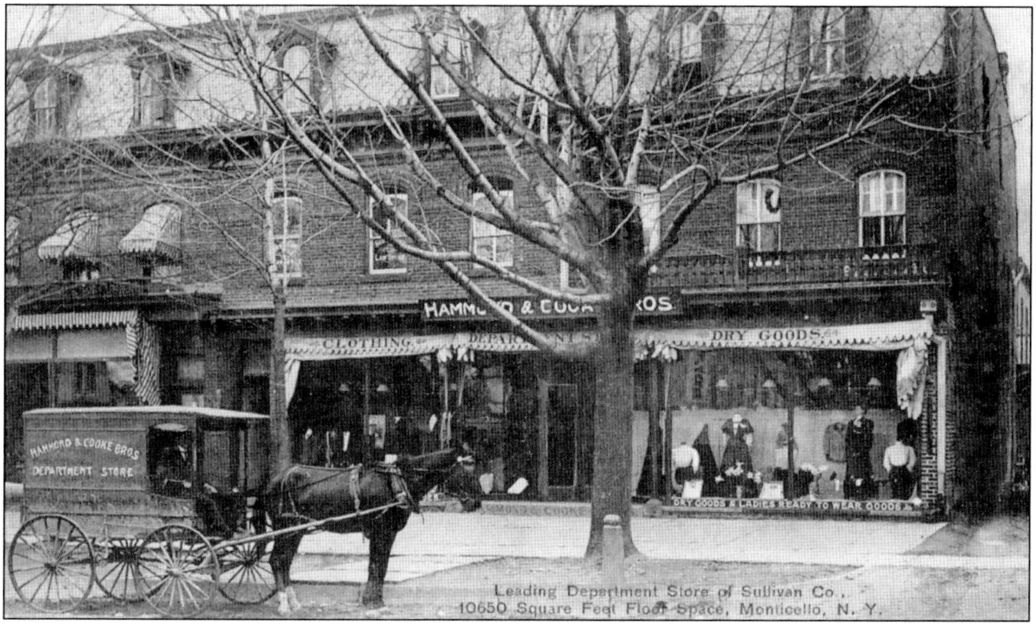

Hammond and Cooke's department store on central Broadway is pictured above with its one-horse delivery wagon idling outside, driver at the ready. Signs advertise "Clothing, Department Store, Dry Goods, Ladies Ready To Wear Goods." A caption printed at the bottom declares it the "leading department store of Sullivan County, 10,650 square feet floor space, Monticello, N.Y." (Courtesy of Richard Benjamin Sr.)

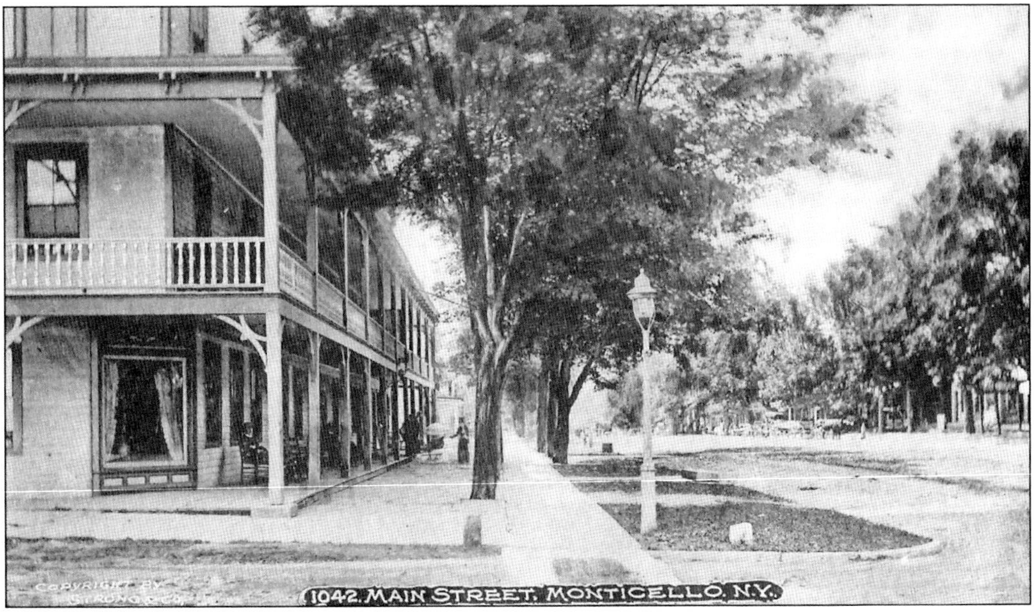

The pre-1909 photograph from the corner of Main (Broadway) and Mill (Saint John) Streets above shows decorative lighting along the main thoroughfare, even in those early days. To the left is the wood-framed high-peaked Hotel Rockwell, which was thoroughly laid to waste by the 1909 fire. The *New York Times* reported that George Rockwell sobbed openly as he watched his hotel's destruction. Another majestic hotel that towered above Main Street was the Palatine, pictured below at the corner of Orchard Street (Landfield Avenue). Although the fire devastated the community, the economy rebounded quickly. (Both, courtesy of Susan Benton Schock.)

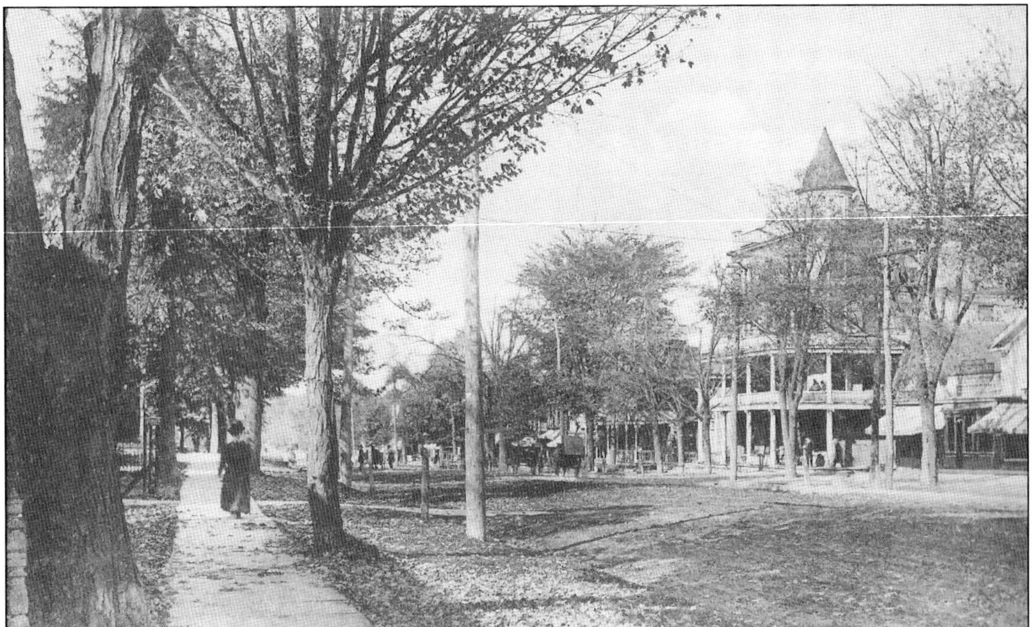

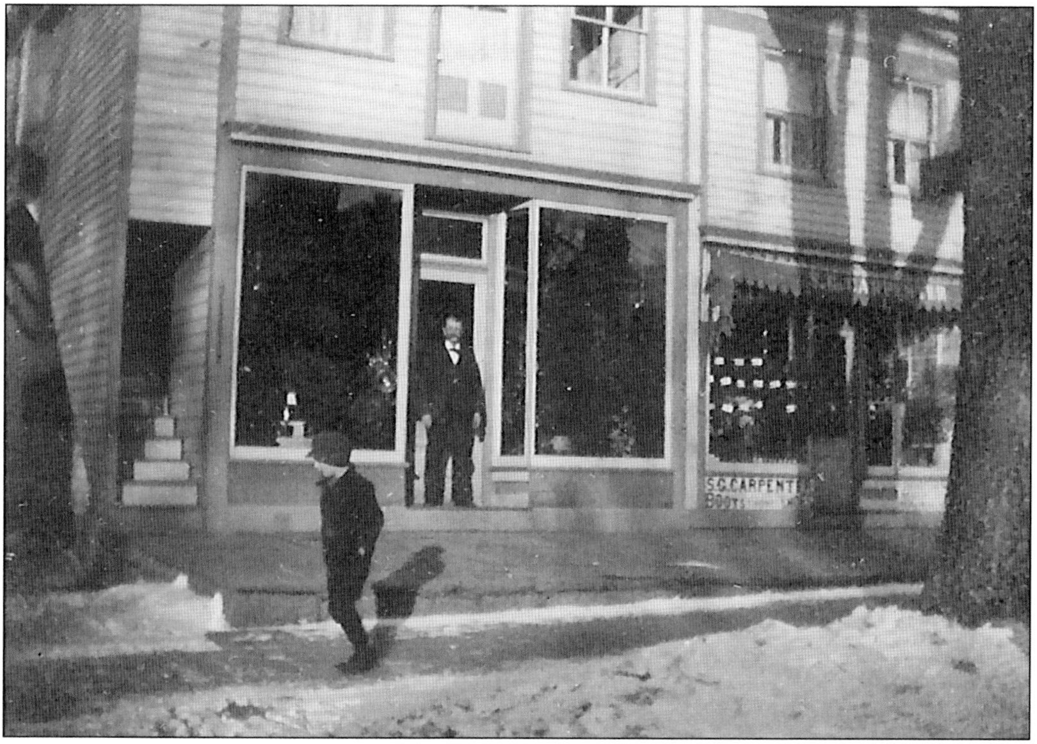

Pharmacist Alpheus A. Crain (1834–1916) is shown in this photograph standing in front of his store across Main Street (264 Broadway) about 1900. Crain's Pharmacy remained an active business well into the second half of the 20th century. (Courtesy of Gary Schmidt.)

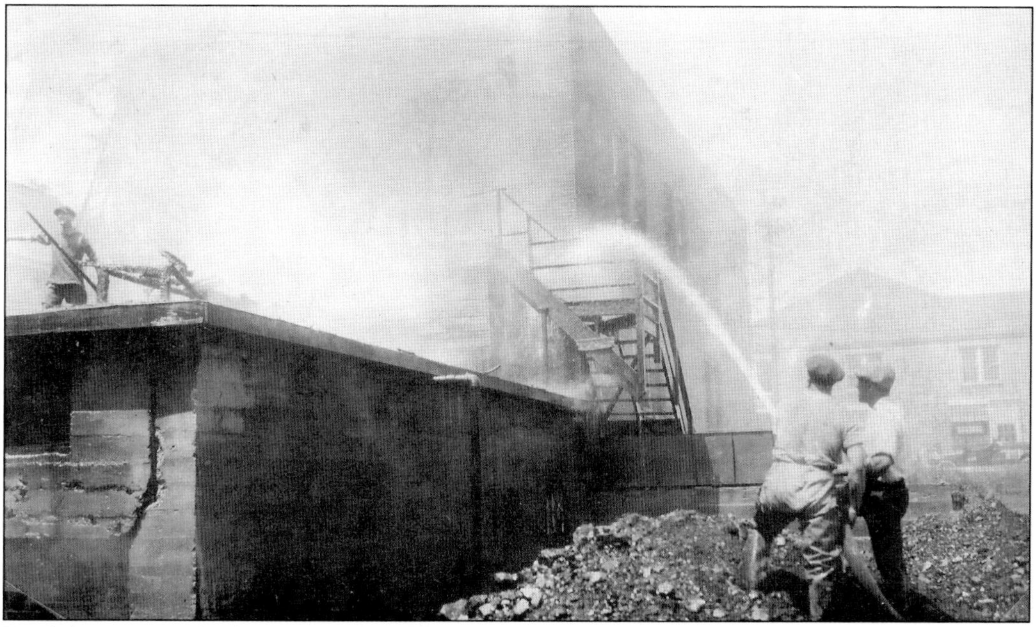

Firefighters spray the burning Monticello Steam Laundry around 1917. This laundry was located near the present-day law offices of Zachary Kelson and Martin Miller at 10 Saint John Street. (Courtesy of William Horton and Monticello Fire Department.)

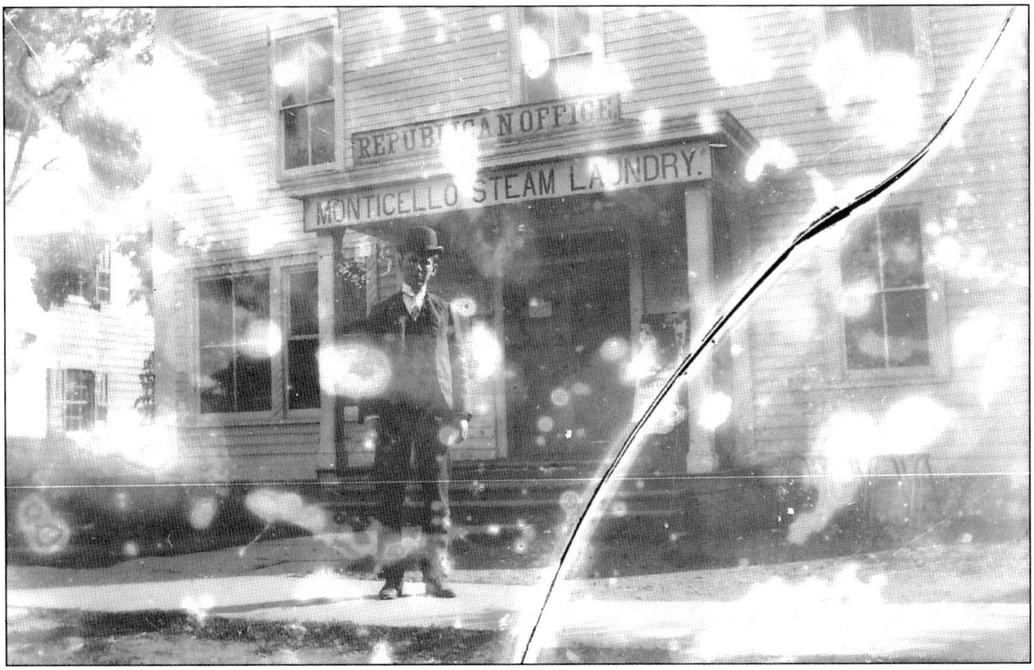

Despite the cracked and stained condition of the glass plate negative, this is an unusual view of the old Monticello Steam Laundry on Saint John Street. In 1899, the establishment advertised in the *Republican Watchman*, "We do hand work. Just the same as you have been getting in the city . . . Domestic finish a specialty. Wagon runs daily . . . Carson and VanLeuver Props." (Courtesy of William Horton.)

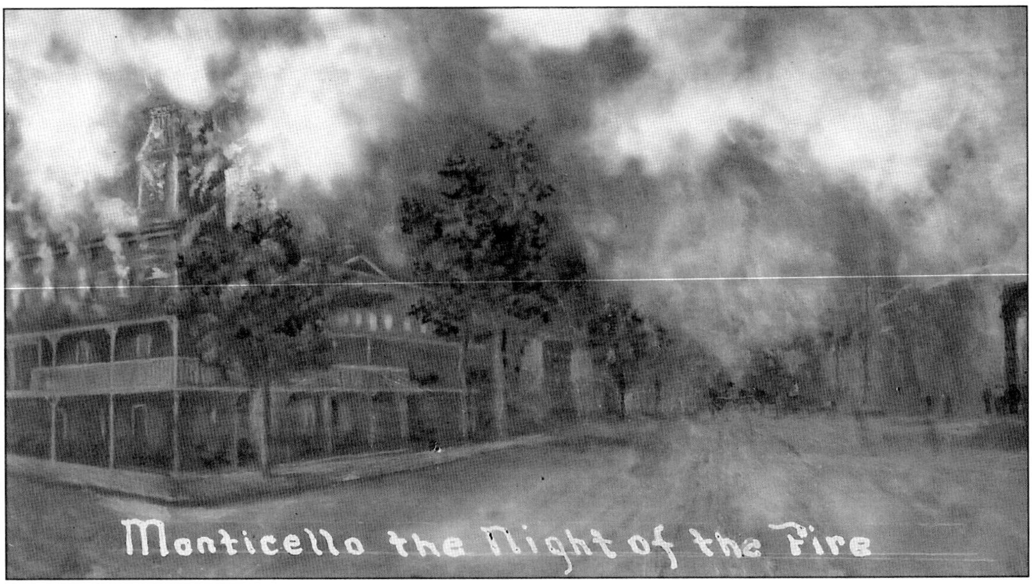

"Monticello the Night of the Fire" hangs at the Monticello Fire House commemorating the fire of August 10, 1909, when "one dread night the villagers awoke; While bells were clanging, dreadful fire and smoke entrapped that mansion in their lurid light, And doomed its ruins to neglectful blight," wrote Arthur C. Butts in 1898 to describe the fire of 1874. His words foreshadowed a larger blaze to come. (Courtesy of Richard Benjamin Sr.)

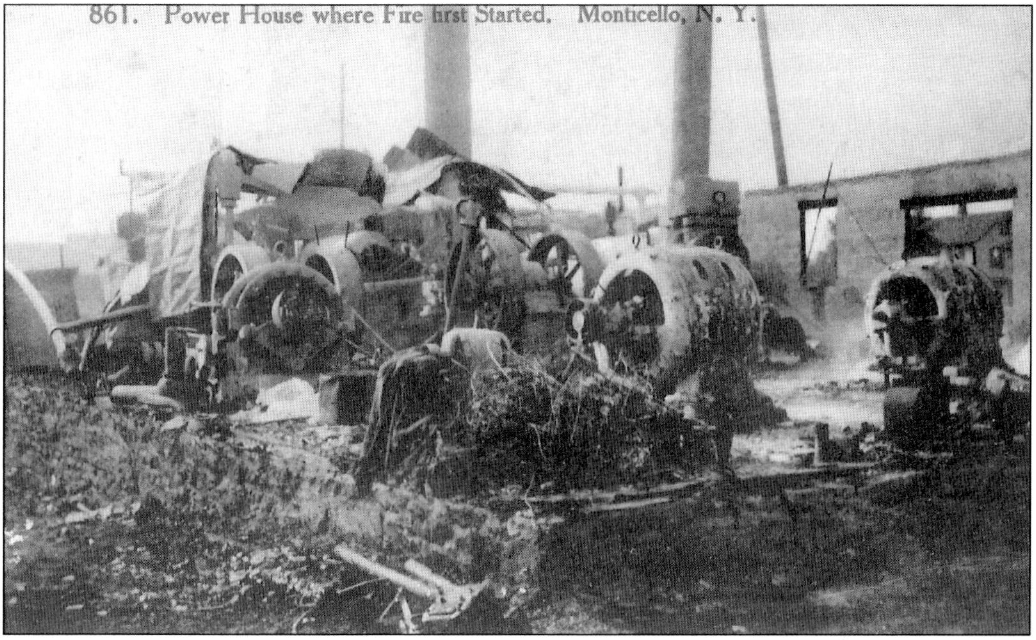

Unfortunately, no one noticed short-circuiting cables at the Murray Electric Light and Power Company on Orchard Street (Landfield Avenue) until it was too late, and Monticello's economy was devastated by the loss of the business center of the village in the fire that ensued. Soon reconstruction began, and within a year or two the community was back on its feet. Murray Electric Light and Power Company rebuilt on lower Saint John Street, and where the power house once stood is now the Landfield Avenue Garage. (Both, courtesy of Richard Benjamin Sr.)

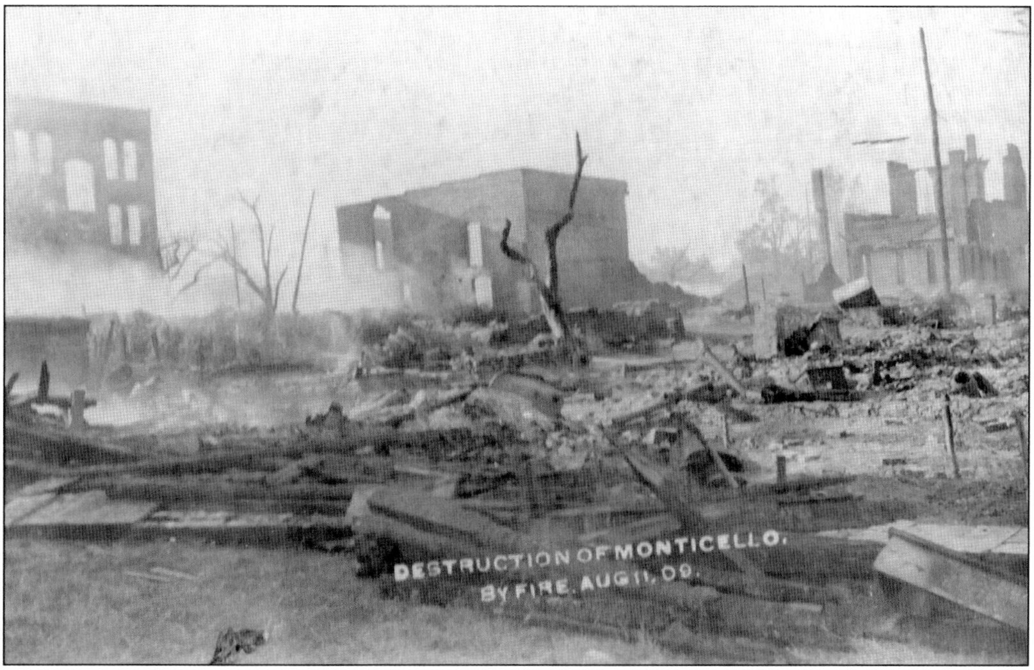

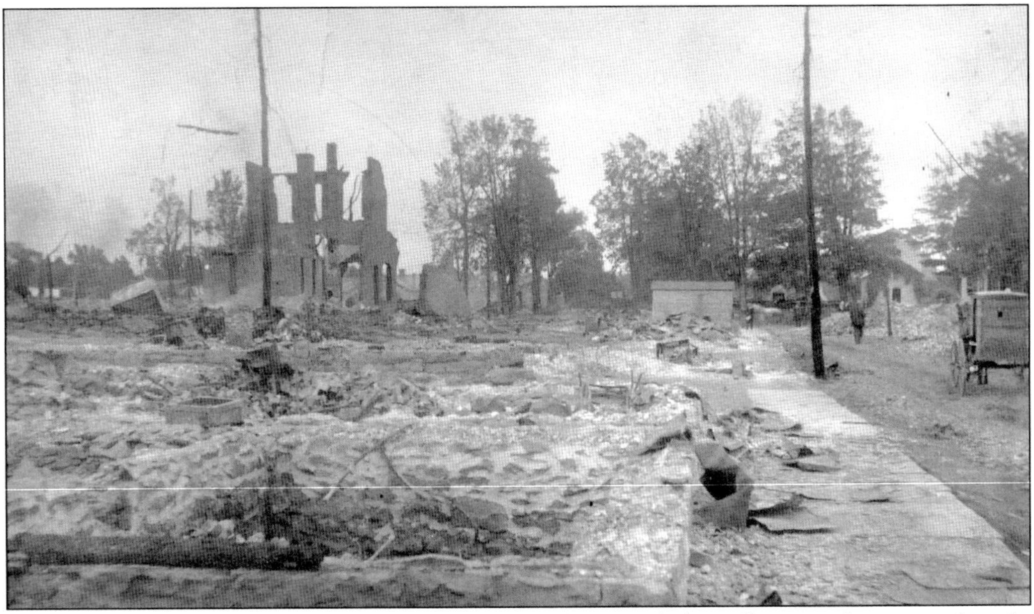

The photograph above appears to show the courthouse, clerk's office, Presbyterian church, and the charred village green, referred to on some maps as Jones Park. In modern times, it is commonly referred to as the courthouse lawn, where no old growth trees remain. Arthur Butts wrote in *Monticello*, "Come, let us sit upon the Village Green / Was fairer lovelier Sylvan Grove e'er seen?" Below is the north side of Main Street (Broadway) facing east. This image was probably taken from the roof of St. Peter's Church at the corner of Liberty Street. (This is the same block as featured on pages 31 and 32.) At the corner of Bank Street, portions that were left standing of the western wall of the ruined National Union Bank are visible. (Both, courtesy of Sullivan County Historical Society.)

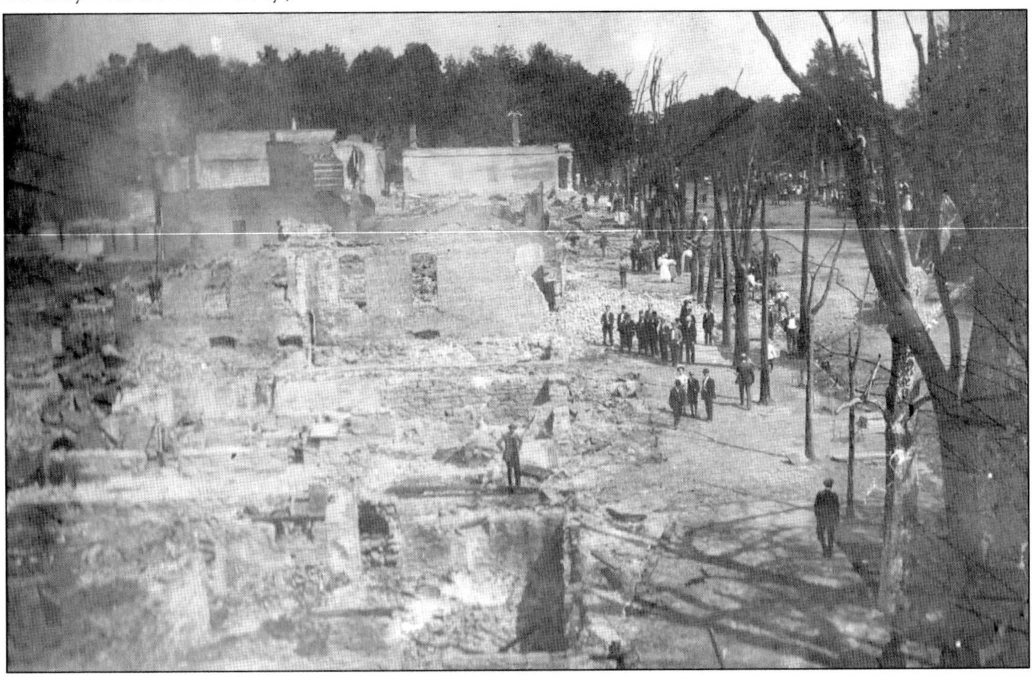

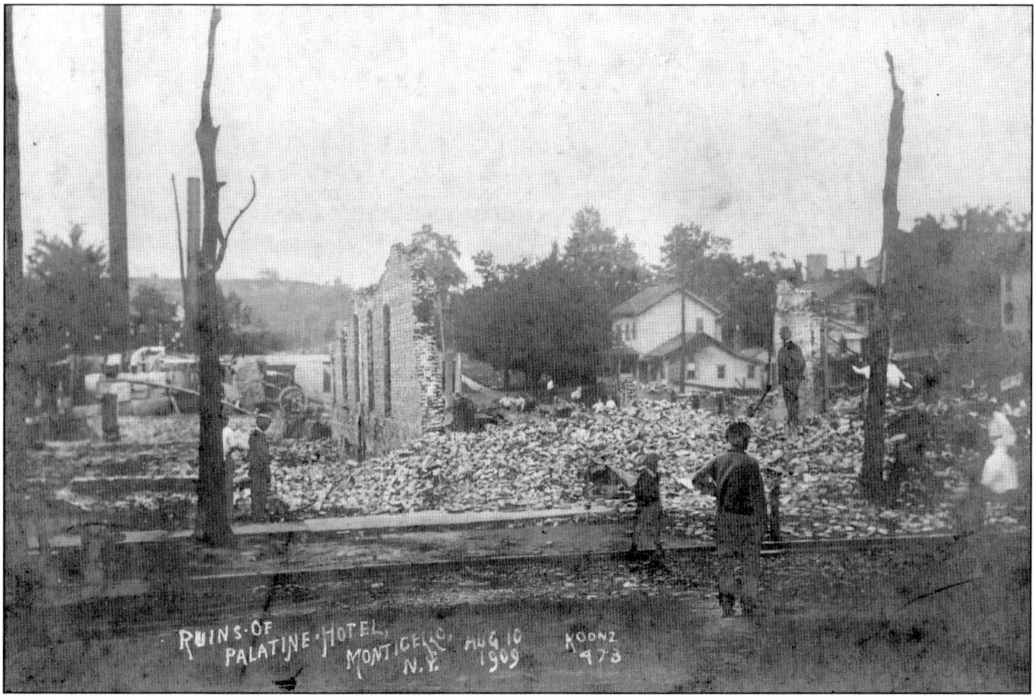

These are the ruins of Palatine Hotel. Below are some of Monticello's bravest, dousing the smoldering heap of ruins that was the village's prosperous business center. The man on the left is firefighter James Kelley, owner of Kelley's Kandy. The identities of the other firefighters and onlookers are not known. (Both, courtesy of Richard Benjamin Sr. and Monticello Fire Department.)

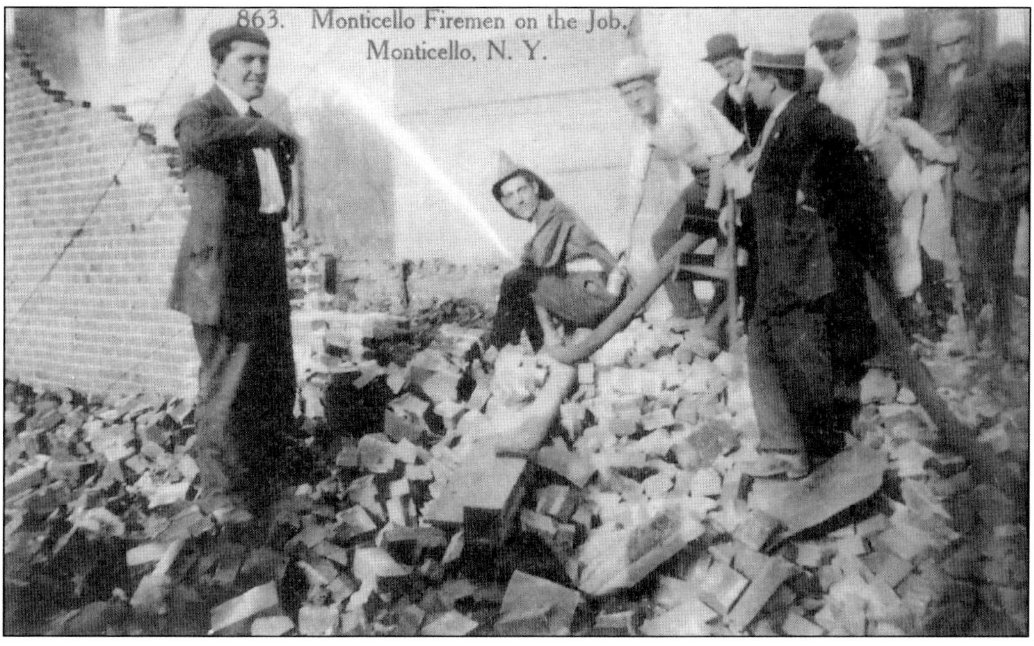

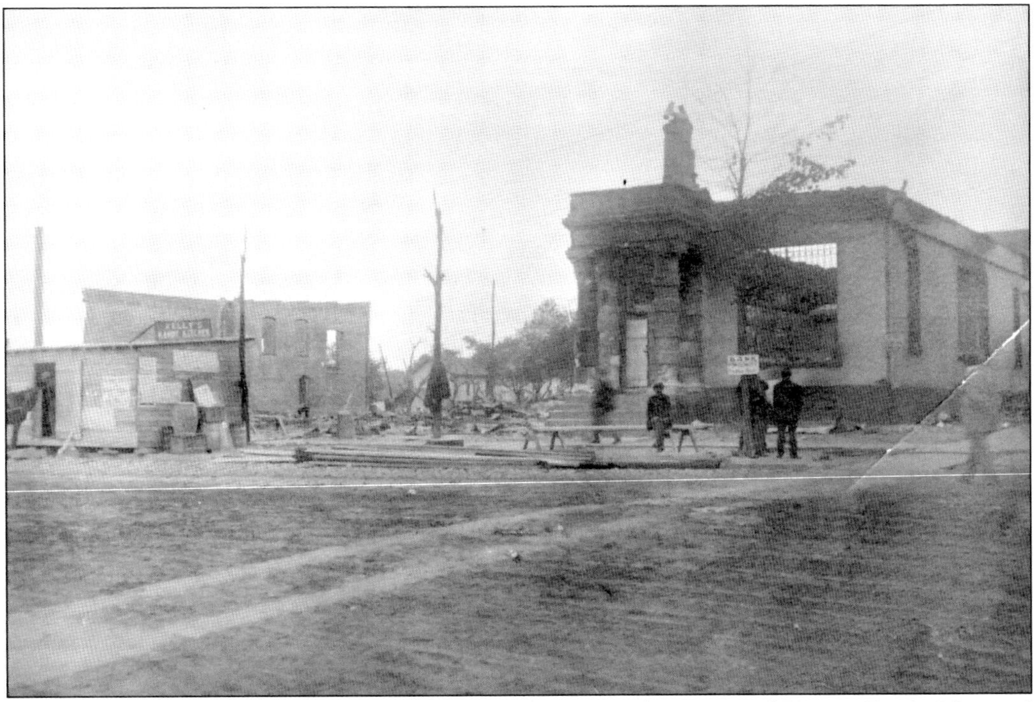

High priority for the firefighters was saving the vault at the National Union Bank. Haggard looking but victorious firemen are shown below, perched atop the charred vault of National Union Bank, its contents preserved. A more distant view of the same bank (above), taken from Mill Street (now Saint John), shows the extent of the surrounding damage. (Both, courtesy of Sullivan County Historical Society.)

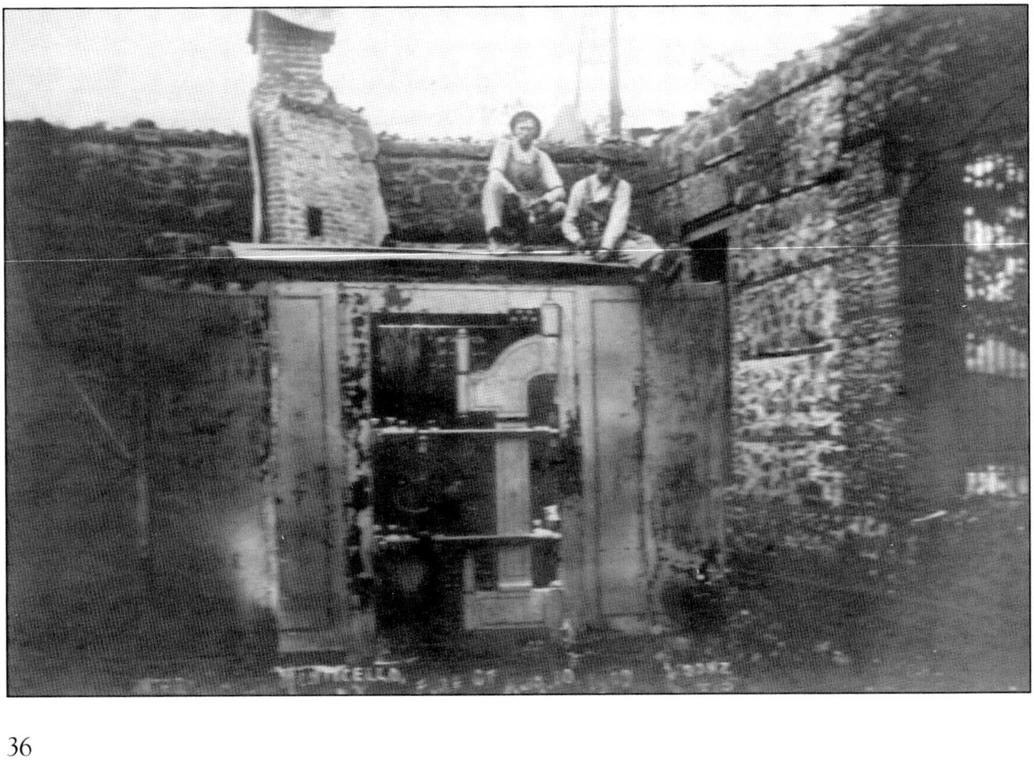

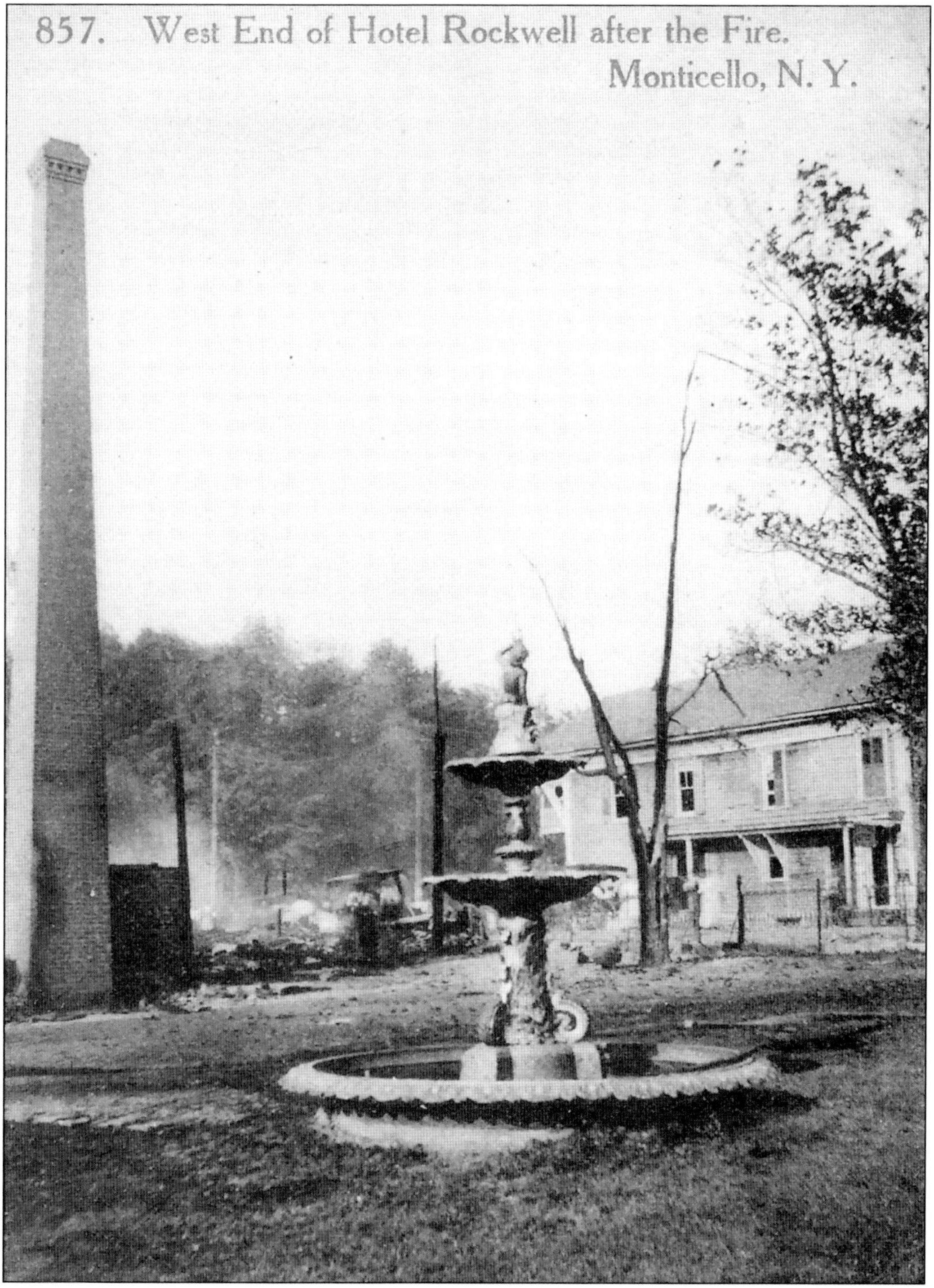

All that remained of George Rockwell's once majestic hotel was its chimney and a decorative fountain on what was once its east lawn. This chimney was still standing into the 1920s (see page 48). It is unknown whether the stack was left in place to serve as a memorial and reminder of that which was lost or if its removal was merely a low priority. (Courtesy of Richard Benjamin Sr.)

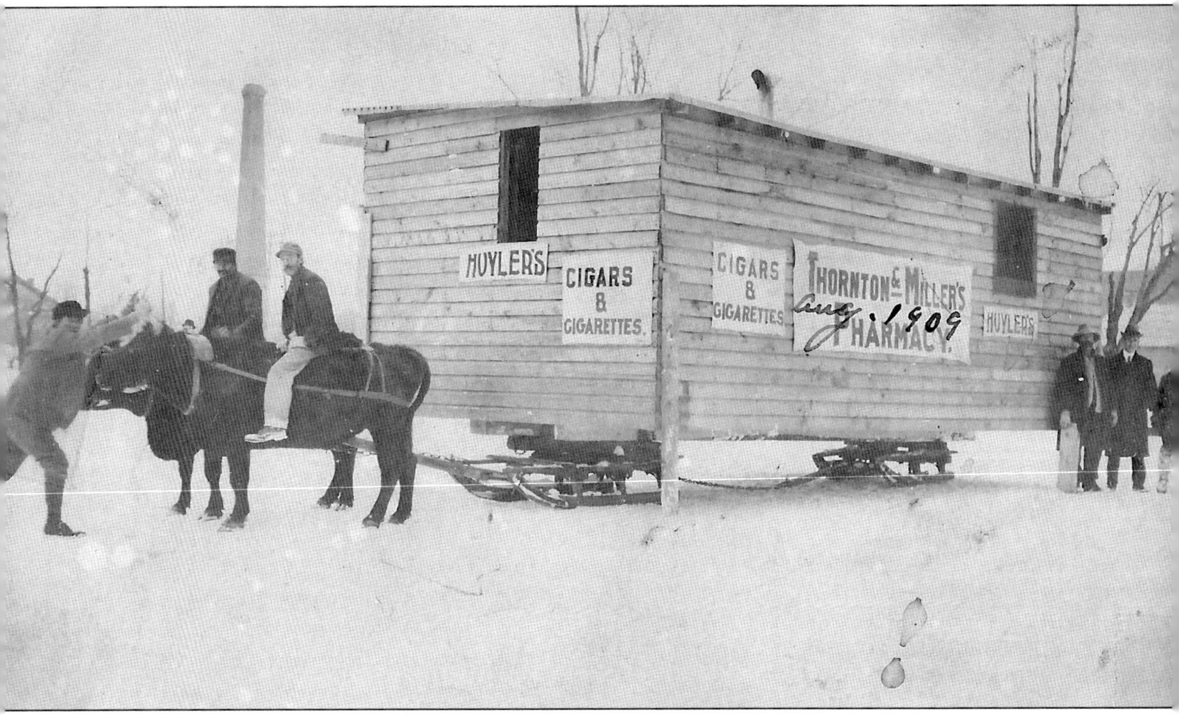

Many establishments set up temporary shanties, like this one, where they conducted business while the owners scrambled to commence the reconstruction effort. Other buildings that opened shanties included Crain's Pharmacy, William Carpenter's shoe store, the Bolsom Café, the Palatine Hotel, and Frank Kennedy's Laundry. (See page 42.) (Courtesy of Richard Benjamin Sr.)

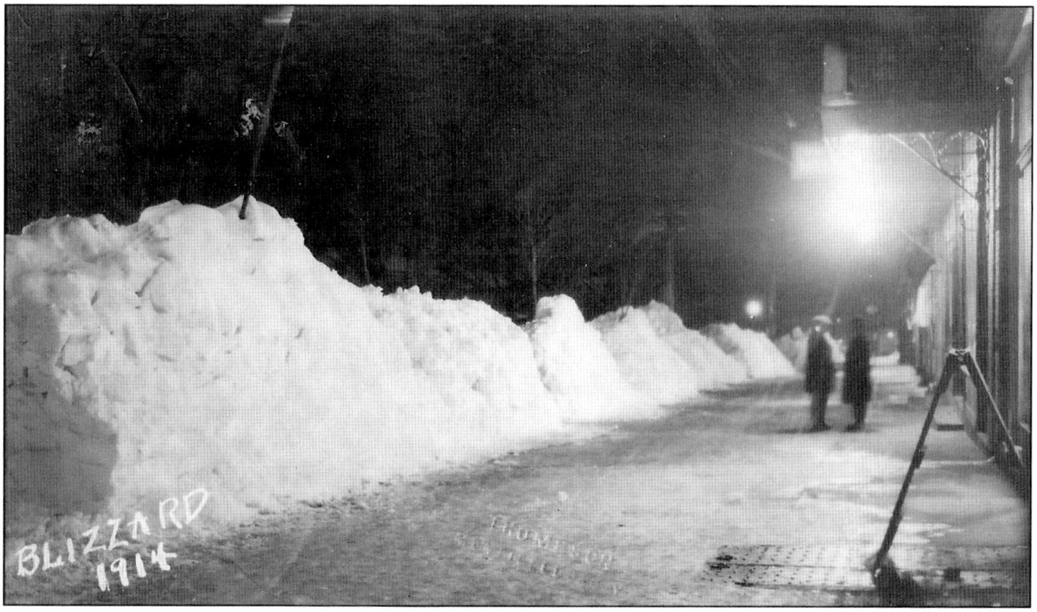

The blizzard of February 1914 dumped snow that drifted higher than most men's heads. Pictured above is a quiet night scene on Broadway, with electric lights brightening the way. Below is a similar scene of the same streetscape and storm taken during daytime. (Courtesy of Richard Benjamin Sr.)

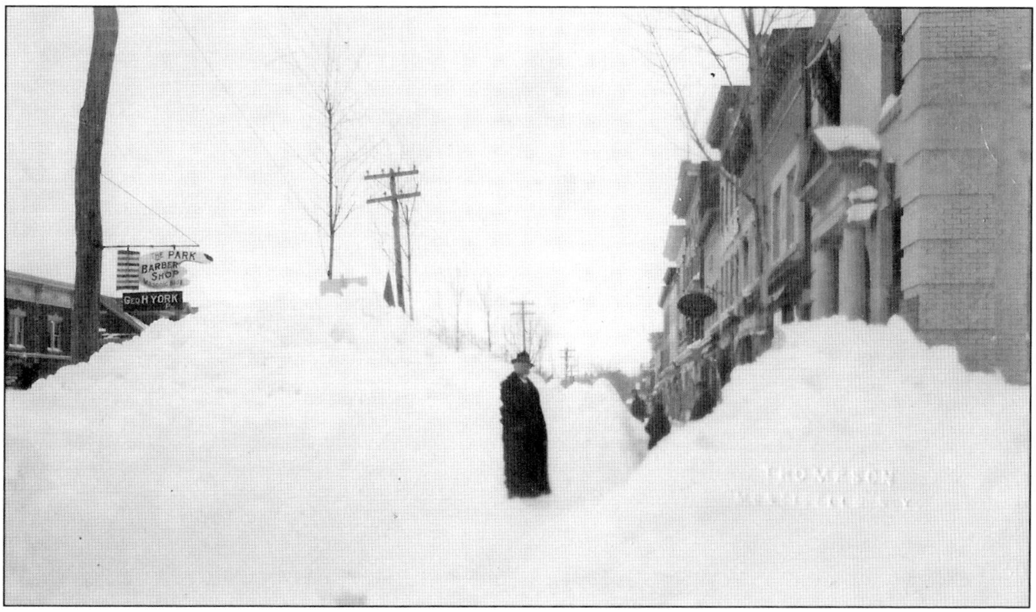

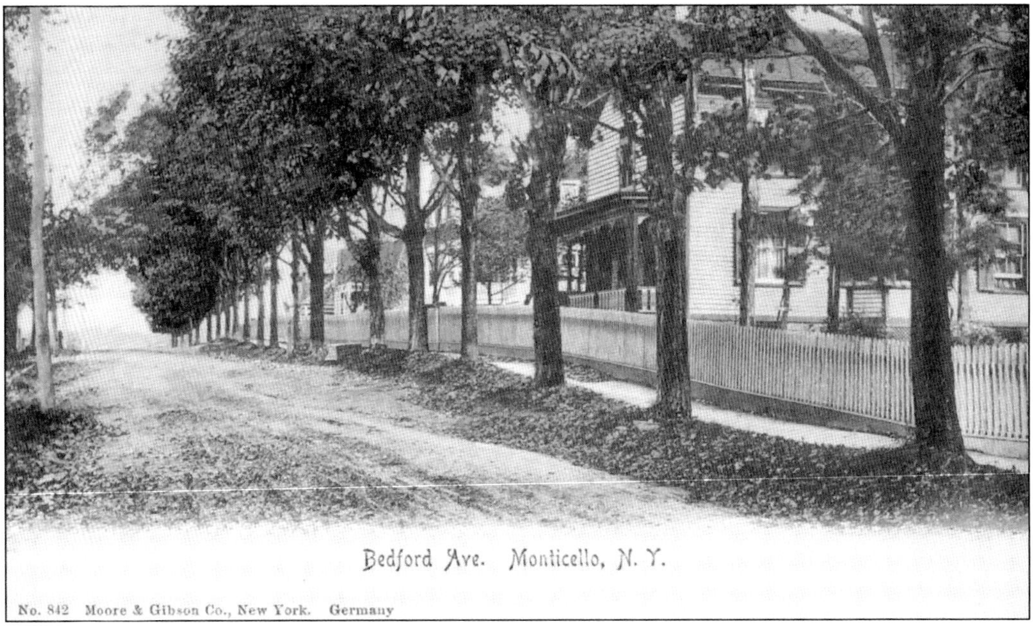

One block south of Broadway, Bedford Avenue connected Mill Street (now Saint John) and Oakley Avenue (now Lake Street). This is a view looking west. Bedford Avenue was earlier called Watkins Avenue, after David Watkins, who was the first station agent at the Monticello railroad terminal and bought the former Bedford property. When Watkins moved to Ellenville around 1895, residents renamed the street after its builder, Joshua Bedford. (Courtesy of Richard Benjamin Sr.)

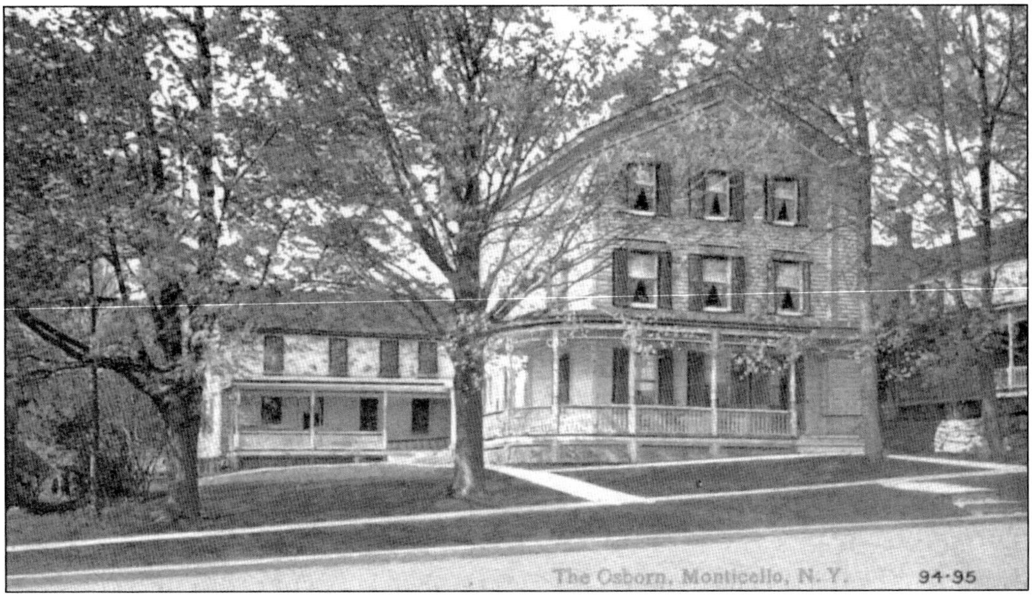

This house was purchased by Emma Osborn in 1897 from Mary Wheeler, who bought it from Frank Hahn, who later built the Hotel Rockwell. Emma and her sisters—Susan, Grace, and Nell—operated the Osborn boardinghouse. Many guests were wealthy New York City clientèle of Emma and Susan, who worked as professional seamstresses. After Nell died in 1954, the house was demolished and replaced by a motel. (Courtesy of Sullivan County Historical Society.)

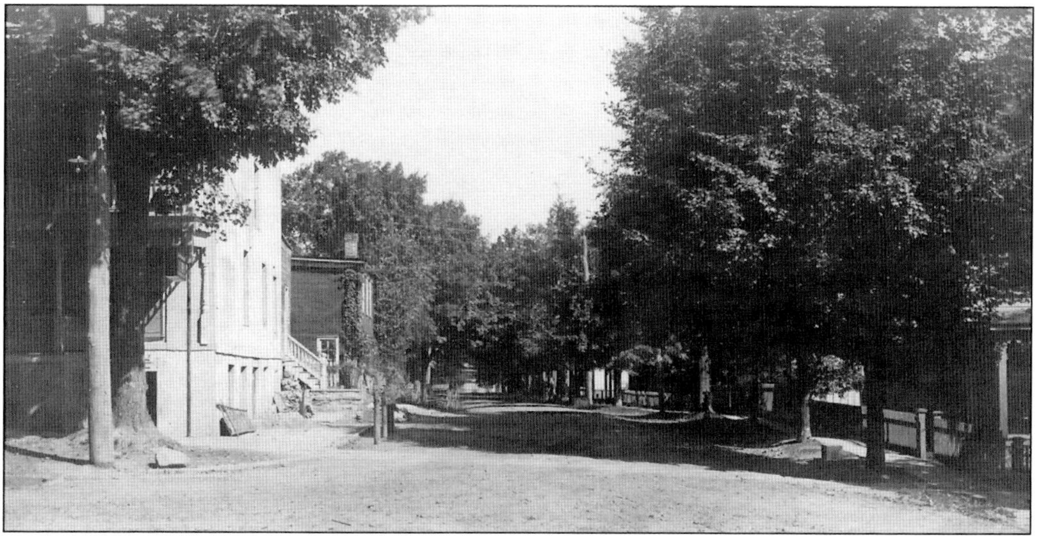

This view of Pleasant Street from Broadway looks toward what was called Pleasant Lake (Kiamesha Lake). At left is the Victoria Hotel (also called the Curley Hotel), and at right is the Presbyterian parsonage, where the village hall and the police station now stand. For a good number of years in earlier days, the third floor of the Victoria Hotel served as Monticello's temporary Masonic lodge. (Courtesy of Sullivan County Historical Society.)

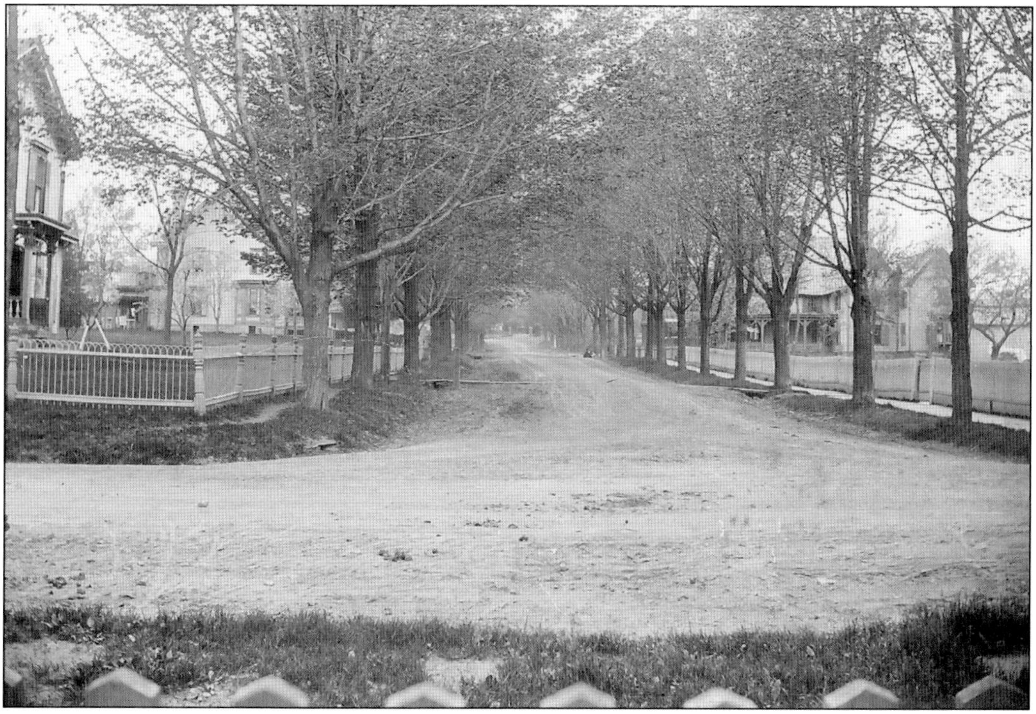

At the corner of Hammond Street, the photographer looks across Pleasant Street west on Hamilton Avenue. At left is the home of Judge Timothy F. Bush and Mary E. Bush. Next to it is the fine Victorian residence of Edith and Mildred Bennett, daughters of George Bennett, who built the house. At the northwest end, behind the courthouse and county jail, is the LaTourette boardinghouse. (Courtesy of Sullivan County Historical Society.)

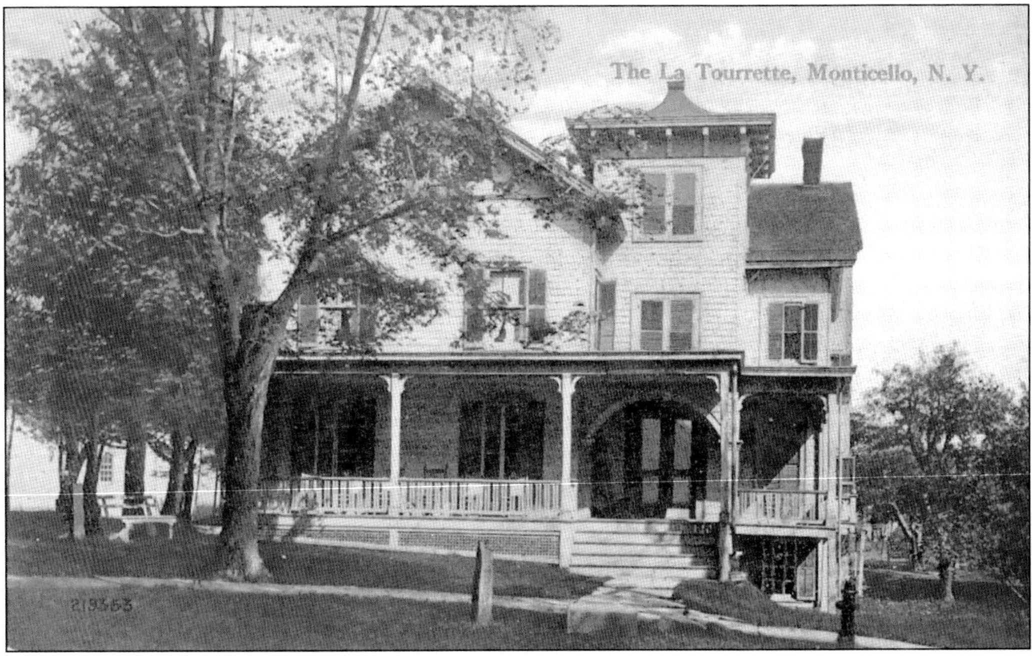

This single-family dwelling was converted to a boardinghouse by Bert LaTourette, later president of the village board of trustees. The home stood approximately where the new Stoloff and Silver law offices now sit at the top of Hamilton Avenue. Prior to LaTourette, the home was occupied by the family of attorney James L. Stewart. (Courtesy of Richard Benjamin Sr.)

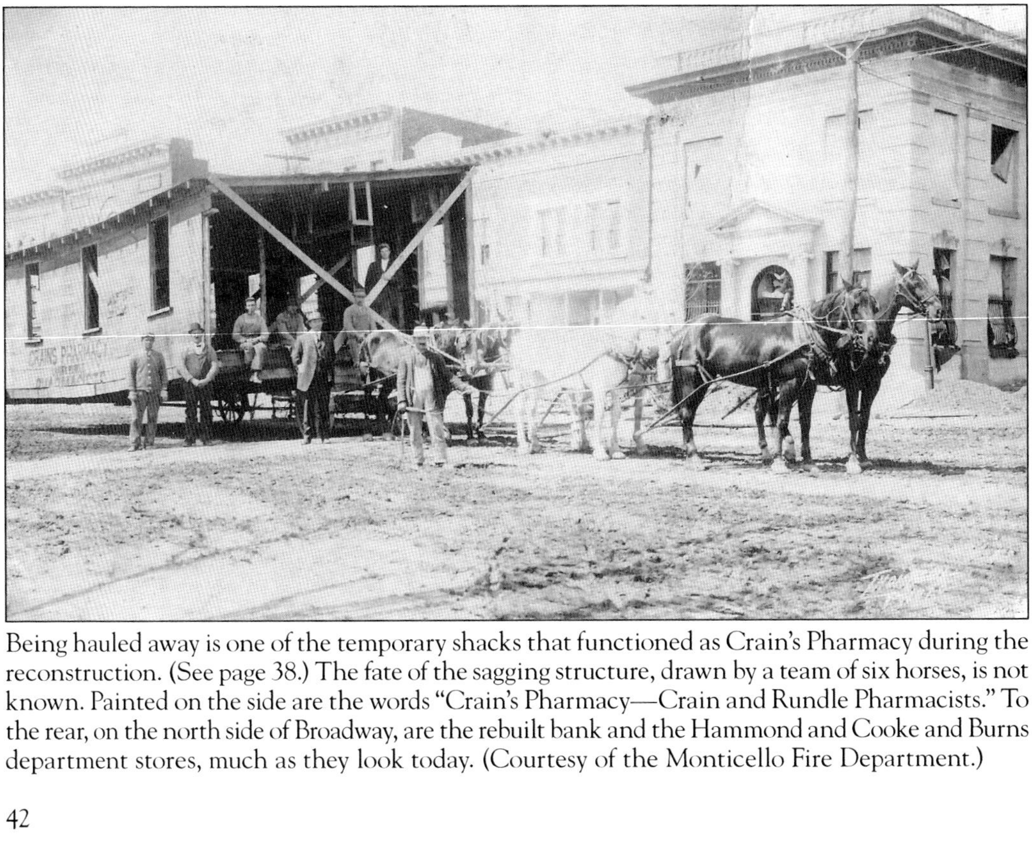

Being hauled away is one of the temporary shacks that functioned as Crain's Pharmacy during the reconstruction. (See page 38.) The fate of the sagging structure, drawn by a team of six horses, is not known. Painted on the side are the words "Crain's Pharmacy—Crain and Rundle Pharmacists." To the rear, on the north side of Broadway, are the rebuilt bank and the Hammond and Cooke and Burns department stores, much as they look today. (Courtesy of the Monticello Fire Department.)

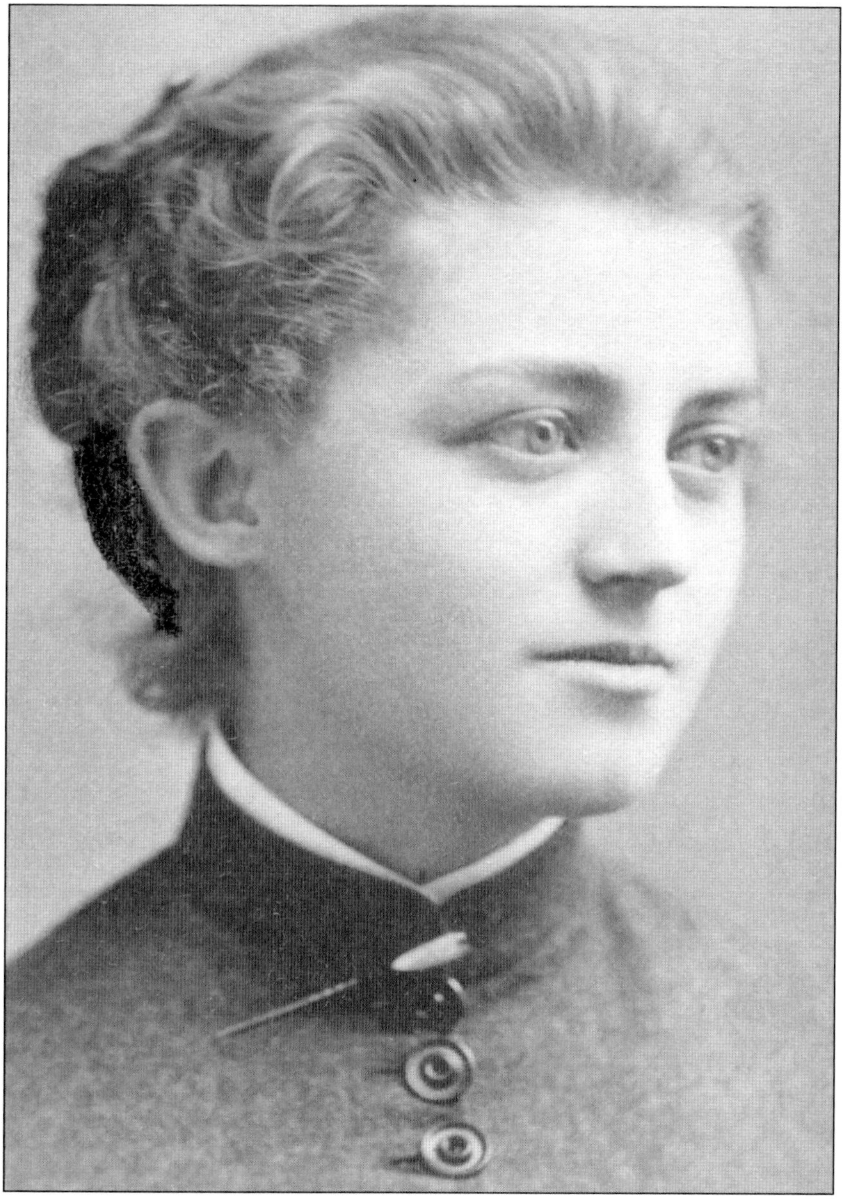

Jennie Lee Niven was born in 1867 and died June 8, 1927. She was the daughter of Thornton Augustus Thompson Niven (1841–1905) and Pluma A. Tremain (1843–1912). Two generations earlier, the surname had been MacNiven. Jennie was a beautiful and talented woman with good business sense, but her behavior was sometimes impulsive, bringing unintended consequences. As owner of the Lyceum Theater (where Kerr's Garage was later built and more recently Miller Automatic), which was the target of arson more than once (see page 20), controversy and tragedy seemed to follow Jennie. The last occupant of the former mansion of Gen. A. C. Niven (built 1805, dismantled 1930), Jennie was married three times. Her first two husbands, Samuel B. Greene and Episcopal vicar David S. Howell II (later a Newark, New Jersey, judge), each died of a self-inflicted gunshot to the head. Advertising man and exhibitor Louis F. Guimond was her third and final husband, with whom she lies buried in the plot belonging to her parents in Rock Ridge Cemetery. (Courtesy of Daniel K. Niven.)

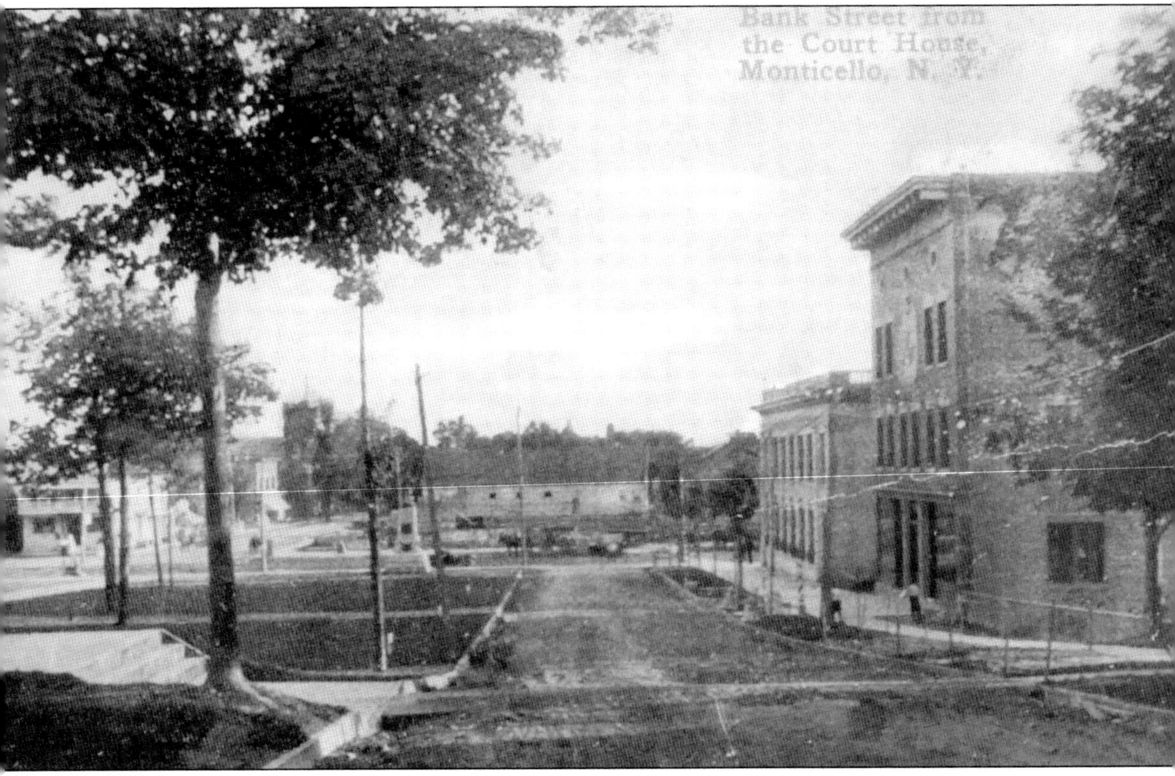

This view looks south down Bank Street toward Broadway sometime after 1910. Across Broadway, only remnants of the burned Rockwell Hotel remain. The Masonic building and National Union Bank, at right, however, have both been rebuilt. After the fire, rather than rebuilding in Monticello, George Rockwell opened a hotel called Liberty House in the village by that name about 10 miles west. (Courtesy of Richard Benjamin Sr.)

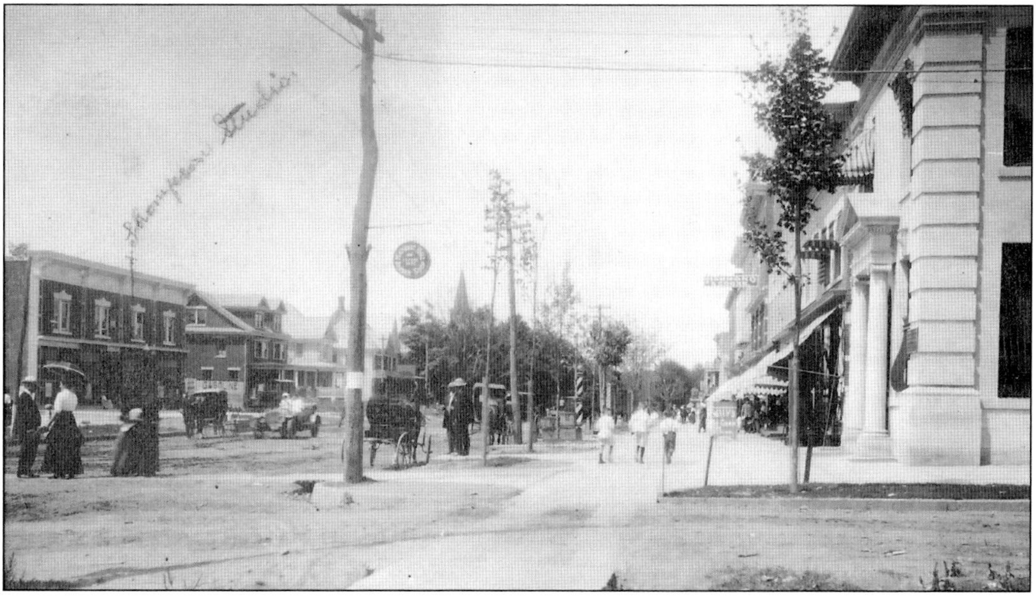

This image shows Broadway and Bank Street, between 1910 (after the fire) and 1912 (when Broadway was paved), looking west. Hammond and Cooke department store can also be seen. Across the street, above the lady with the parasol, someone has written in pencil, identifying the location of Howard Thompson's photography studio in the *Republican Watchman* building. Next door, gasoline was sold. A round sign mounted on the rough-hewn utility pole points up Bank Street to "Masonic Hall Barber Shop, G. York, Prop." Below, a February 1914 winter view shows an ox at rest after plowing Broadway. (Both, courtesy of Richard Benjamin Sr.)

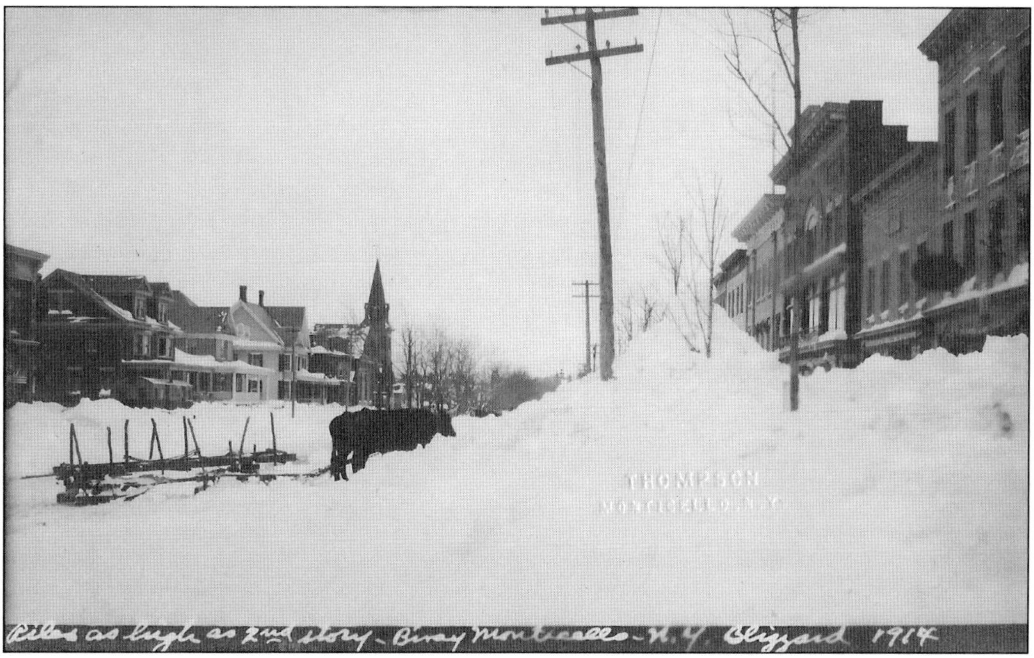

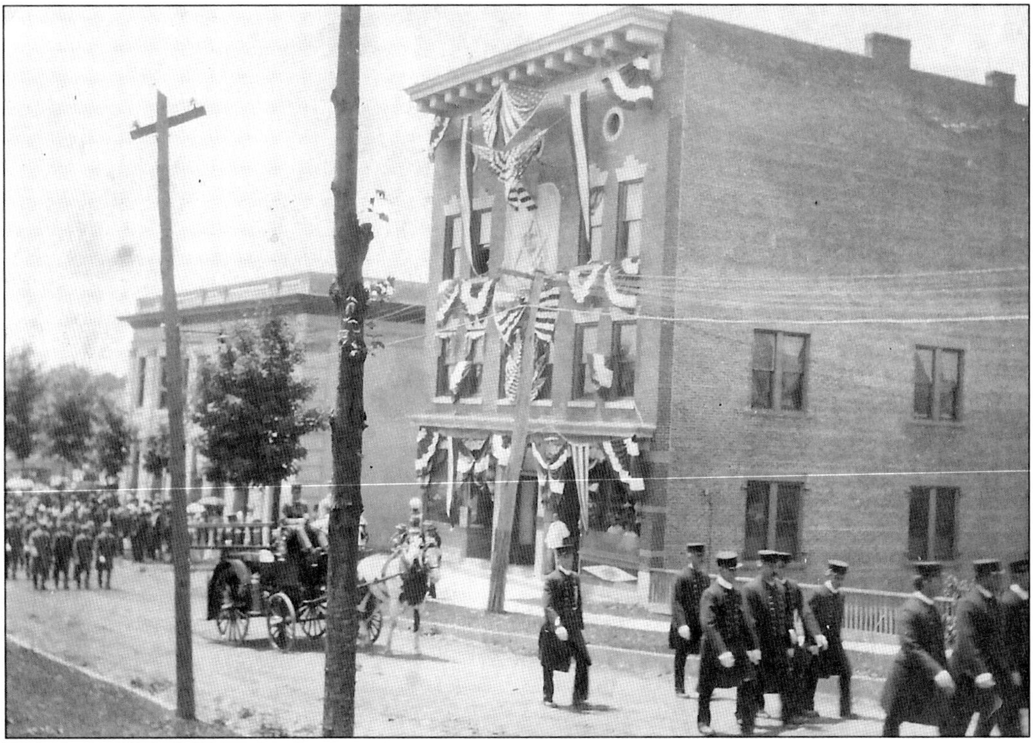

Firemen roll past the reconstructed Masonic temple. Although Monticello's Masons now meet in Liberty, a stone at the northeast corner of the Masonic Building at 5 Bank Street (above) still attests: "This cornerstone with its Archives taken from the ruins of the Temple burned Aug. 10, 1909 was relaid in the new with Masonic honors Nov. 18th following." (Courtesy of Susan Benton Schock.)

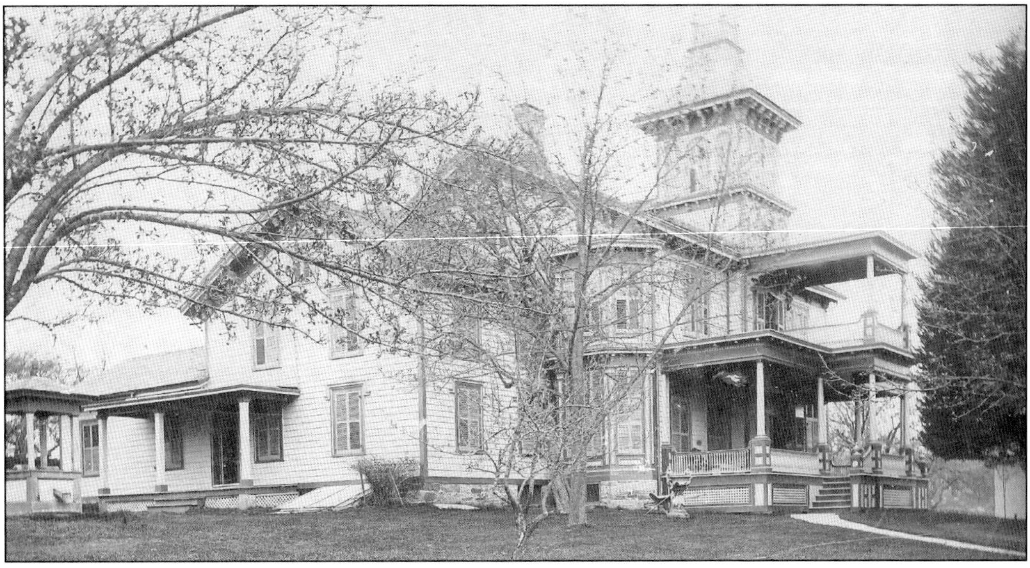

The above picture is of the Bushnell building, taken December 14, 1898. This property is one of the historical landmarks of Monticello. Names from the Bushnell family are connected with the early history of Monticello. The building now houses the Sullivan County sheriff's office. (W. Milliken photograph, courtesy of Sullivan County Historical Society.)

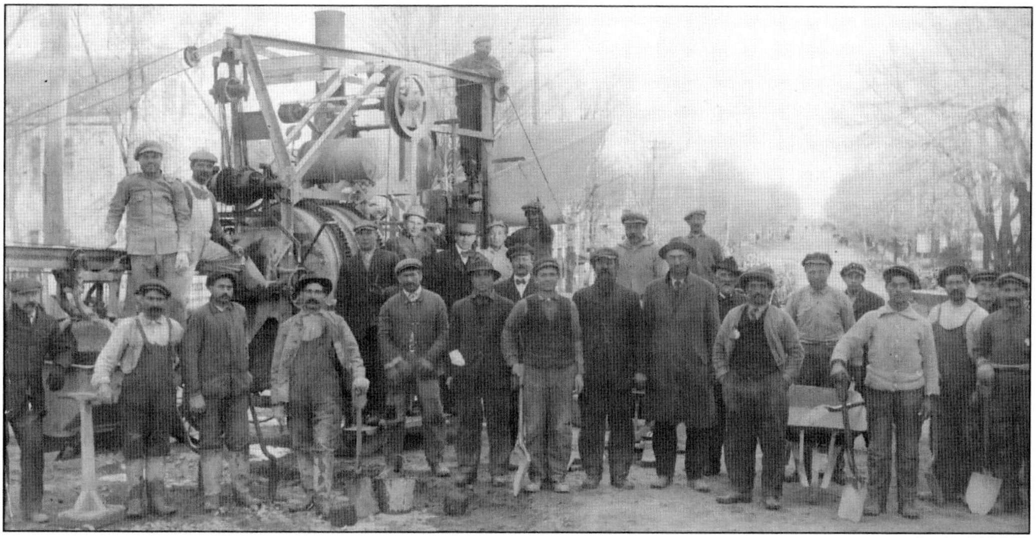

Following the devastating fire of 1909, the first paving of Monticello's main thoroughfare took place in 1912. Previously, Main Street (Broadway) was a dirt road riddled with potholes. Above the men appears to be a portable cement mixer. Workmen may have found it most productive to have a machine in which to mix cement and then spread it on a one-lane width. Since the closest thing to a loader in those days was a wagon, sand, stone, and cement were presumably shoveled by hand. From the stack in the background, it appears the drum may have been steam-driven. The original survey of the Newburgh-Cochecton Turnpike, measured and recorded by Samuel F. Jones and filed at Kingston before Judge William A. Thompson (ironically), measured Broadway as 99 feet (six rods) wide and about 1 mile long. (Courtesy of Monticello Fire Department.)

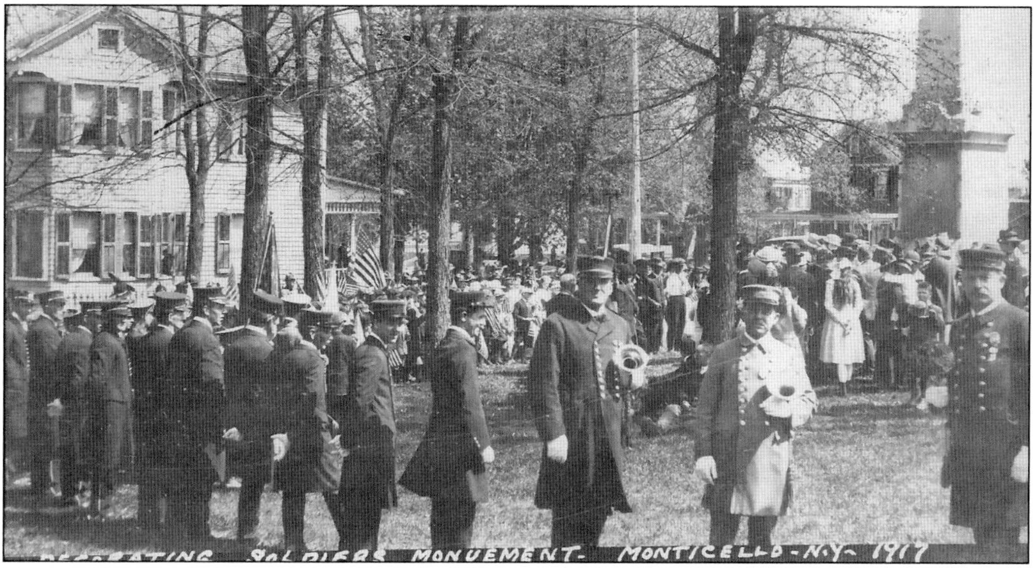

Shown here are members of Monticello's fire companies and civilians decorating the *Soldiers and Sailors Monument* at the three-way corner of Jefferson and Young Streets and Broadway. In addition to depicting an annual community rite, this photograph gives a rare view of a vanished neighborhood around Young and Wheeler Streets. It was demolished in the 1970s to construct a municipal parking lot and the Sullivan County Government Center. (Courtesy of Monticello Fire Department.)

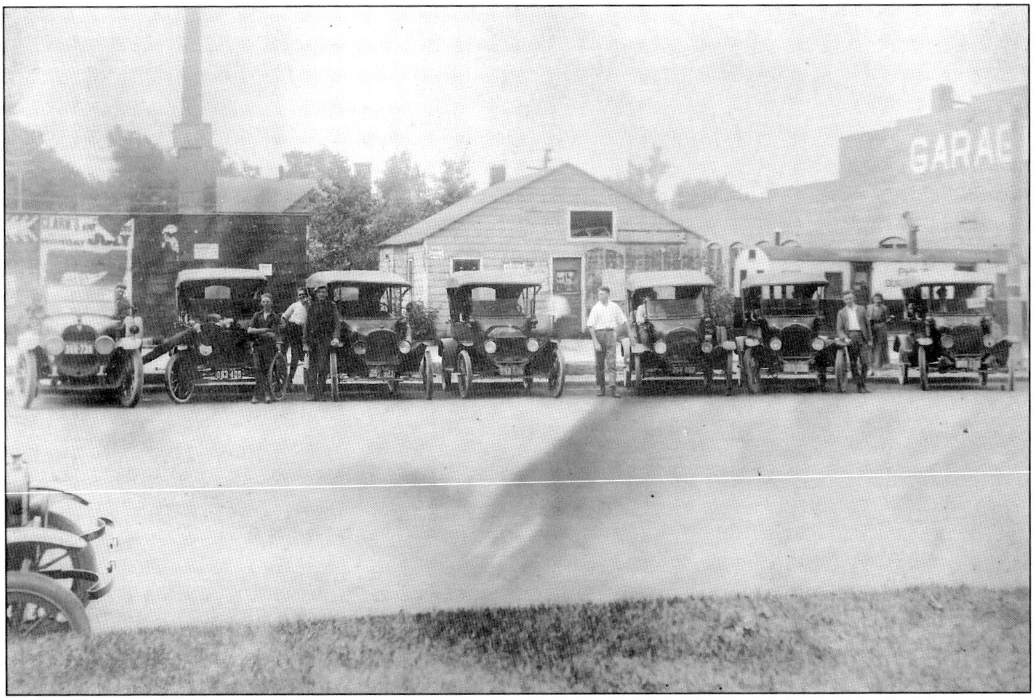

Where the Hotel Rockwell once rose, by 1920 only the chimney remained. A broadside tells of Clark's Animal Circus on a Monday in July. Another announces a masquerade ball. A small sign advertises Packard autos. The door says "Rockwell Office" or "Rockwell Café." Above at left, a sign papered over seems to read "Lyceum Theatre." Phil Scheuren's Quick Lunch wagon is at right. (Courtesy of Richard Benjamin Sr.)

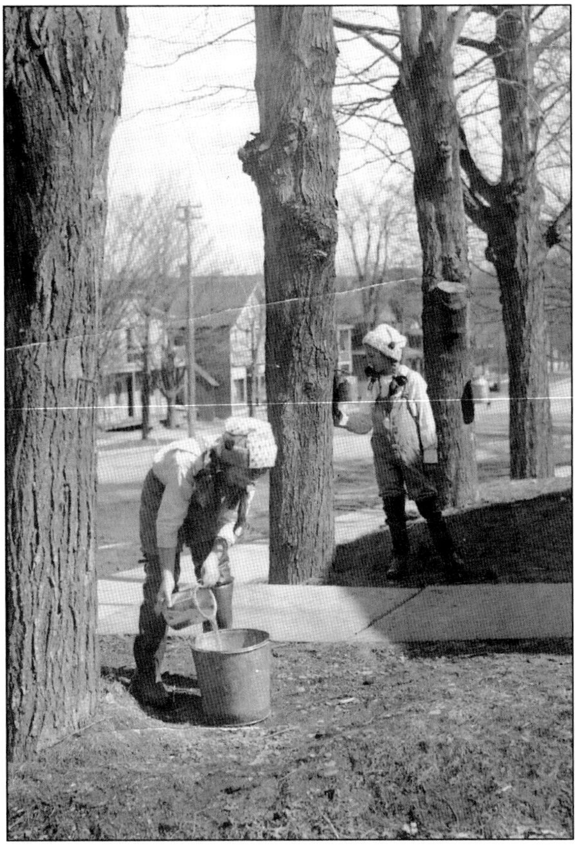

Stately maples that once lined Broadway served as more than just shade trees, as this c. 1913 photograph attests. Elizabeth and Emma Jean Scriber (daughters of *Republican Watchman* editor and publisher A. M. Scriber) tap sap from one such tree, in front of the Scriber house on West Broadway, close to Jefferson Street. All these trees are gone now. (Courtesy of Susan Benton Schock.)

Virginia Thompson Niven lived in a large single-family house on East Broadway across from Rock Ridge Cemetery. Shown here feeding chickens, Virginia was born August 4, 1867, in Monticello to John Alexander Thompson and Agnes Nancy Dunham of Thompson Ridge (Orange County). A graduate of Columbia University, she taught art at the Seguin Physiological School for "weak-minded and weak-bodied children" in New Jersey. She married Kenneth Duncan Lozier Niven on June 27, 1907, and died February 22, 1957, in Monticello. (Courtesy of Daniel K. Niven.)

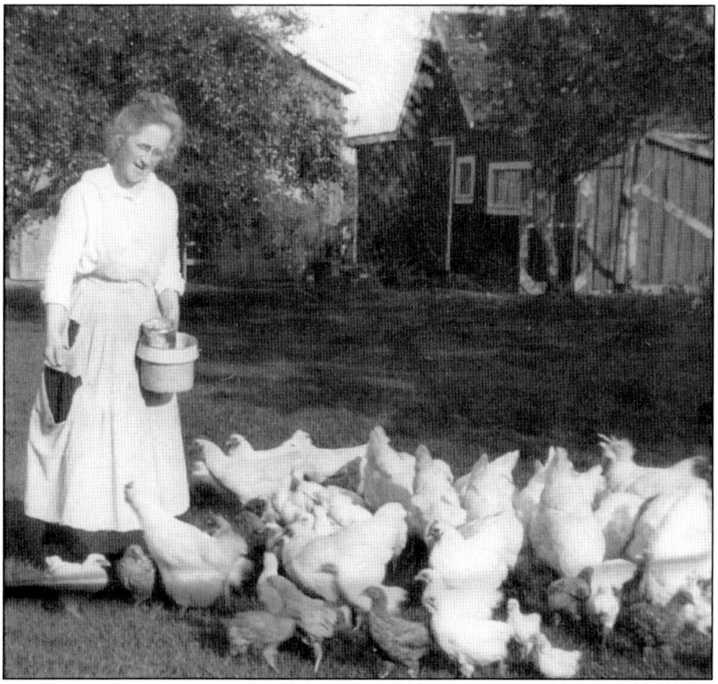

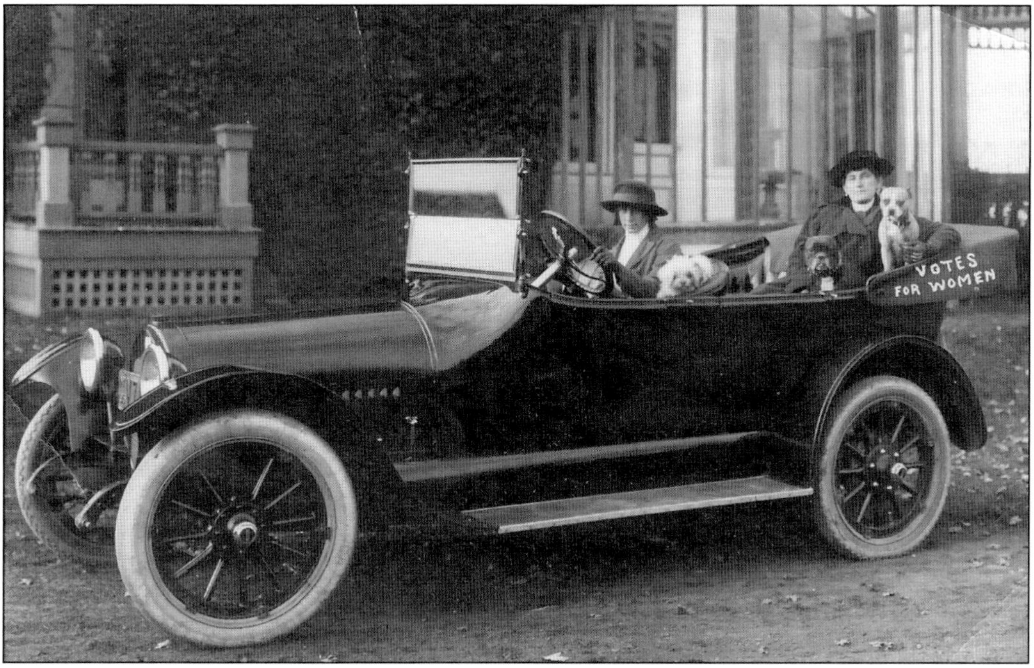

With daughter Alma at the wheel, Elisabeth Muller is pictured here in 1917, leaving their castle in a black Buick convertible for 1,500 miles to crisscross New York and Canada. The pair campaigned for the New York State Assembly, advocated for woman suffrage, and opposed the war against Muller's native Germany. Accompanying them were three canine companions, French bulldog Napoleon (center), an English boxer (in Muller's arms), and a fuzzy dog with Alma. (Courtesy of Susan Benton Schock.)

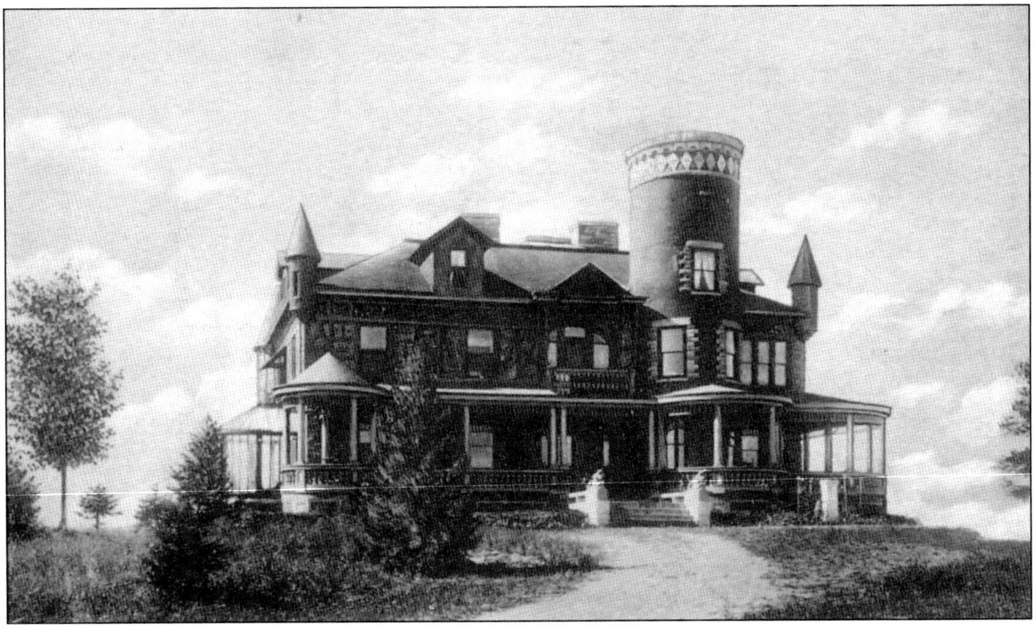

Muller Castle, built of stone, stood on Monticello's Egg Hill near Varnell Road. Boasting 18 large bedrooms, 4 baths, 6 toilets, 3 dining rooms, a salon, and a foyer used as an office, the estate also had several outbuildings. They included a wagon house, shed, large chicken house, a six-room bungalow, a seven-room stone lodge, and a stone barn with running water. The estate later became part of Lazar's Bungalow Colony, also known as Lazar's Castle. From 1958 through the 1970s, it was Castle Country Club. The photograph below shows the castle in the early 1960s. An earlier photograph appears above. (Above, courtesy of Valerie Yaros; below, courtesy of Shari Parson.)

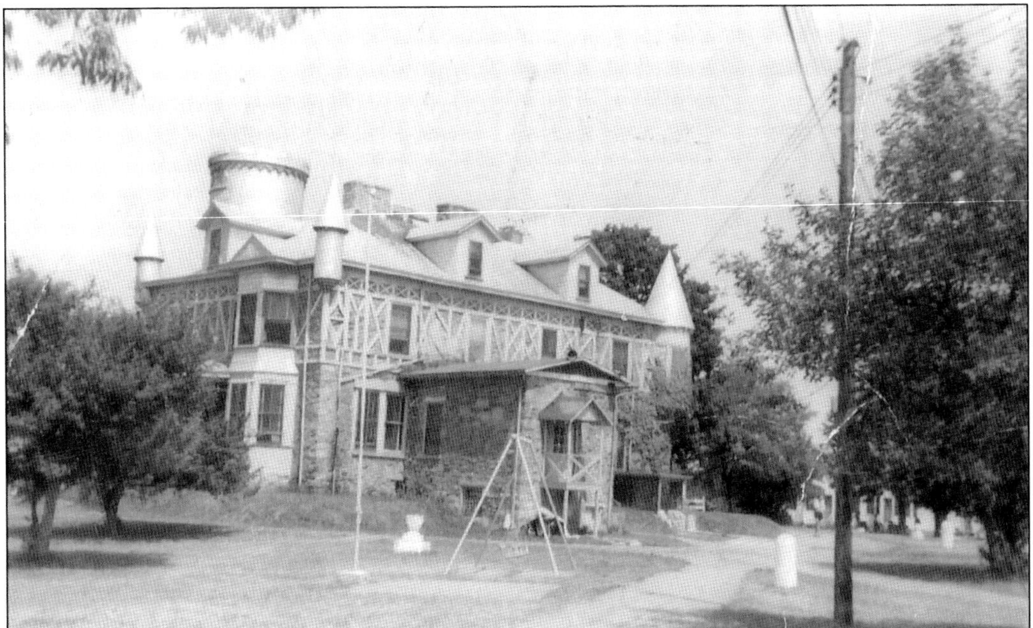

Elisabeth Marie (Worth) Muller graduated in 1903 from the women's law class at the Heidenfelds and Meisner institutes in New York City. She was a delegate to the National American Woman Suffrage Association, which met in Philadelphia in 1912. Allied with Theodore Roosevelt, she made multiple runs for the New York State Assembly as a Progressive. (Courtesy of Susan Benton Schock.)

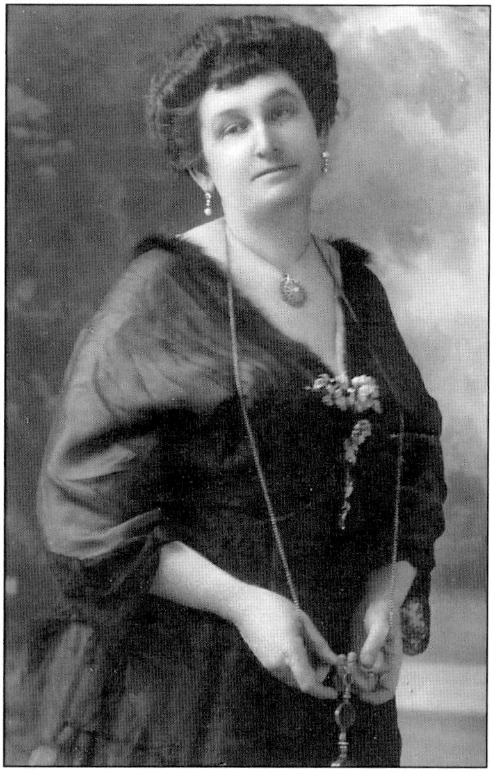

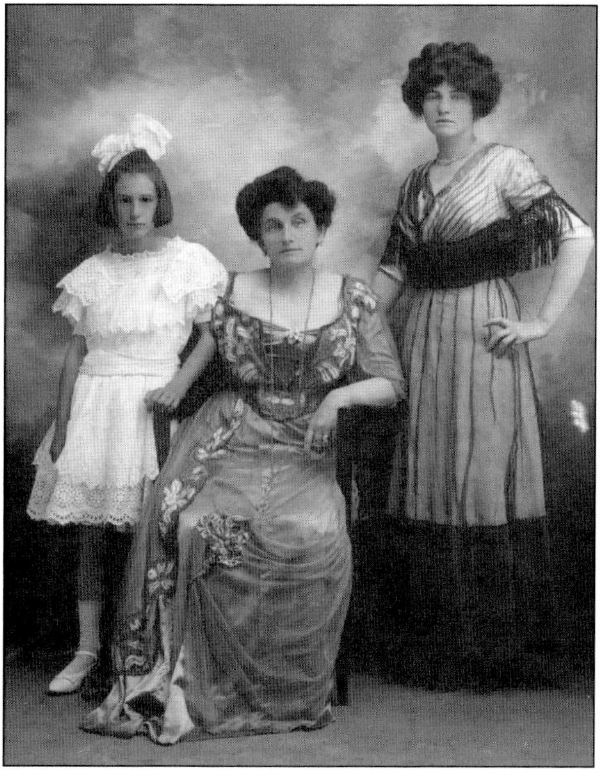

Elisabeth Muller's daughters Alma (right) and Phyllis Muller (left) supported their mother's crusade for women's voting. Alma was an athlete and fine horsewoman, once riding from the family's Long Island home to Monticello in two days. She married Frank Morgan (born Frank Wupperman), who played the wizard in the *Wizard of Oz*. (Courtesy of John Conway.)

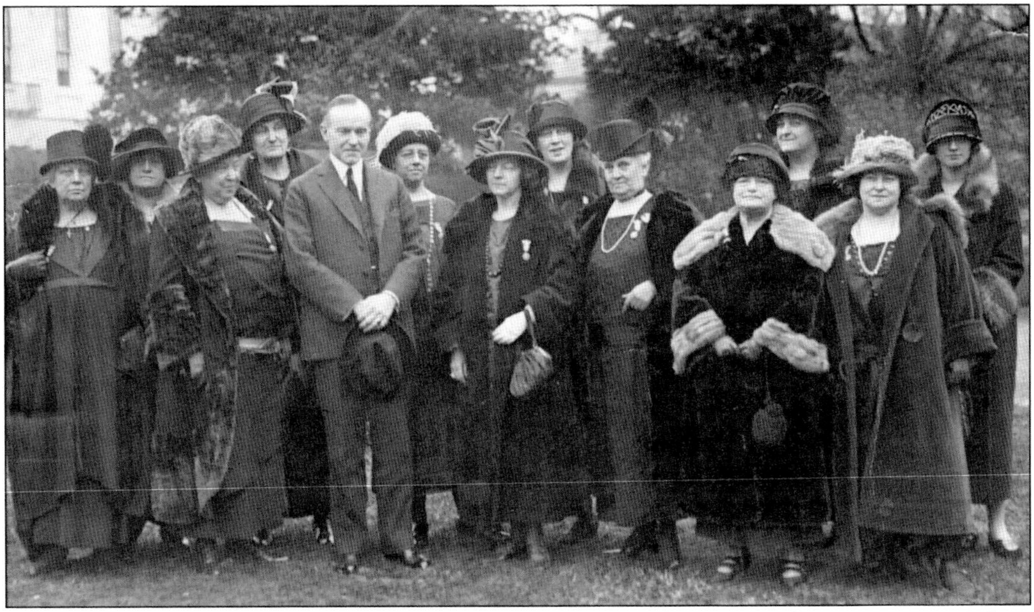

Elisabeth Muller (second row, second from left) of New York is pictured next to Pres. Calvin Coolidge with representatives of the oldest women's Republican club in the United States. The women met with the president and his wife, Grace (first row, fourth from left). "I attended four meetings yesterday, and on Monday . . . I attended the meeting of the New Yorkers . . . a dinner to the Women's Lawyers Club; Tuesday four club meetings; two dinners Wednesday, and Thursday the Legislative League," she wrote for the *Republican Watchman*. (Courtesy of John Conway.)

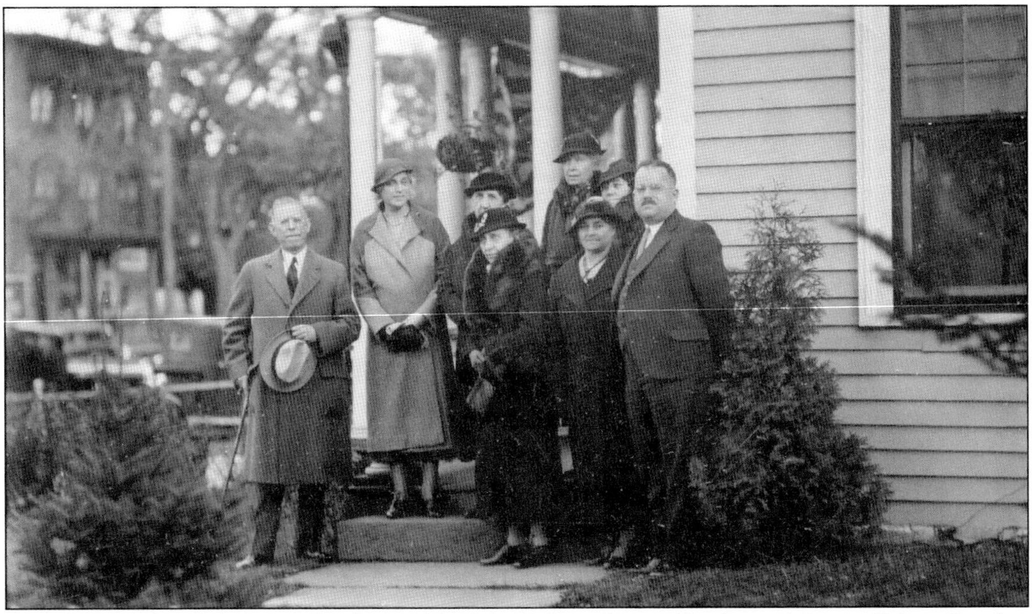

From left to right on the ground in front of the John P. Jones house (the first in Monticello) on October 12, 1934, are Dr. Julius Rosenthal, Harriett Jones, Agnes Fairchild, and Rev. Dr. William Arrowsmith Crawford. Standing on the steps are Renee Rosenthal, Edith Bennett, Carolina (Mrs. J. P.) Roosa, and Mildred Bennett. They all lived close by, and many had old Monticello surnames. The Rosenthals and Harriett Jones occupied the building behind them. (Courtesy of Daniel K. Niven.)

William B. McMillan coauthored a history of the 143rd Regiment and commanded Post 205 of the Grand Army of the Republic. In 1907, he cofounded the Sullivan County SPCA and conducted lectures for the Bureau of Farmers Institute. McMillen told a Methodist congregation in 1915 of meeting Abraham Lincoln at Camp Chase, Maryland, in November 1862, calling Lincoln "a very sympathetic man . . . easily moved by the afflictions of others." McMillan told of Hannah Hammond of Monticello, whose son ran away to be a Confederate officer and was taken captive. Yielding to pleas of Methodist clergy, Lincoln ordered the prisoner set free rather than shot, allowing a "happy reunion" back home in Monticello. McMillan served 30 years as treasurer of Monticello Freemasons. He died at age 83, June 14, 1926. Pictured below is his funeral at Rock Ridge Cemetery. (Right, courtesy of Richard Benjamin Sr.; below, courtesy of Monticello Lodge No. 532.)

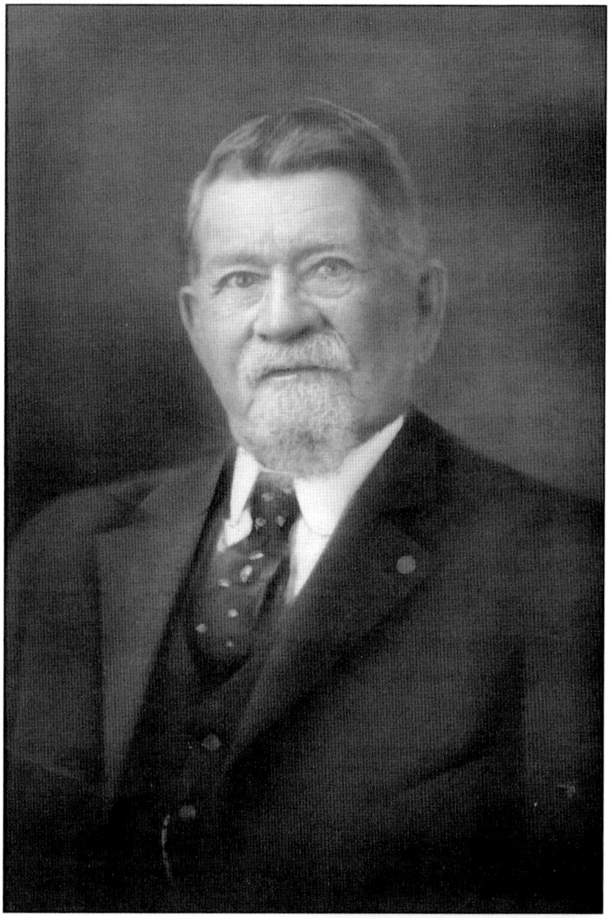

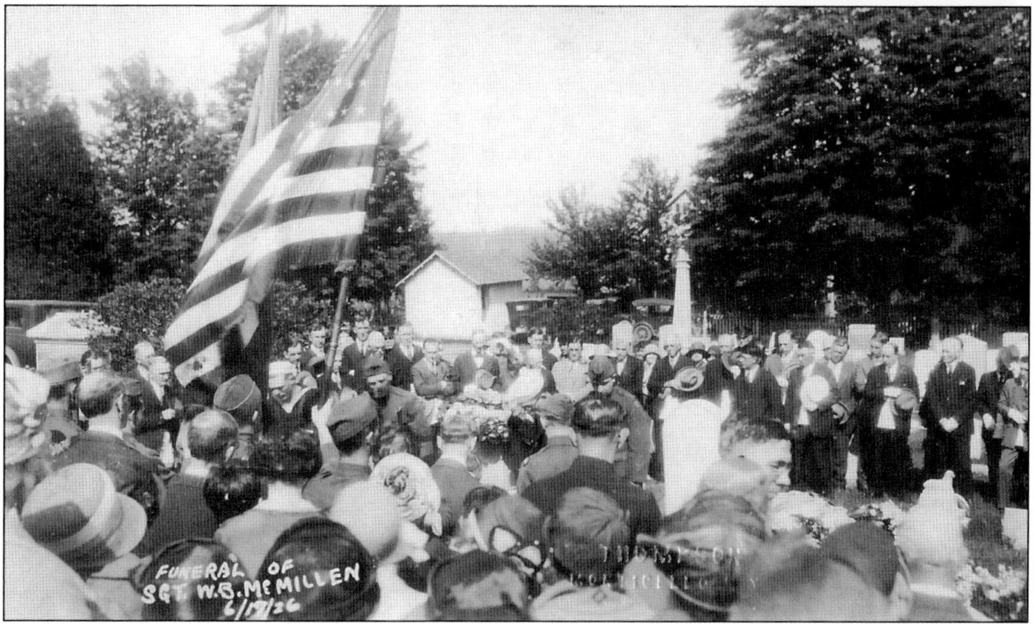

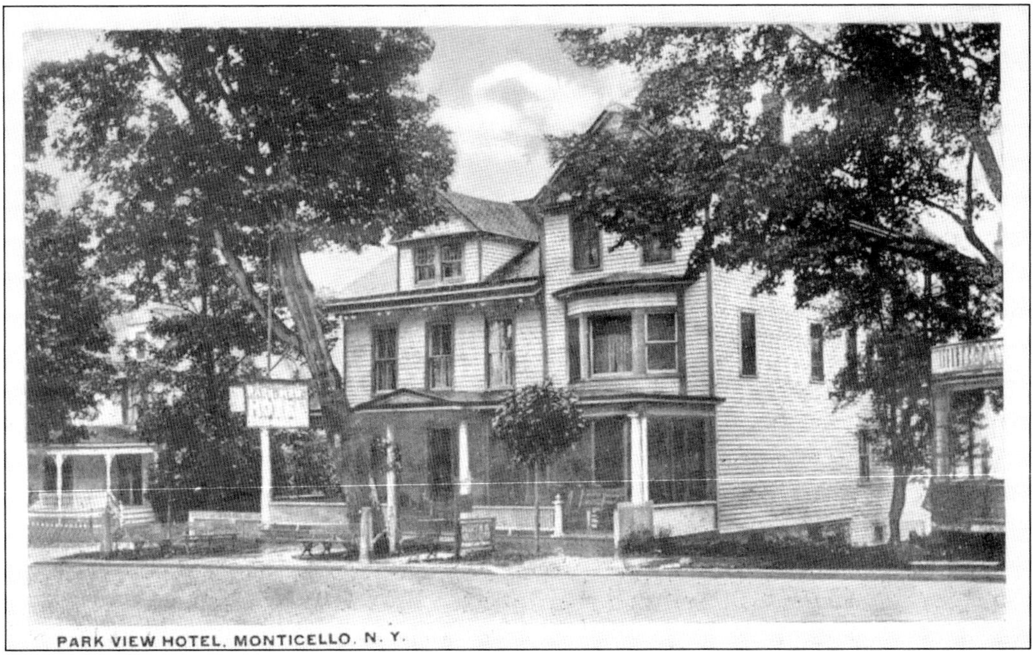

The Park View Hotel, opposite the village park, also called the village green and occasionally Jones Park (nowadays known as courthouse lawn), at 197 Broadway was then owned by M. A. Turner. It advertised "Large airy rooms, well heated, modern improvements. Special rates for fall and winter. First-class table." (Courtesy of Richard Benjamin Sr.)

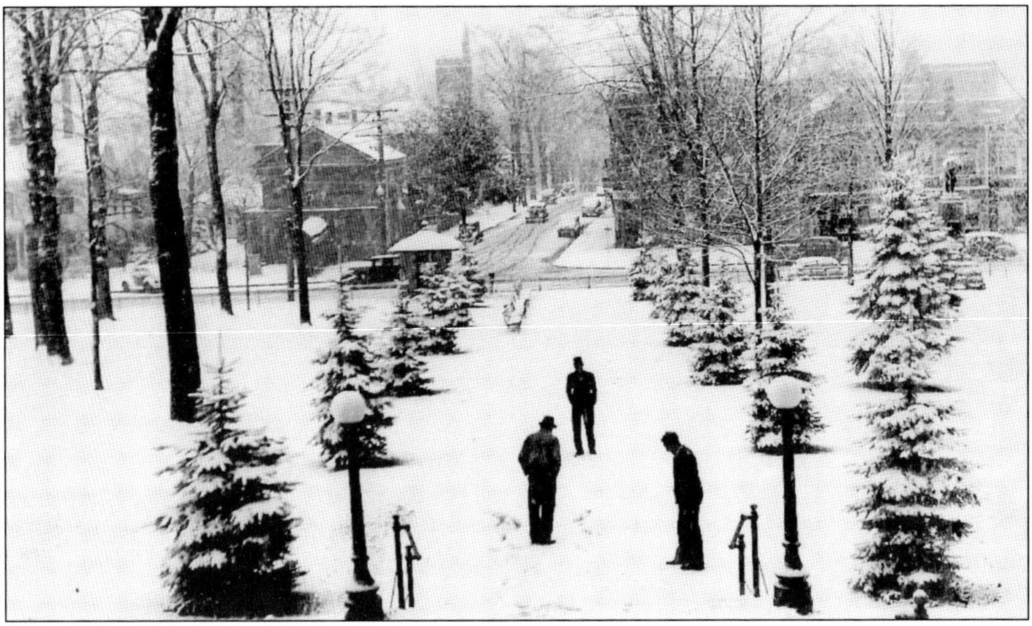

From the steps of the courthouse on November 4, 1934, this photograph looks north up Saint John Street toward the train station. At left is the Park Restaurant, owned by George and Alexandra Karamechedis. The one-time residence of village founder John P. Jones is to its left. Two of the three men shown are longtime Sheriff Harry Borden and Deputy Sheriff Ed Lane. (Courtesy of Helen Karamechedis Oliva.)

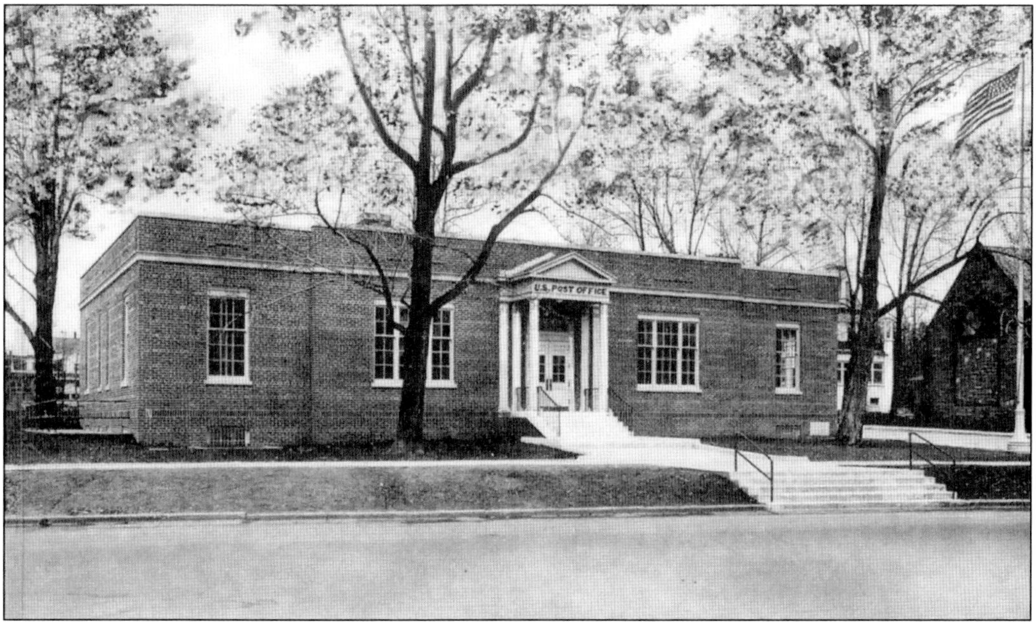

The present Monticello Post Office was started in 1934 under the federal Works Progress Administration and dedicated May 19, 1935, by Franklin Roosevelt's postmaster general, James A. Farley, who was also the New York State Democratic committee chairman and ran for president. The U.S. House of Representatives Committee on Buildings and Grounds heard extensive testimony as early as 1916 on Monticello's need for a new post office. (Courtesy of Richard Benjamin Sr.)

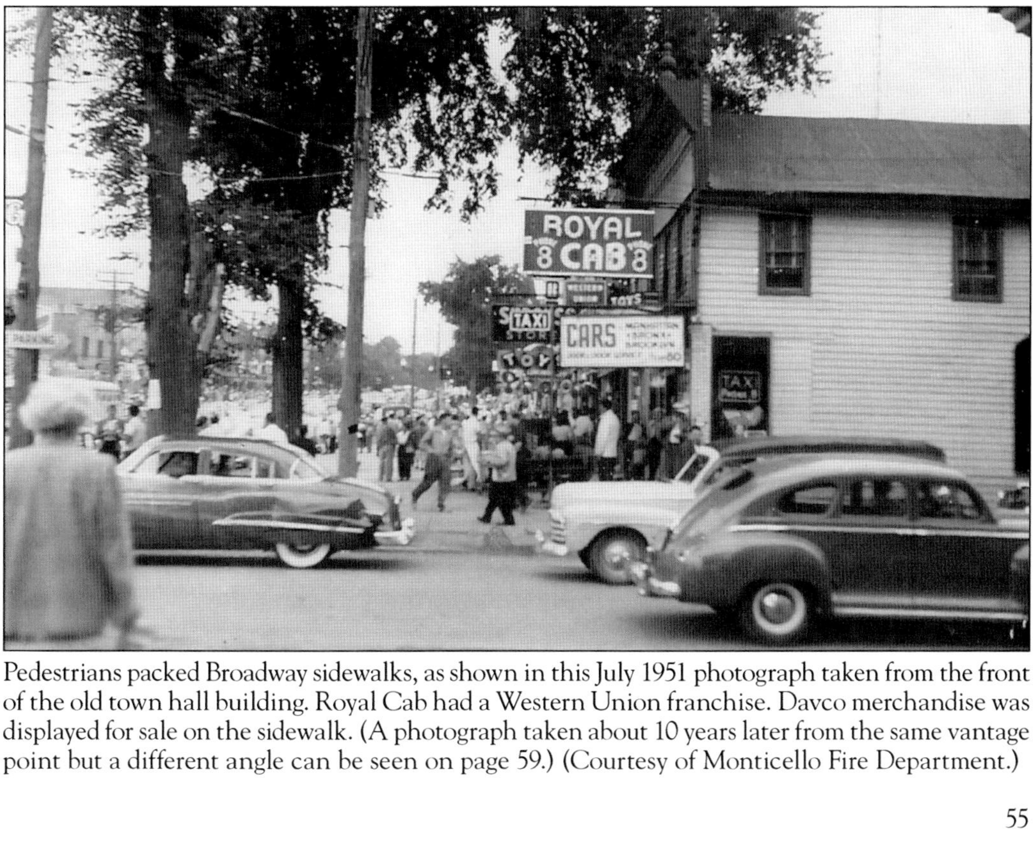

Pedestrians packed Broadway sidewalks, as shown in this July 1951 photograph taken from the front of the old town hall building. Royal Cab had a Western Union franchise. Davco merchandise was displayed for sale on the sidewalk. (A photograph taken about 10 years later from the same vantage point but a different angle can be seen on page 59.) (Courtesy of Monticello Fire Department.)

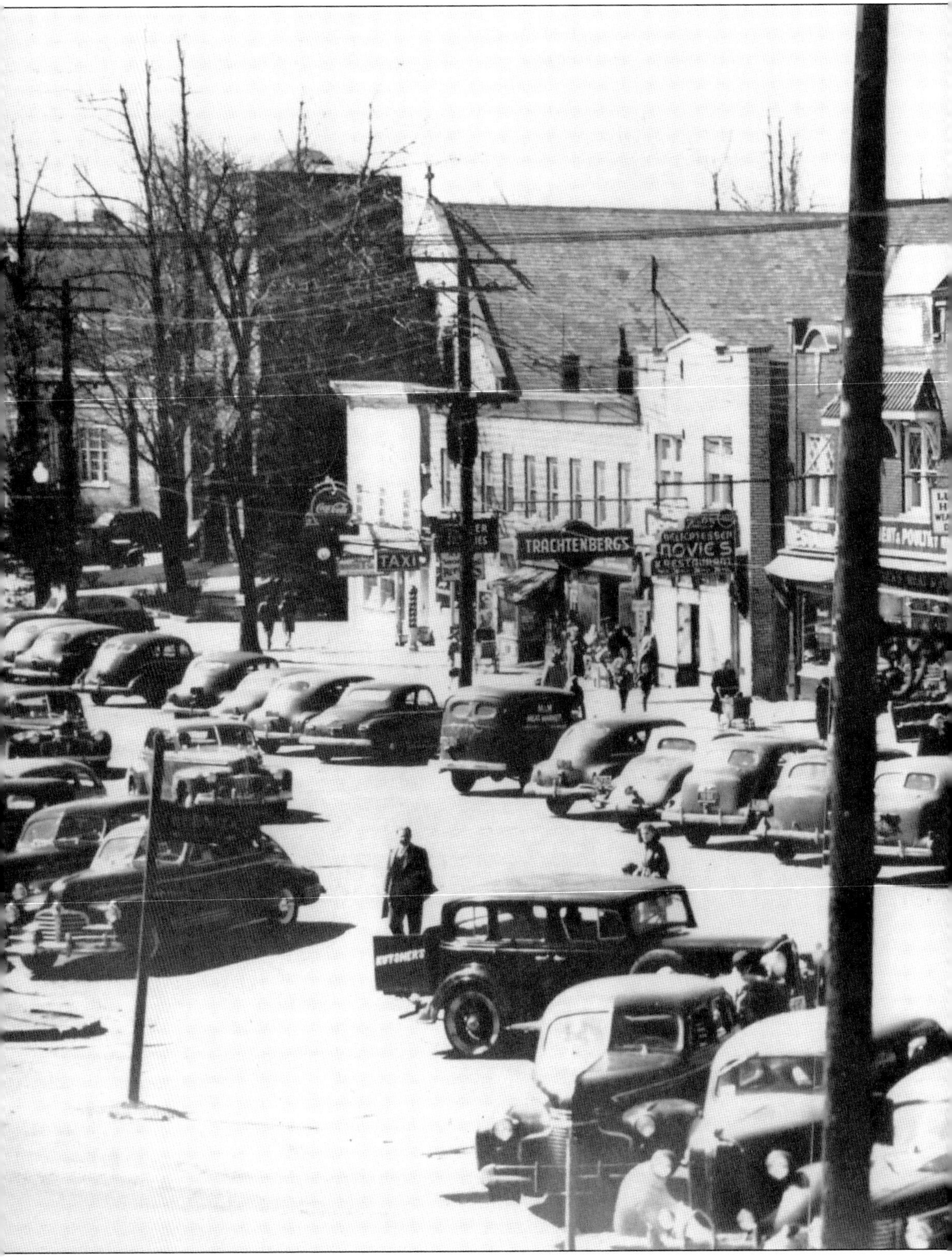
TAXI
TRACHTENBERG'S

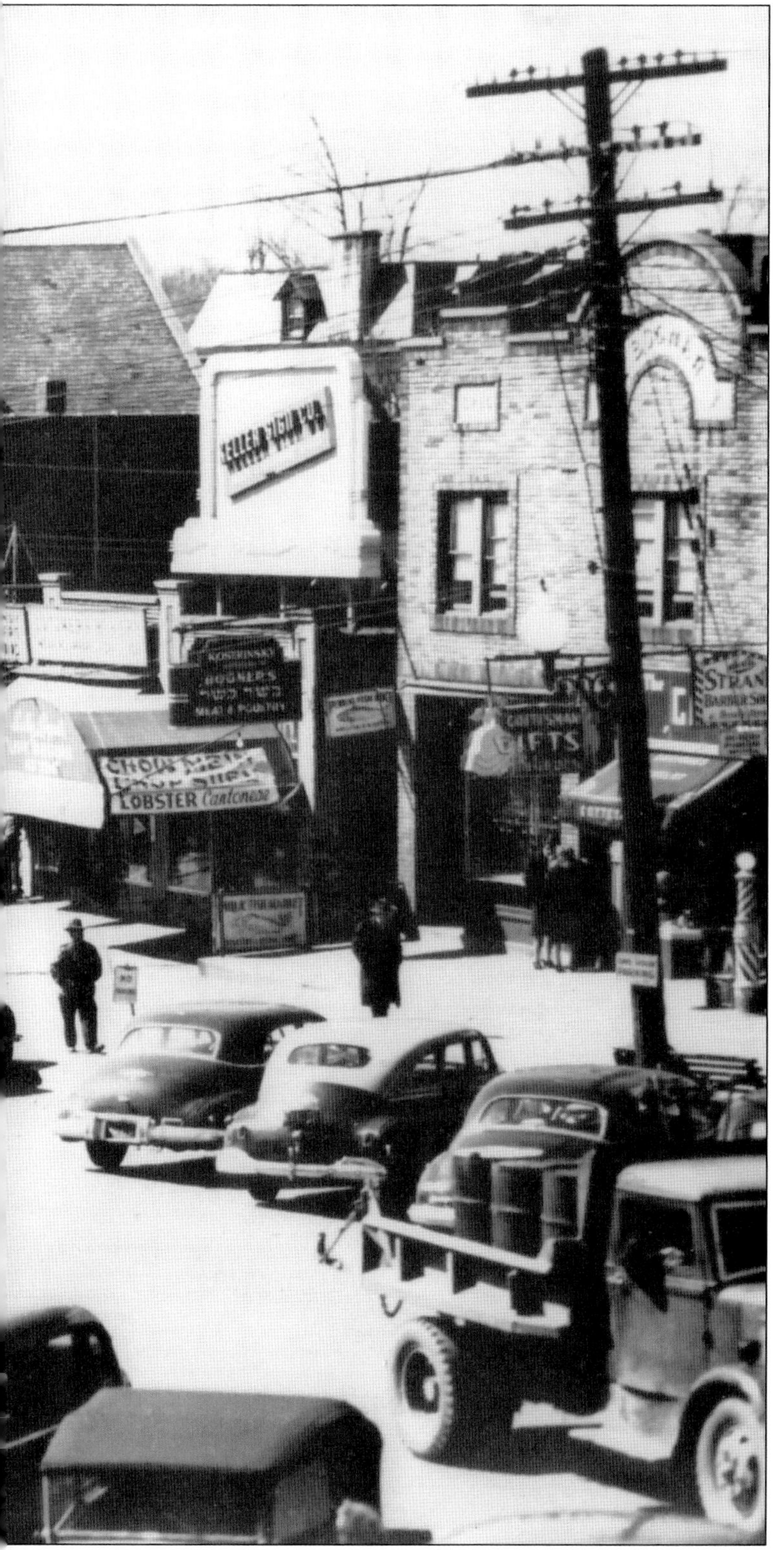

This springtime photograph shows Broadway (Route 42) from above the corner of Oakley (now Lakewood) Avenue. The image may be more recent than the newest automobiles shown because production was curtailed during the war years. Mayor Luis DeHoyos opposed elimination of diagonal parking, but parallel parking on Broadway became mandatory in 1946 when the village sought the state's permission to install parking meters. At right, in the Bogner building, is the Sol Strand Barber Shop and Beauty Parlor (later David's Fast Photo), Gottesman's Gifts (now Crown Chicken), Bogner's Meat and Poultry, the Green Door Bar and Grill, and Keller Sign Company. Next is Lutzker's Hosiery, Trachtenberg's (now Chinatown Kitchen), Joe Hertz's shoe repair, a taxicab company, and another barber. At the corner is St. Peter's Roman Catholic Church (minus its steeple), then the post office. (Courtesy of Ralph Cutler.)

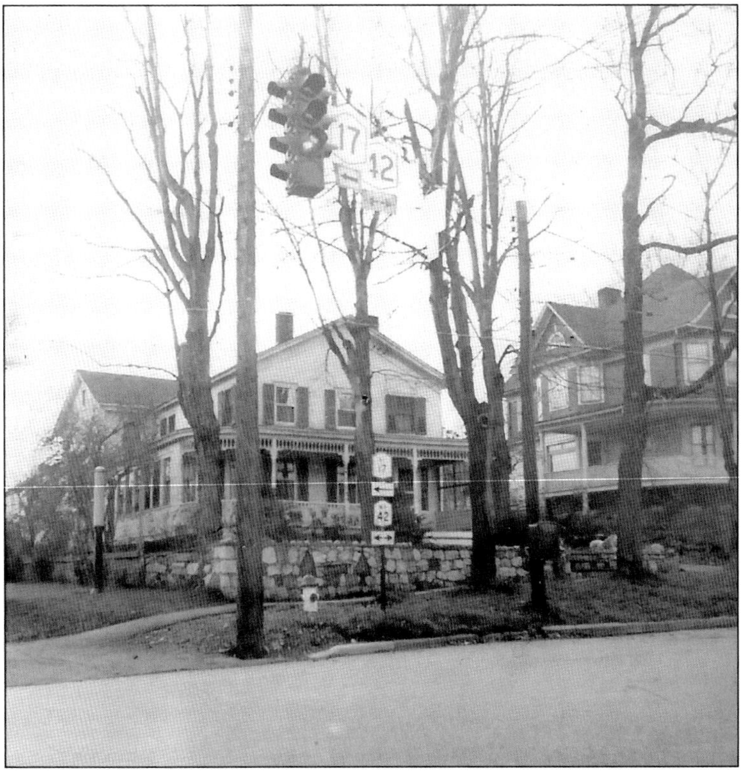

This house is pictured in 1963, when it was home to Alvin O. and Elizabeth Scriber Benton, owners of the *Republican Watchman*. They bought it from Henry and Lilly Mauer, who inherited it from their parents, Elizabeth and William. The Mauers bought it from district attorney George L. Cooke, later elected judge of Sullivan County. It still stands at 531 (formerly 373) Broadway. (Both, courtesy of Susan Benton Schock.)

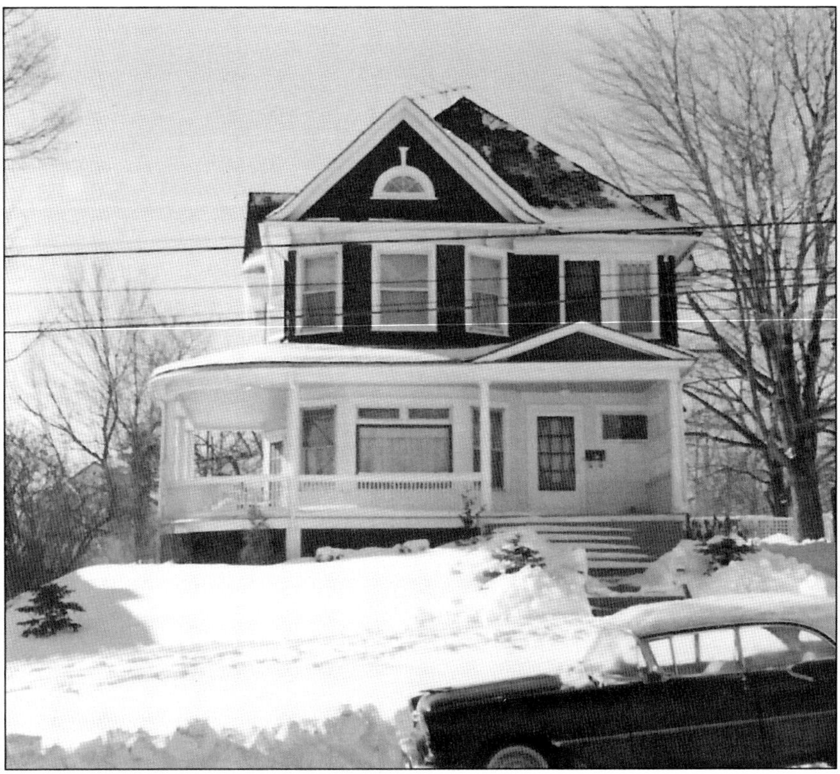

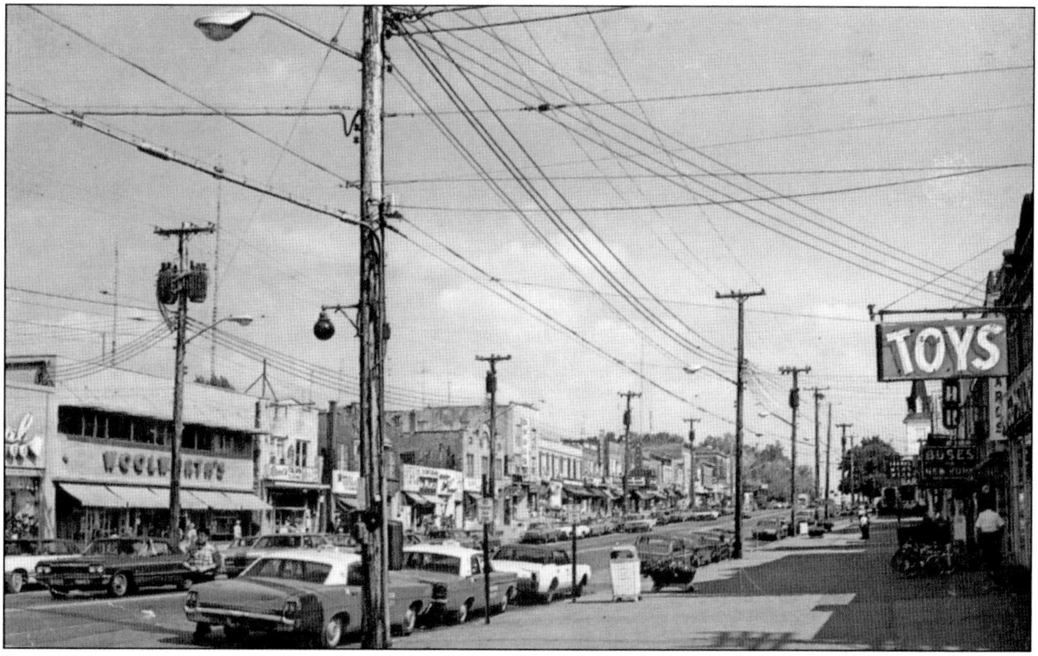

At the northwest corner of Prince Street with a slightly different camera angle than the photograph taken about 10 years earlier (see page 55), this vantage point shows the south side of Broadway, including Woolworth's. At right is Davco with bicycles lined up outside, the Short Line bus company, and the Methodist church in the distance. Business owners took pride in maintaining flowers along the sidewalk. (Courtesy of James Steinberg.)

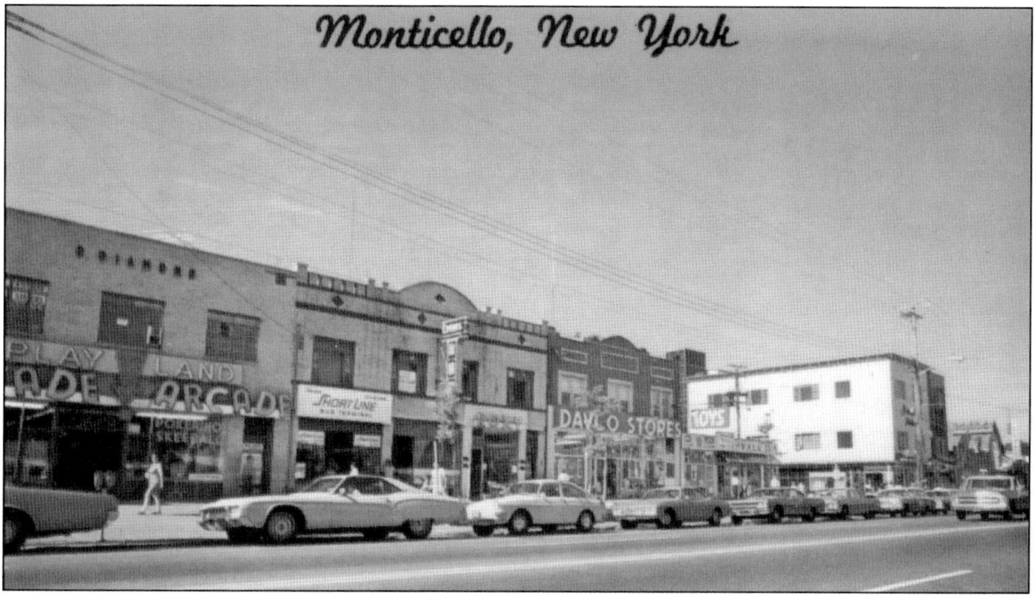

In the 1960s, Broadway businesses were still booming. Playland featured Pokerino and Skee-Ball. Phil Walter gave free games to children who had good report cards. Short Line buses carried commuters east to Manhattan, west to Binghamton, and points beyond. Davco sold toys, scout uniforms, bicycles, and more. On the far corner of Prince Street, new structures took the place of the old municipal building. Canton served Chinese food. (Courtesy of John Conway.)

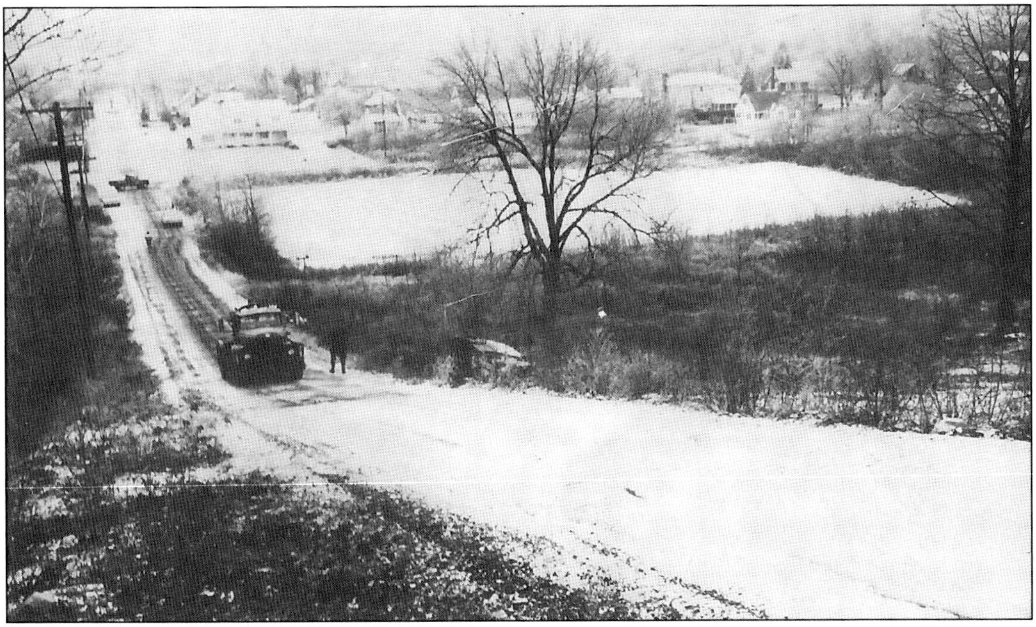

This image of Fraser Avenue was taken from the crest of Starr Hill, December 11, 1967. (The same road is shown more than a century earlier on page 15, looking north instead of south.) At right is the present-day Fraser Pond. At one time, all of this land was sown with hay. Sometimes closed to traffic in winter, it is still a favorite sledding spot for children. (Courtesy of Monticello Department of Public Works.)

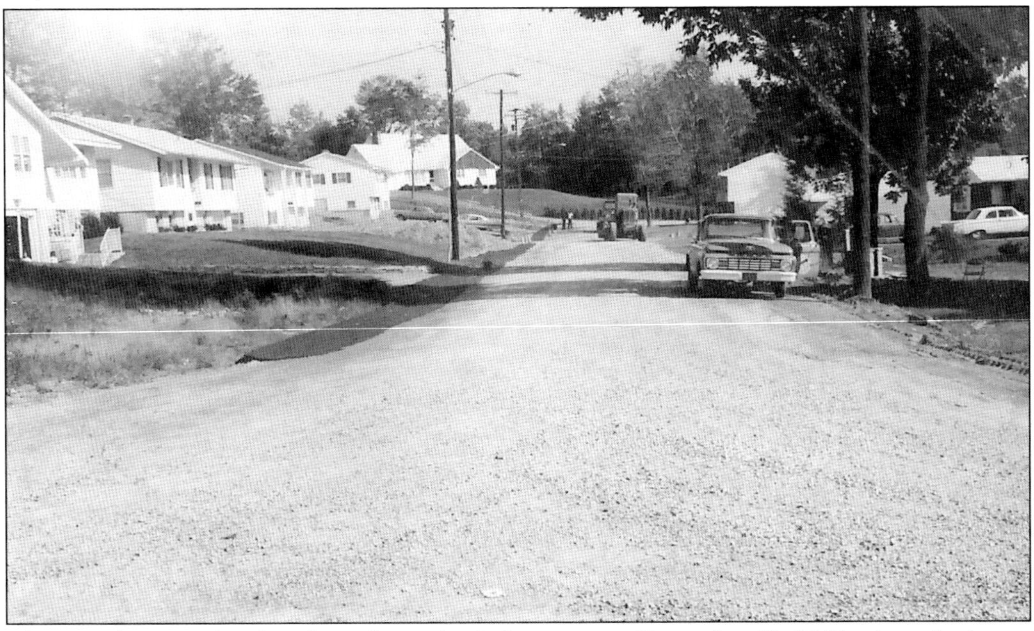

This is a photograph taken from the author's driveway on December 12, 1967, when the house was owned by George and Bertha Streifer. The view looks across Fisk Avenue east down Rupp Avenue. This neighborhood was constructed about 1958. Road resurfacing by the Village of Monticello was under way when the photographs on this page were taken. (Courtesy of Monticello Department of Public Works.)

Two

TRANSPORTATION

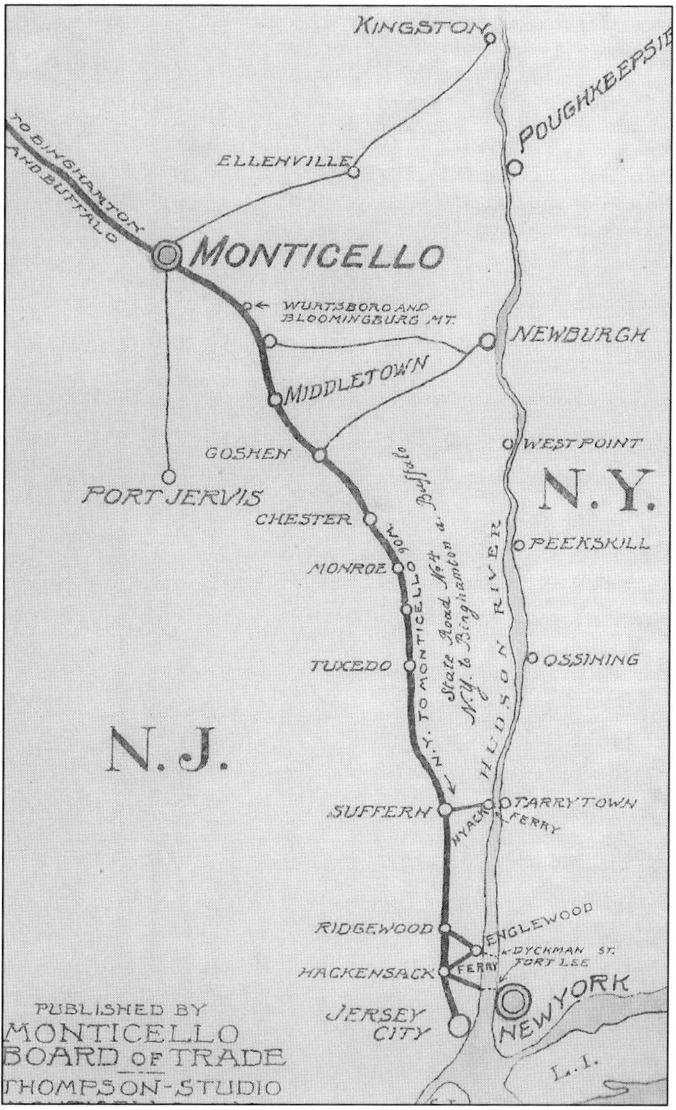

This map, from an early tourism booklet entitled "Monticello the Beautiful" by the Monticello Board of Trade, depicts Monticello as the center of the region. The Monticello and Port Jervis line was a spur connecting from the Port Jervis terminal. The Monticello and Port Jervis Railroad beckoned tourists from the city to come and enjoy the health benefits of fresh mountain air and water. (Courtesy of Susan Benton Schock.)

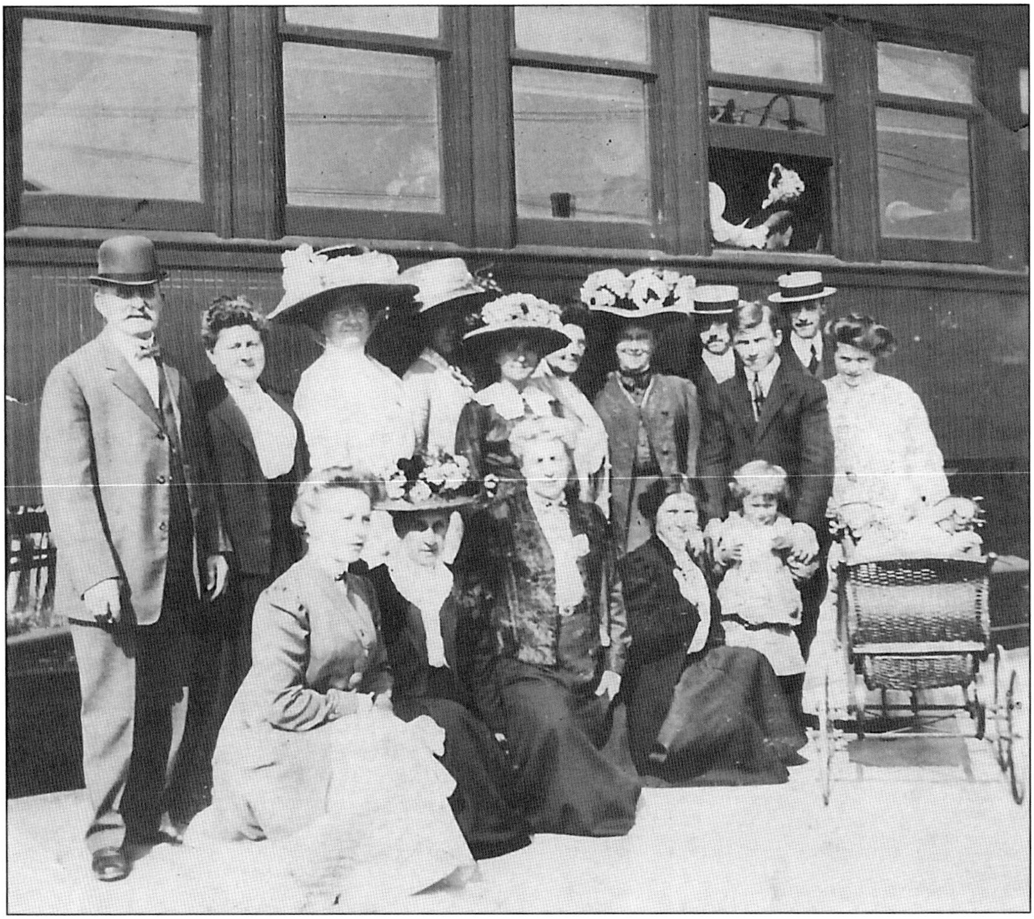

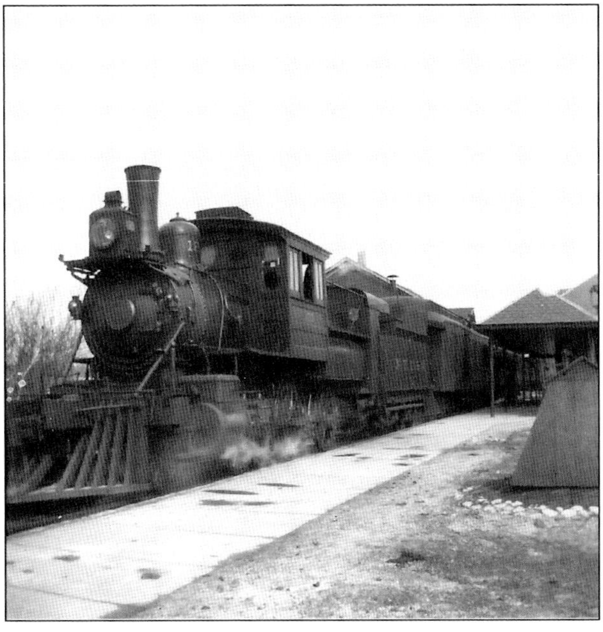

The last passenger train to Monticello was an excursion on March 16, 1941, though Monticello's last hurrah for regular passenger service was the summer season of 1935, after which it was used for freight only. At right, a Monticello and Port Jervis and Western train idles at the Saint John Street depot. Railroad historian John Taibi reports that this engine, No. 128, was a Mogul (2-6-0) built by the Dickson Locomotive Company and received by the Ontario and Western Railroad (O&W) to be in their Class R in 1890. Steam locomotives are classified by wheel arrangement. A 2-6-0 has a pair of leading wheels, followed by six driving wheels. This engine was sold for scrap in 1917, most likely to aid the war effort in Europe. (Courtesy of Susan Benton Schock.)

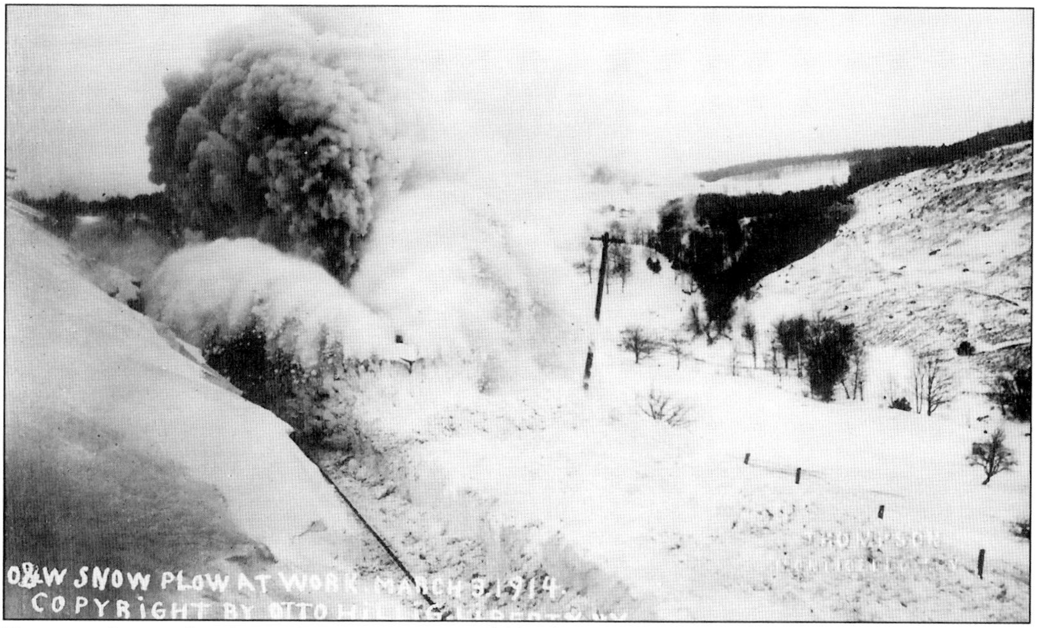

Keeping the tracks clear of snow was more difficult in some Catskill winters than others. An especially heavy snowfall was not too much to stop this plow from chugging along. O&W plow engineers were careful that windrows of snow did not block highways at railroad grade crossings. This Otto Hillig photograph is dated March 3, 1914. (Courtesy of Richard Benjamin Sr.)

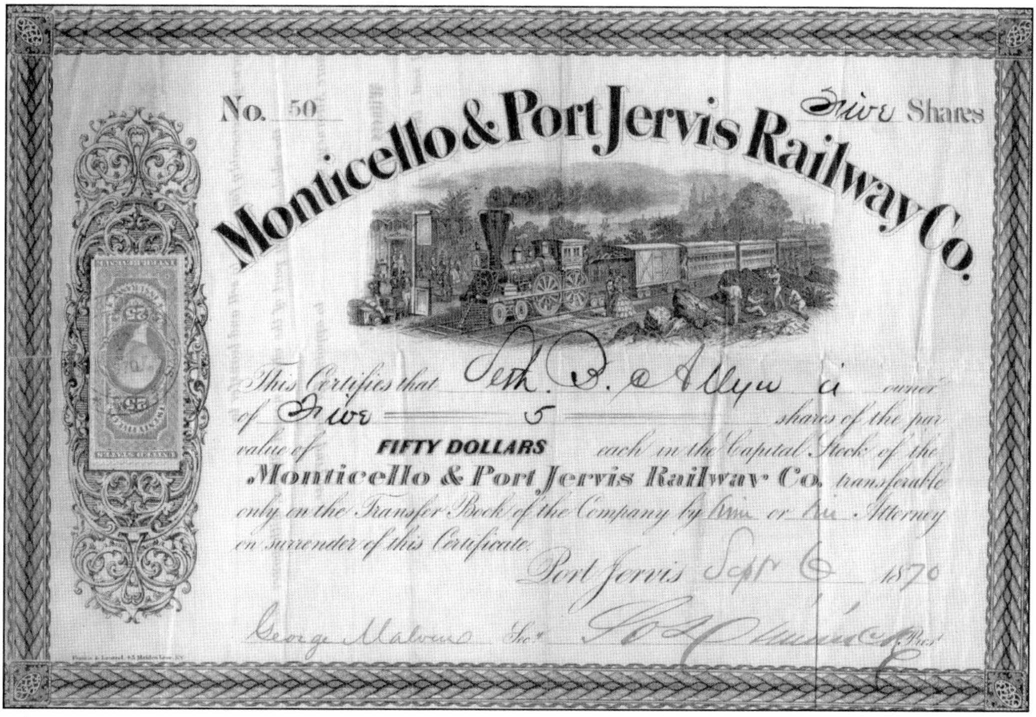

No. 50 Five Shares

Monticello & Port Jervis Railway Co.

This Certifies that Seth B. Allyn is owner of Five 5 shares of the par value of FIFTY DOLLARS each in the Capital Stock of the Monticello & Port Jervis Railway Co. transferable only on the Transfer Book of the Company by him or his Attorney on surrender of this Certificate.

Port Jervis Sept 6 1870

George Malone Sec. Pres.

Above is a reproduction of a stock certificate issued to Seth B. Allyn for five shares of par value stock in the Monticello and Port Jervis Railway Company, dated September 6, 1870, valued at $5. (Courtesy of Daniel K. Niven.)

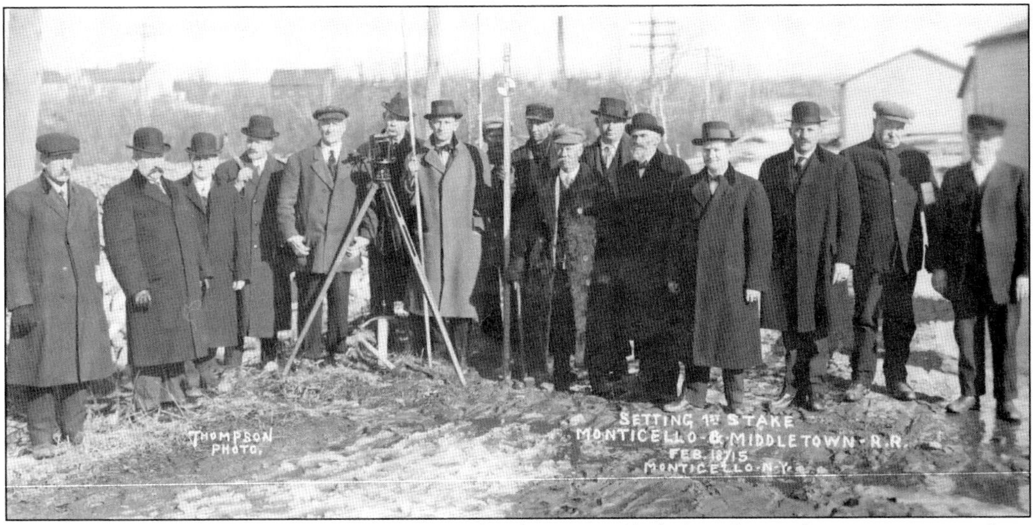

Interest generated by the Fallsburg-Monticello electric trolly led to this stake-setting scene for a Monticello-Middletown Railroad on February 18, 1915. Behind this doomed project, from left to right, are Charles Martin, Walter "Butch" Smith, Louis Guimond, Fred Grain, project mover Blake Mapledoram, Walter Prince, Arch Carey, unidentified, Fred "Wick" Sprague, Martin LaTourette, Russell Ross, Sanford Ostrium, Gus Stone, Henry Stratten, William Trowbridge, and John Heath. (Howard Thompson photograph; courtesy of Daniel K. Niven.)

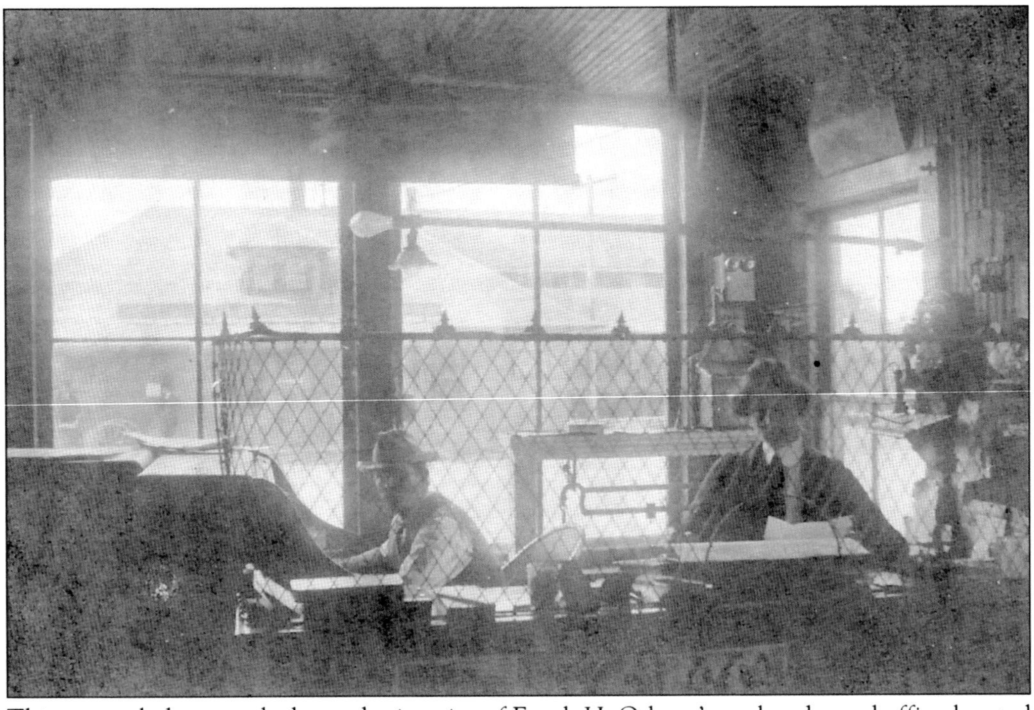

This unusual photograph shows the interior of Frank H. Osborn's coal and wood office located directly across Saint John Street from the railroad depot. Workers at the present-day Van Etten Oil Company office, currently on the same location as this building, may feel they are looking out their office window a century or more ago. (See the building's exterior on page 74.) (Courtesy of William Horton.)

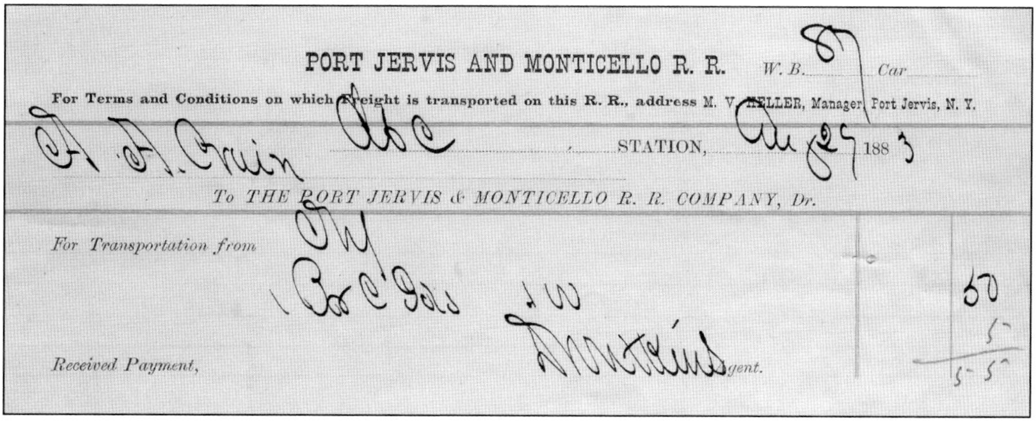
PORT JERVIS AND MONTICELLO R. R. W. B. 87 Car

For Terms and Conditions on which Freight is transported on this R. R., address M. V. HELLER, Manager, Port Jervis, N. Y.

A. A. Crain STATION, Aug 29 1883

To THE PORT JERVIS & MONTICELLO R. R. COMPANY, Dr.

For Transportation from

Received Payment, Agent.

The ticket above for the Port Jervis and Monticello Railroad, dated August 29, 1883, acknowledges receipt of $55 from Monticello pharmacist Alpheus A. Crain (see page 31) for transportation of a boxcar of unidentified freight. The passenger ticket below indicates that fare from Monticello to Port Jervis was $1.32 in 1874. (Above, courtesy of Lynn Sullivan; below, courtesy of Richard Benjamin Sr.)

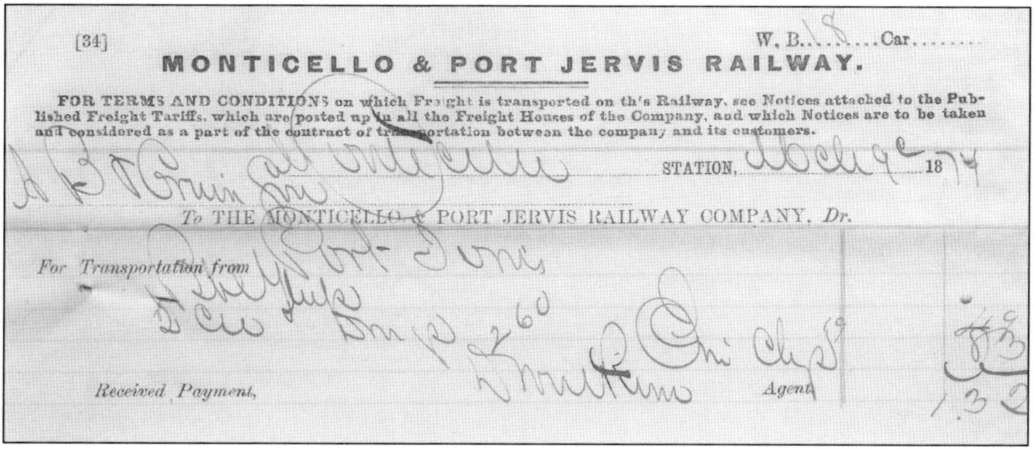
[34] W. B. 18 Car

MONTICELLO & PORT JERVIS RAILWAY.

FOR TERMS AND CONDITIONS on which Freight is transported on this Railway, see Notices attached to the Published Freight Tariffs, which are posted up in all the Freight Houses of the Company, and which Notices are to be taken and considered as a part of the contract of transportation between the company and its customers.

STATION, 18 74

To THE MONTICELLO & PORT JERVIS RAILWAY COMPANY, Dr.

For Transportation from

Received Payment, Agent

1.32

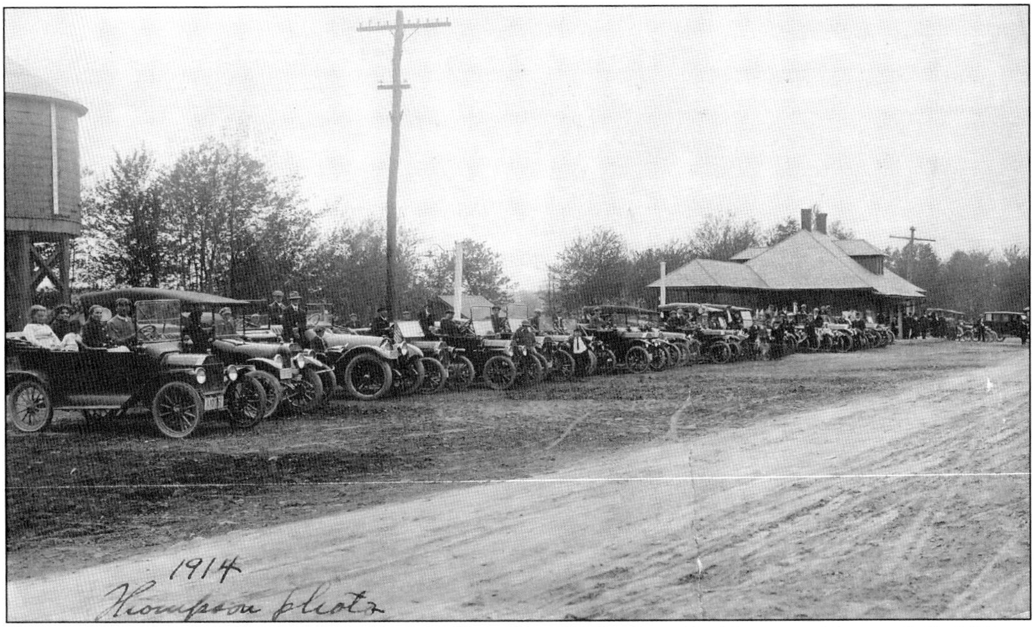

By 1904, the population between Cornwall and Delhi had swelled by an additional 80,000, in large part due to improved the road and rail systems. The O&W Railroad collected $300,000 in fares, half for Monticello, Fallsburg, and Hurleyville. Commuter trains were so crowded that passenger cars were coupled to milk trains on Friday evenings. Dubbed the "Silly Hubby's" train, passengers rode in a parlor car where they played cards and enjoyed beverages. It is clear from these photographs that there were times when parking was scarce at the Monticello depot. (Above, courtesy of Richard Benjamin Sr.; below, courtesy of Sullivan County Historical Society.)

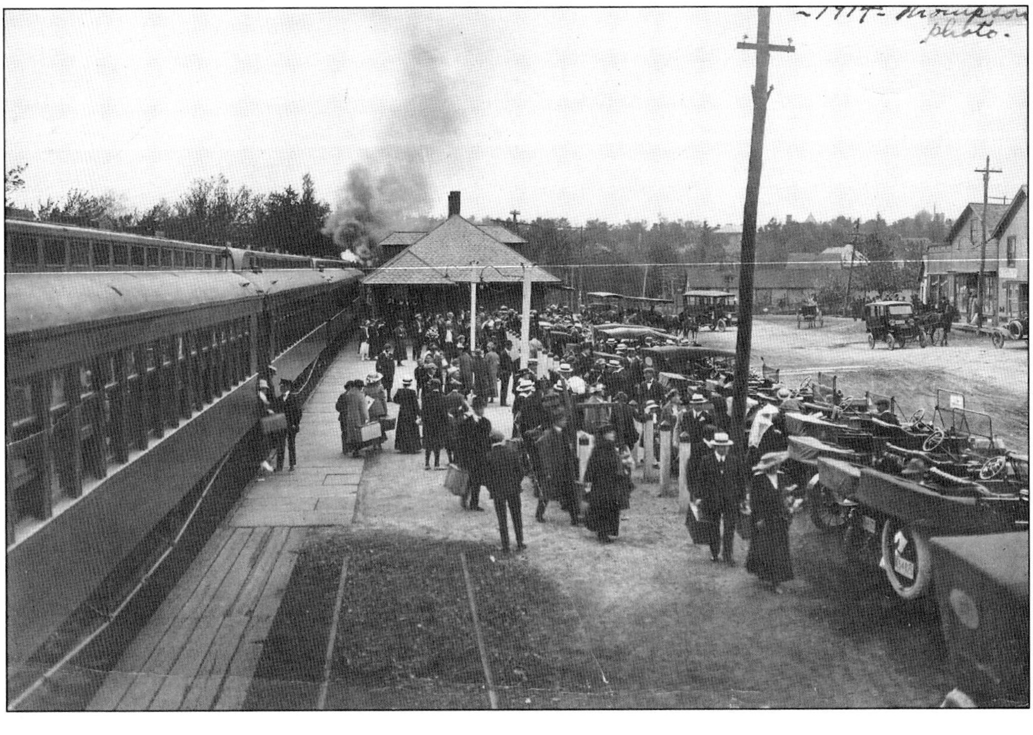

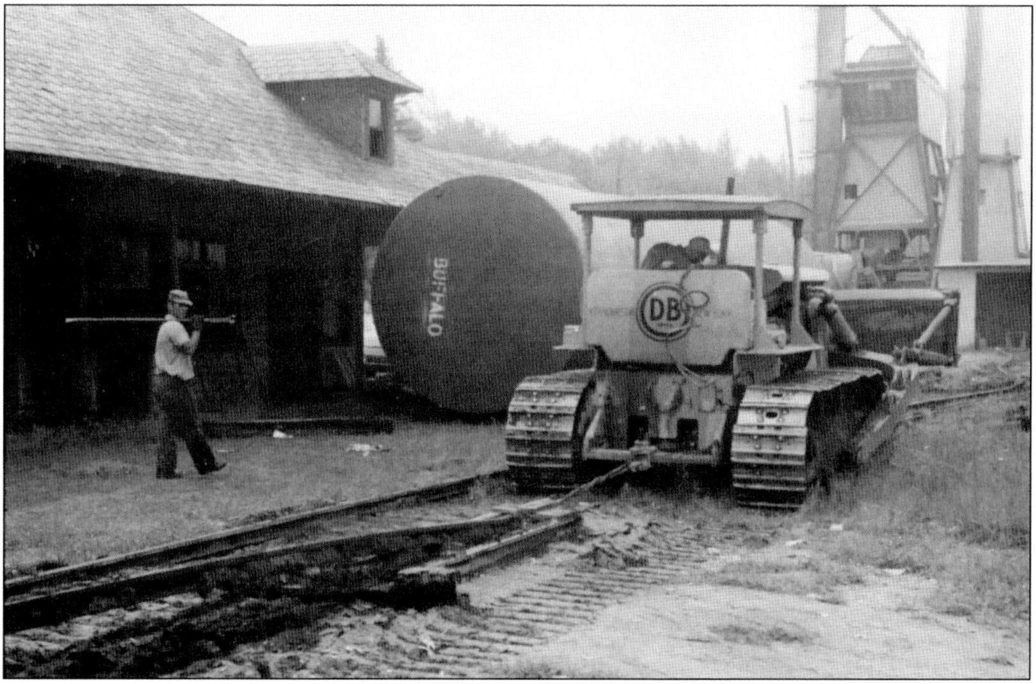

After the Ontario and Western Railroad ceased operation of the Monticello line on March 29, 1957, the removal of the abandoned tracks punctuated the end of Monticello's railroad era. Presumably the tracks were sold as scrap. A laborer with a long crowbar perched on his shoulder approaches a bulldozer owned by a Kerhonkson excavator. (Courtesy of Van Etten Oil Company.)

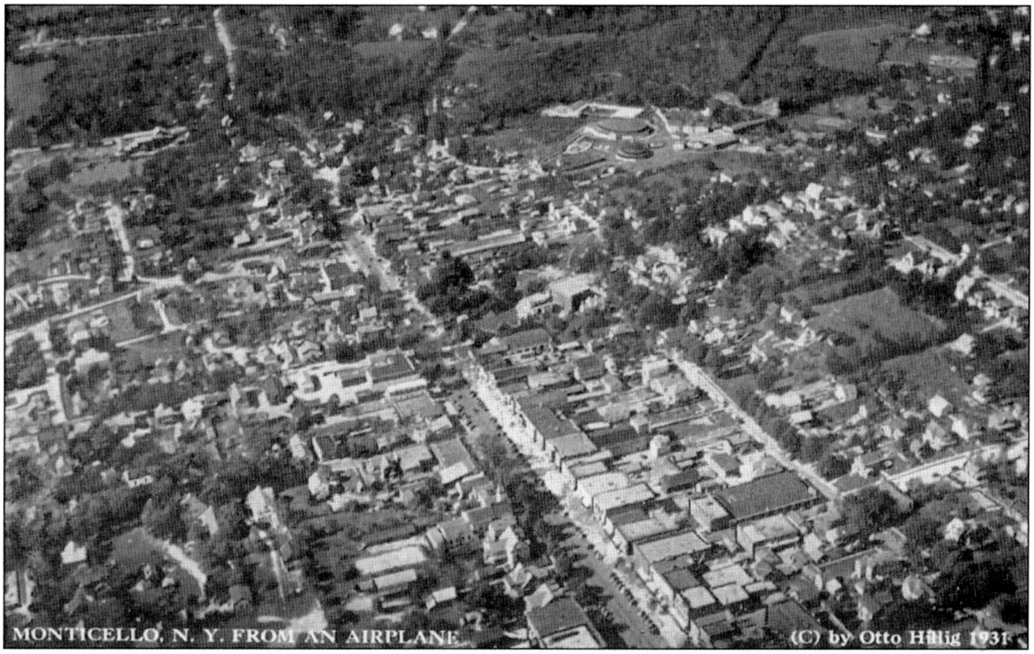

Otto Hillig provided a view of Monticello during the 1930s from *The Liberty*, the aircraft he flew on his long-distance solo flights. The image gives a broad perspective of the village, including the Monticello Amusement Park to the northwest. (Courtesy of Richard Benjamin Sr.)

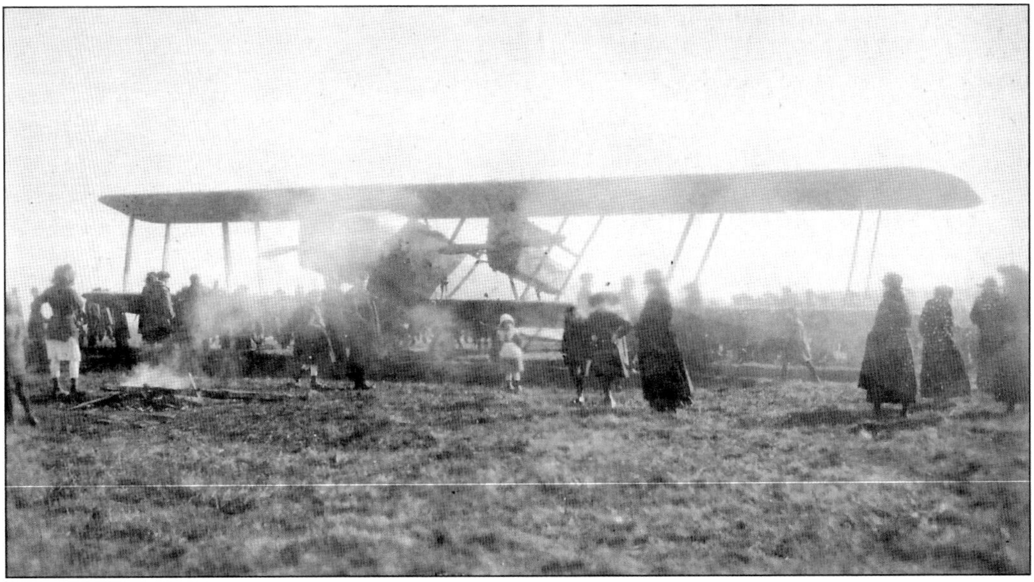

The landing of a twin-engine biplane in Monticello around 1919 generated much excitement in town. It is not known which airfield is shown here. It seems more likely to be in the area of Wood Avenue, but it could also be the Heins Airport on Cantrell Road. (Howard Thompson photograph; courtesy of Richard Benjamin Sr.)

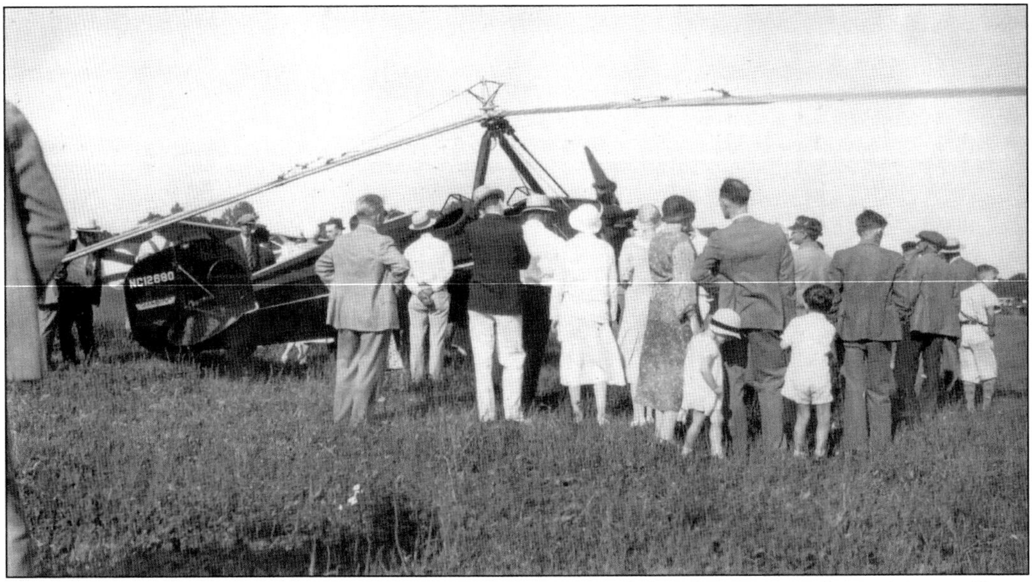

Neither helicopter nor airplane, the craft pictured above—exhibited at a county fair in Monticello—is an autogiro. Manufactured by Pitcairn-Cierva Autogiro Company, only 19 of this mid-sized model PA-18 (NC12680) were sold. In 1931, Amelia Earhart set a world's altitude record for autogiros, climbing to 18,415 feet. Military historian Robert Debs Heinl Jr. called the autogiro "an exasperating contraption." (Courtesy of Daniel K. Niven.)

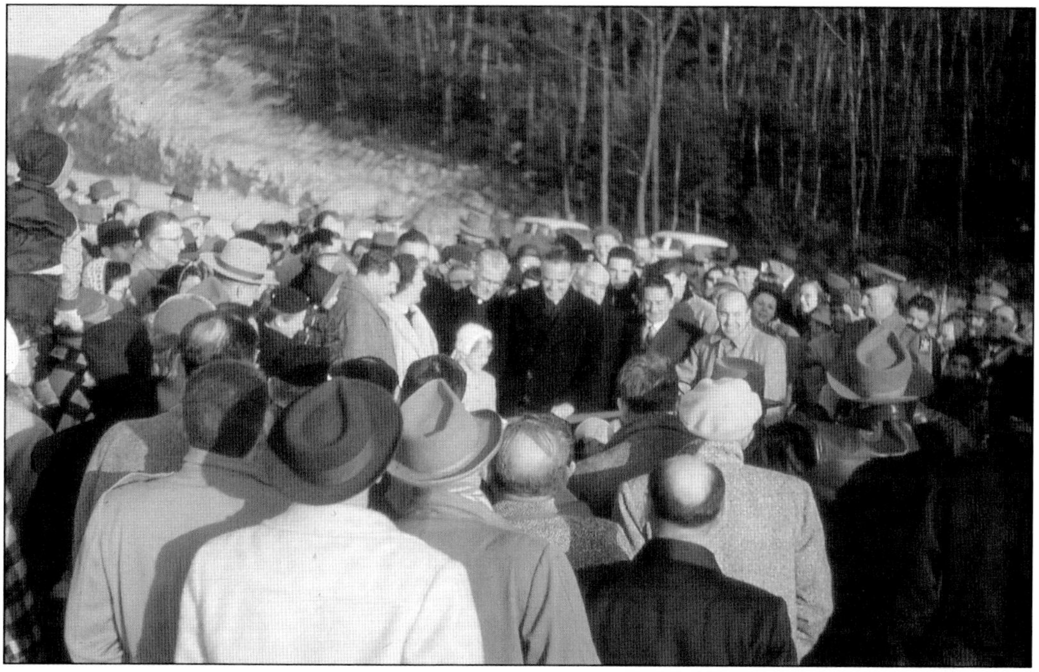

A red ribbon cut in November 1957 atop one of the tallest natural barriers between Monticello and New York City (above) celebrated the carving through Wurtsboro Mountain of a lifeline of commerce and comfort. Gov. Averill Harriman is credited with constructing arteries like State Route 17, building upon the old Newburgh-Cochecton Turnpike. Engineering of modern highways brought Monticello within easy driving range of city-dwelling motorists. (Above, courtesy of Daniel K. Niven; below, courtesy of Van Etten Oil Company.)

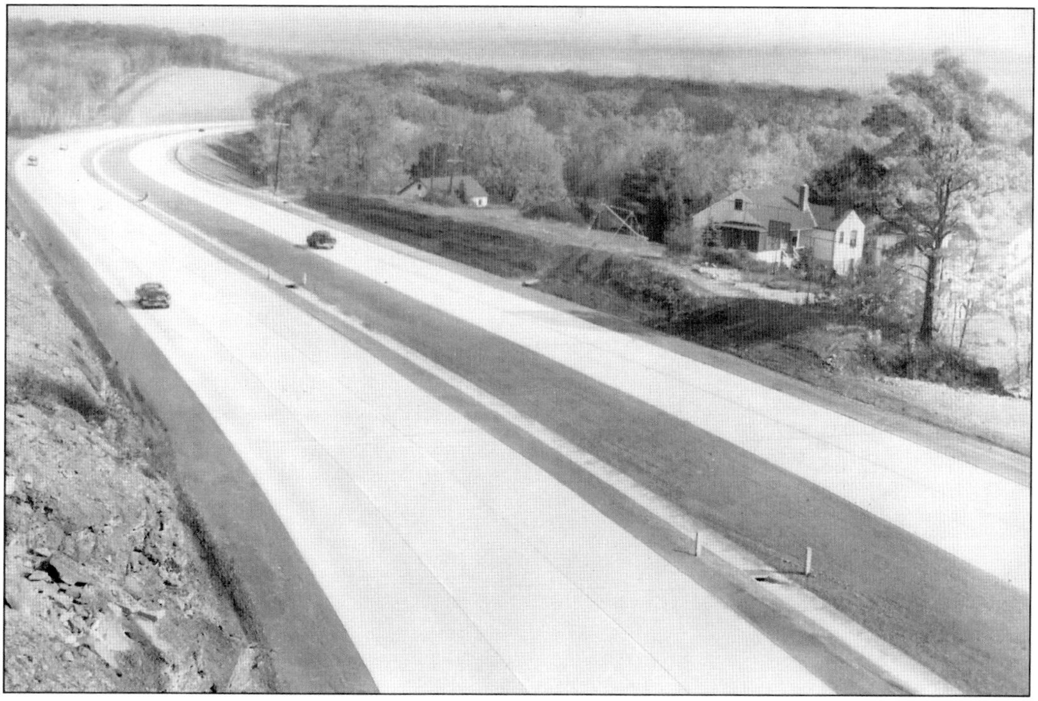

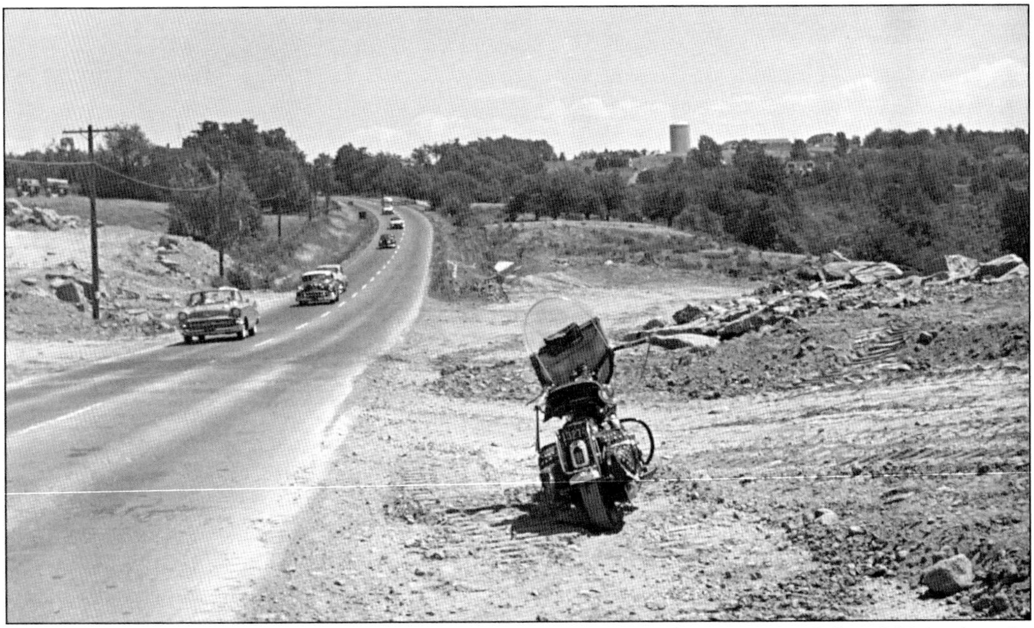

With construction of the Monticello Raceway, also in 1957, the portion of the old Newburgh-Cochecton Turnpike that was Route 17 (today known as Route 17B) was widened to allow increased traffic. The area shown below is west of the village of Monticello. The water tower visible at right still exists near Dunbar Road in the village, though today it is obscured by trees. In the view below, standing in front of Daitch Shopwell store looking north up Jefferson Street toward Routes 17 and 17B, the Dunbar Hill water tower is visible. At left is what was the town hall in 1966 and is now the town highway garage. Prior to that, the building housed Pargas propane. The photograph is dated December 22, 1965. (Above, courtesy of Van Etten Oil Company; below, courtesy of Village of Monticello Monticello Building Department.)

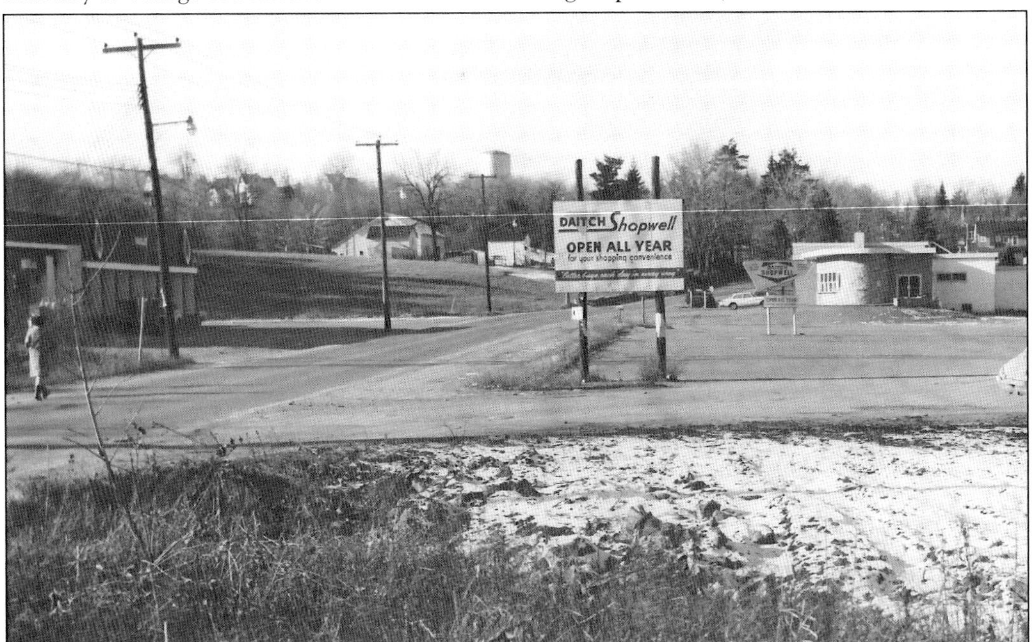

Three

BUSINESS AND INDUSTRY

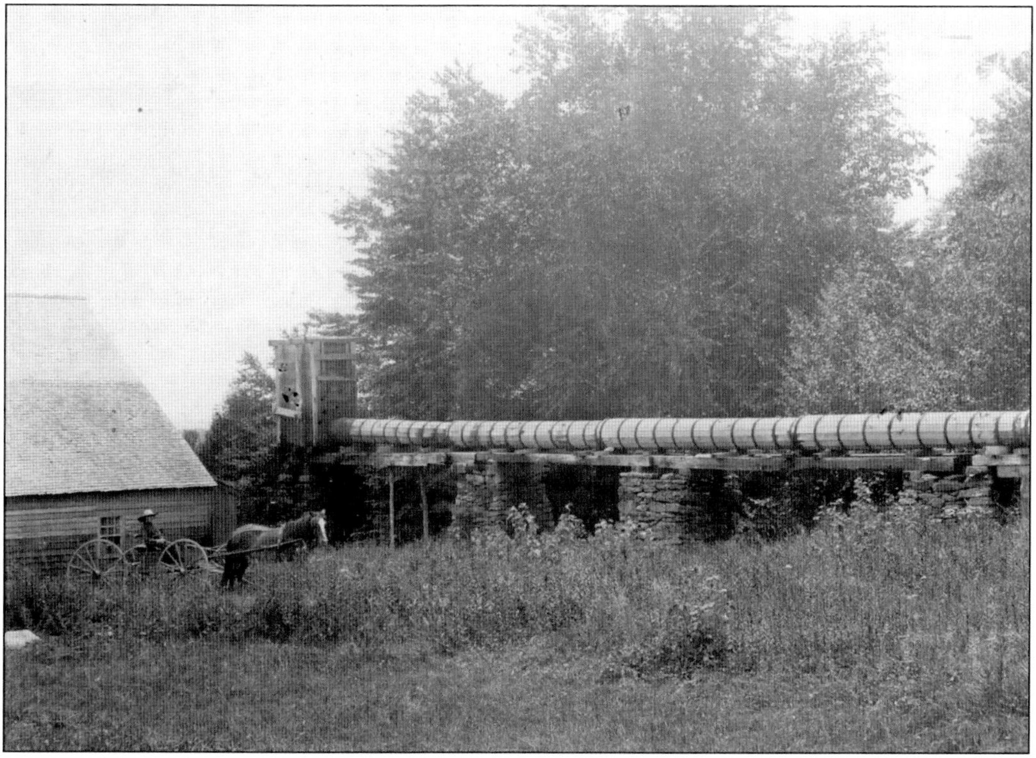

" 'Tis said, his riches bursting coffers fill; / Yet toils he humbly, daily, at the mill, / Where through the race the Old Pond's waters steal / With power to turn the moss-grown water wheel," wrote Arthur C. Butts in 1898. Pictured above is Eli Fairchild's gristmill, later owned by English-born George Billings and Lucien Hatch, pioneer feed merchants of Monticello. (Courtesy of Daniel K. Niven.)

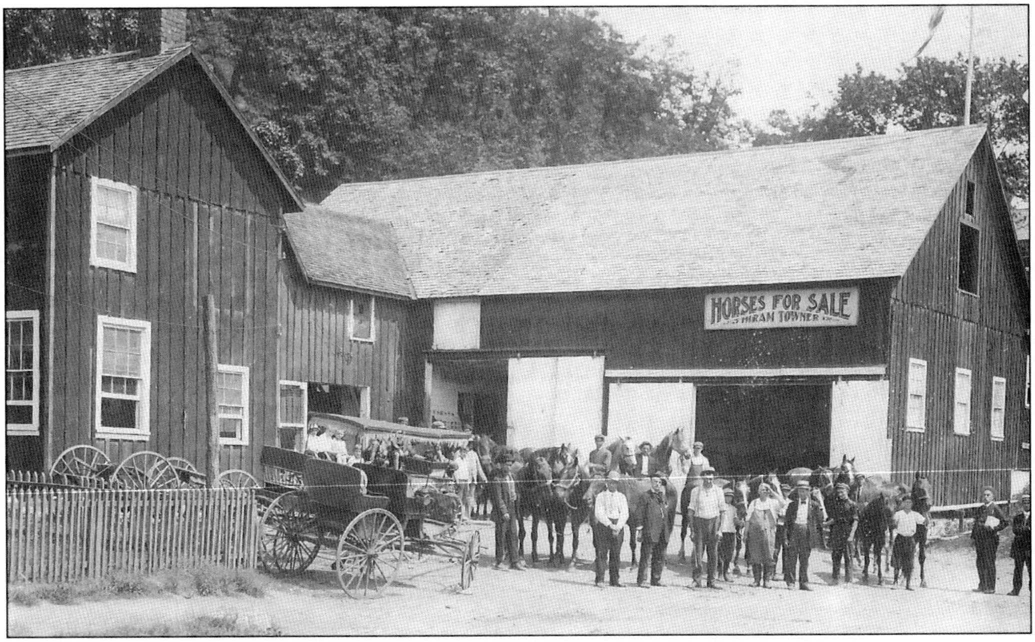

Hiram "Hipe" Towner conducted this horse market on the east side of the southern end of Prince Street. He is said to have bought and sold more horses than any other man in this section, making trips to the West to purchase and ship carloads of wild horses back through Port Jervis by rail. The barn garaged the stagecoaches that ran from Monticello to Middletown and served as Monticello's first amusement auditorium. The Towner house stands on the north side of Broadway, on a slope above the intersection with Port Jervis Road. The family owned property on both sides of Broadway at this intersection, including the land on which Chief Judge Lawrence H. Cooke, his wife, Alice McCormack, and their neighbors later lived. (Both, courtesy of Richard Benjamin Sr.)

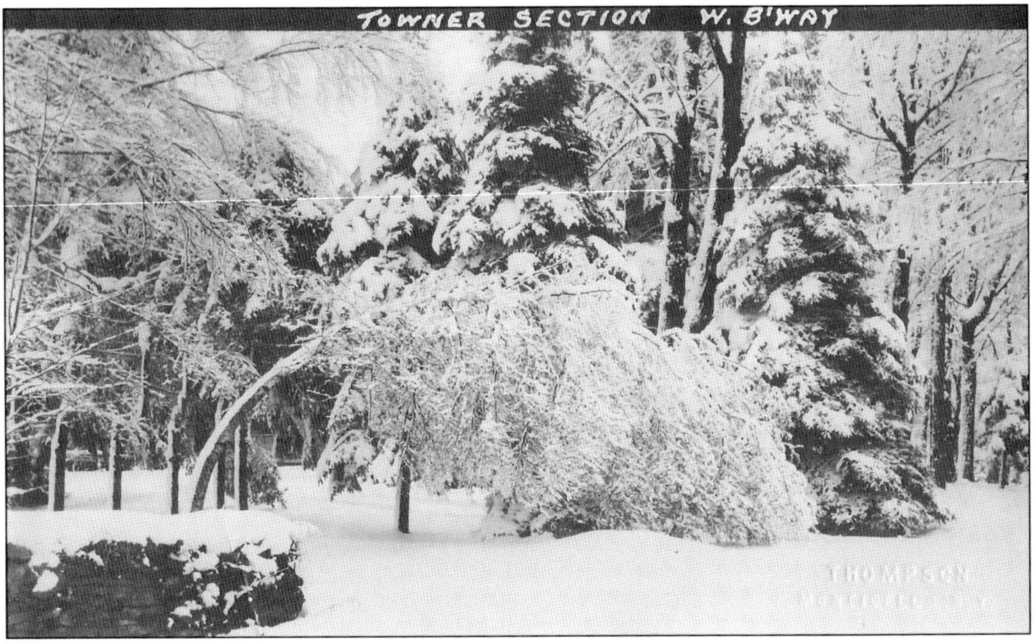

Zilla Towner was a skilled rider in late 19th-century Monticello. She was born November 6, 1889, to Hiram Towner and Virginia Lawrence and died October 22, 1983, at age 93, in Riverside, California. Zilla married Edwin Allabough Sr., who lived to see 94 years of age. Young Zilla is mentioned a number of times in published accounts of coaching day parades. It is no wonder, considering she grew up around Hipe Towner's often unbroken horses fresh from the Wild West. During winter months, the Towners sometimes boarded at the center of the village, such as at the Bushnell house behind the courthouse. (Courtesy of Richard Benjamin Sr.)

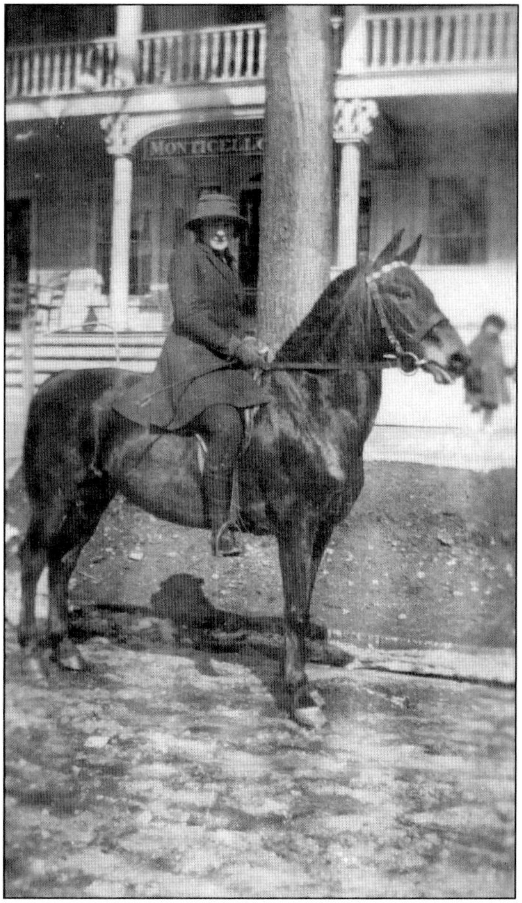

The photograph below shows the sheepskin tannery, which mostly specialized in book leather, on Tannery (Spring) Street. Built by Ephraim Burnham, it was later taken over by John H. Campbell and Company, a New York City firm. When managed by Robert McNickle (see page 102), he oversaw 60 men. Originally relying on once-plentiful hemlock bark native to much of Sullivan County, it burned down in 1924. (Courtesy of John Conway and Monticello Fire Department.)

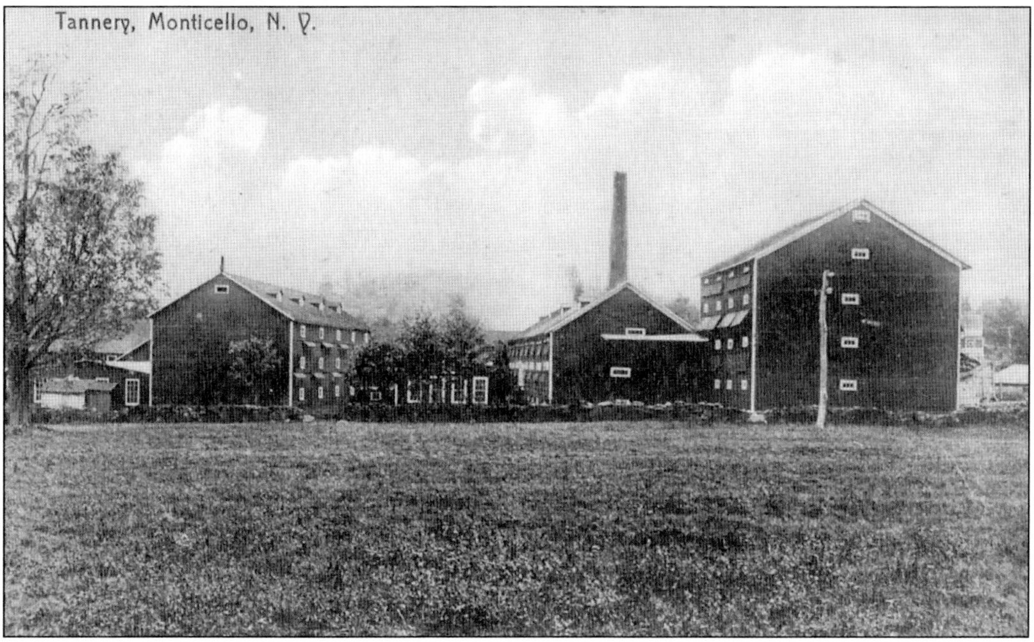

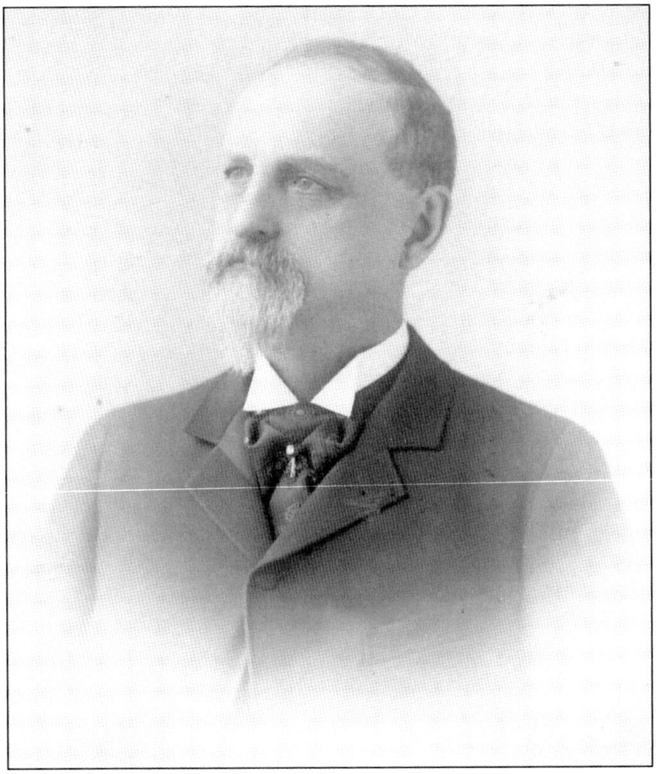

George Monroe Beebe (1836–1927) practiced law in Monticello in 1857, was appointed secretary to the Territory of Kansas in 1859, and was acting governor in 1860–1861. He practiced law in St. Joseph, Missouri, and Virginia City, Nevada. He returned to Monticello in 1863 and edited the local *Republican Watchman* newspaper in 1866 before serving in the New York Assembly 1872–1873 and in Congress 1875–1879. He left Monticello in 1892, died in Ellenville, and is buried in Newburgh. (Courtesy of Susan Benton Schock.)

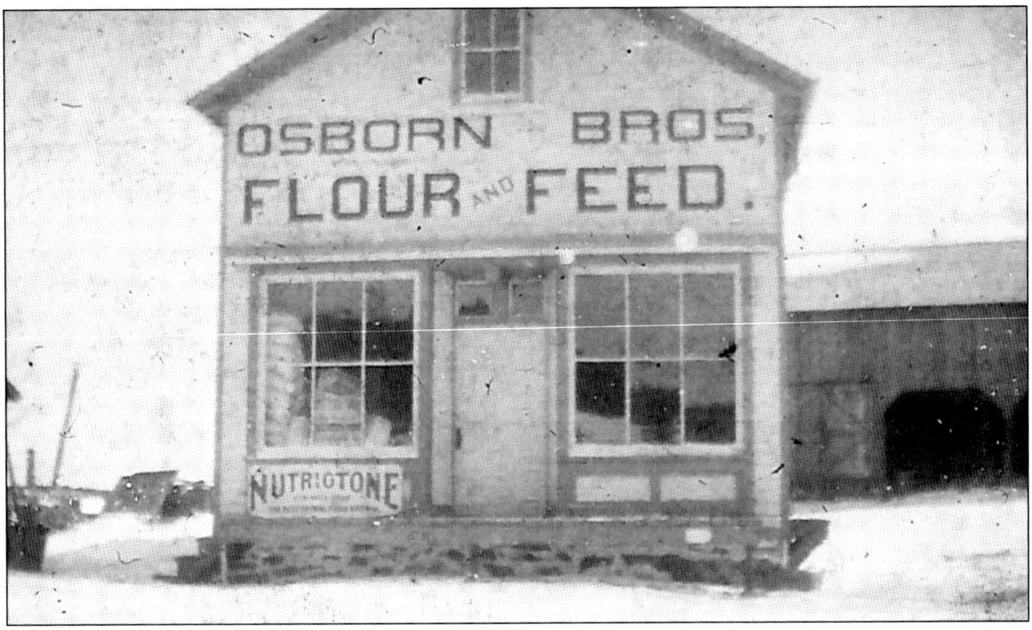

Osborn Brothers Flour and Feed stood on Mill Street (now Saint John) near the present site of Van Etten Oil Company. This store is believed to be the exterior of the one on page 64. Nutriotone, advertised in the sign on the storefront, was a tonic, or condimental food, for livestock. A 1916 study by the Vermont Agricultural Experiment Station questioned the manufacturer's claims that it increased milk production. (Courtesy of William Horton.)

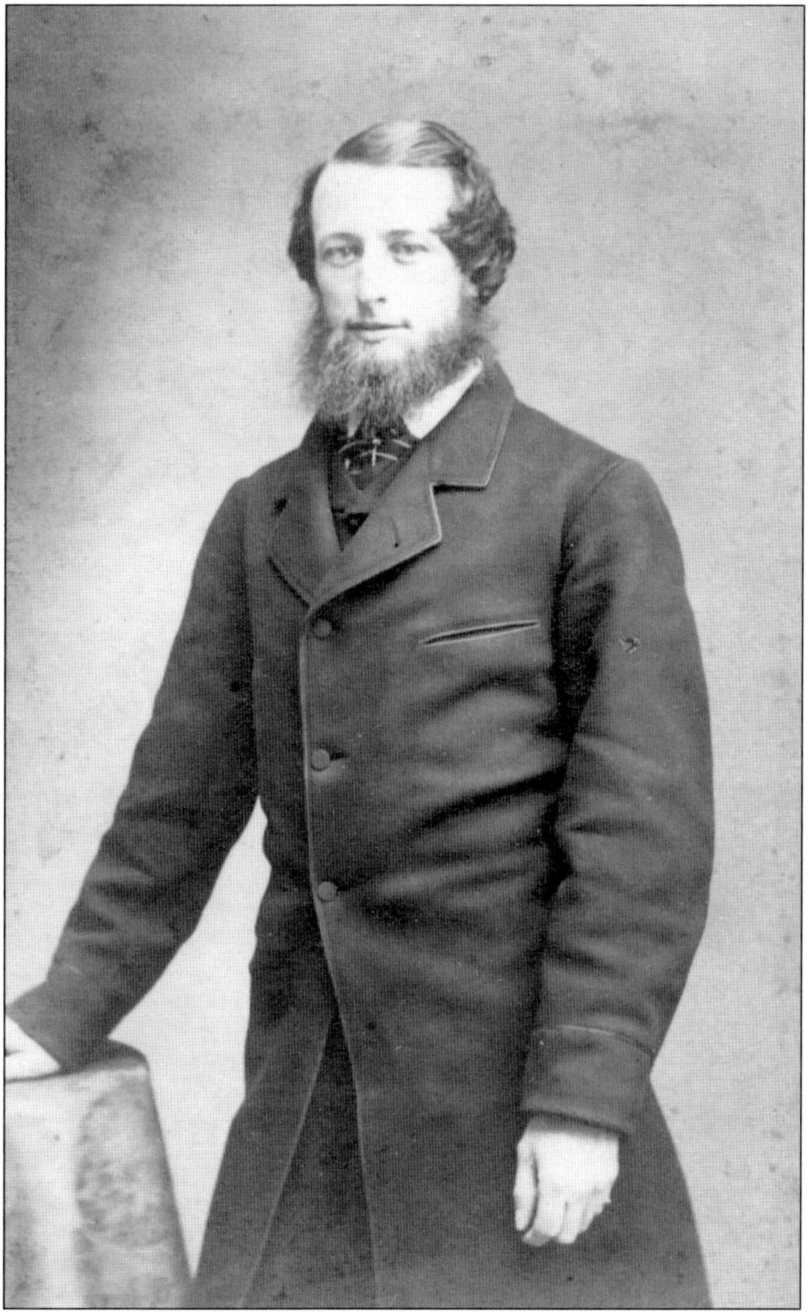

Pictured above is William H. Cady, a prominent Monticello merchant. He was director of the Monticello and Port Jervis Railroad, treasurer of the Monticello and Wurtsboro Turnpike Company, and village clerk. The W. H. Cady Company business was located in A. C. Niven's brick building on Broadway, currently the Trotter's Bar. Cady owned a number of properties in Monticello, some of which were developed as money-making ventures. At one time, he owned the J. P. Jones residence, but his most admirable home stood on the location of what would later become the Victory store, currently The Recovery Center, next door to the Niven office. That beautiful house was destroyed by fire in 1876. (Courtesy of Daniel K. Niven.)

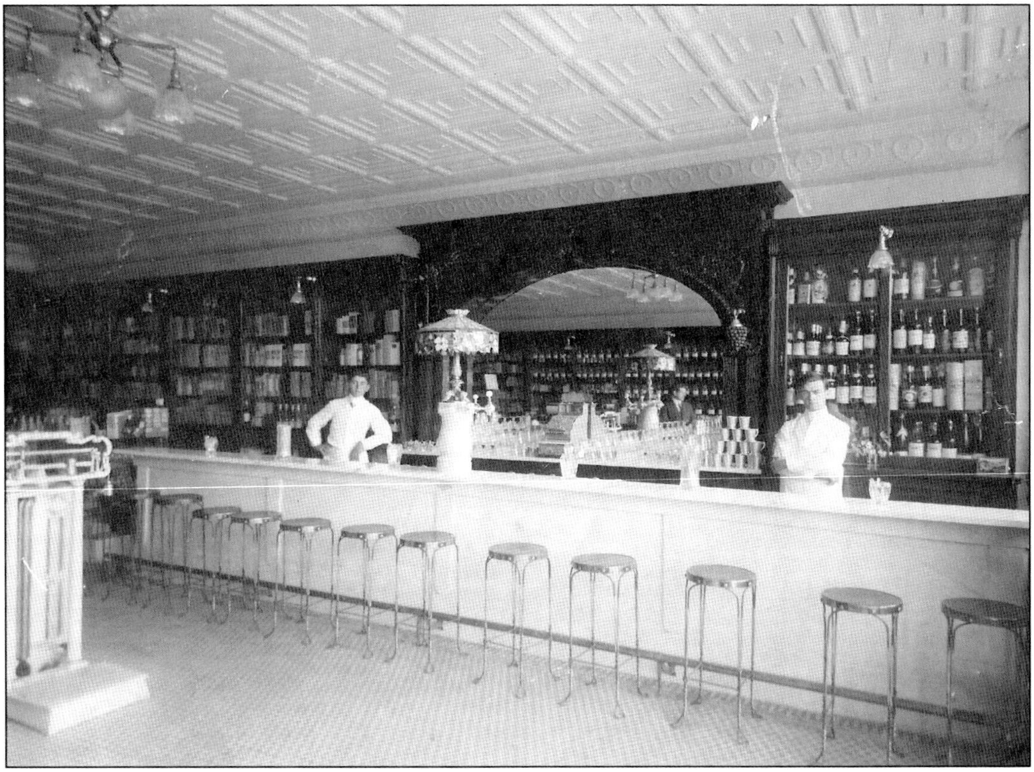

"Fine stock of wines and liquors at Thornton and Miller's drug store" advertised the store shown in the picture above. The photograph below shows Monticello after a heavy snowstorm, in front of Hammond and Cooke. At right is the exterior of Thornton and Millers Pharmacy located on Broadway, east of Hammond and Cooke's department store; by the 1950s, the facade was completely altered to approximate a law office at 228–230 Broadway. (Courtesy of Richard Benjamin Sr.)

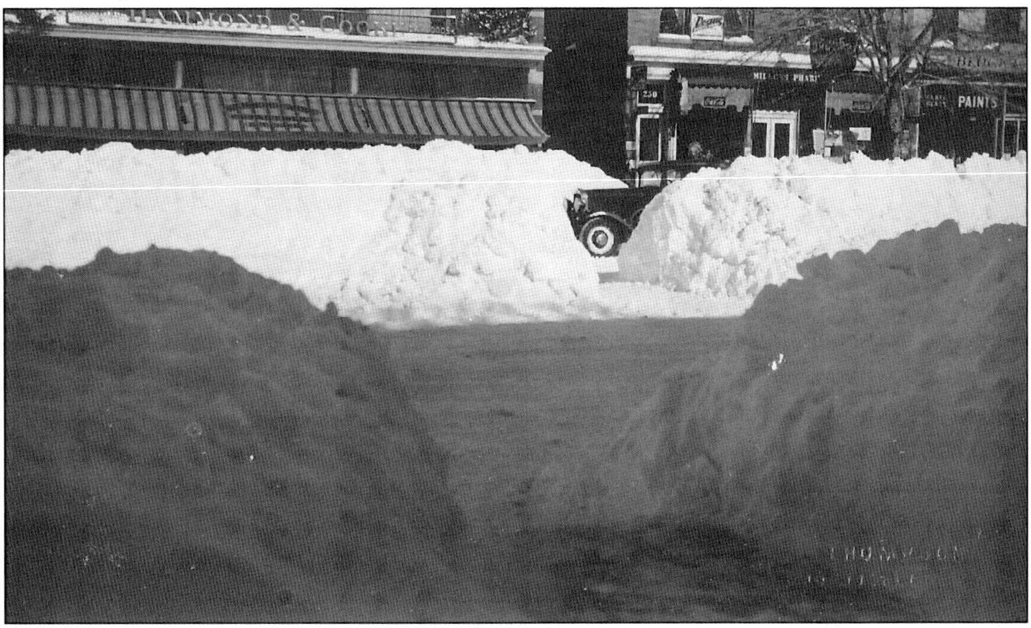

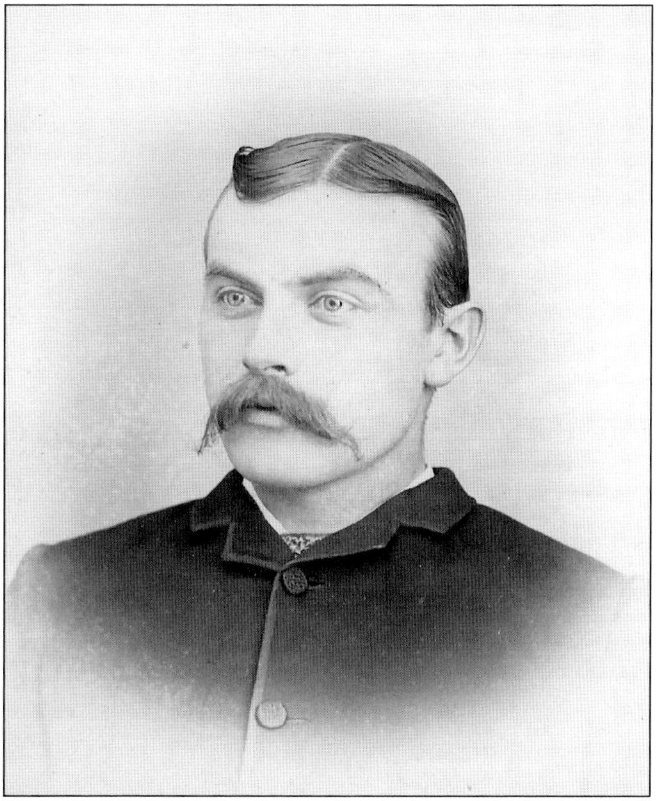

Pictured here is Adelbert M. Scriber (1865–1948), owner, editor, and publisher of the *Republican Watchman* and author of the historical novel *Old Jed* (a saga of mid-Hudson/Delaware valley pioneers and Native Americans). He was director of Sullivan County Trust Company, president of Sullivan County Historical Society, and charter member and president of Monticello Rotary. He was also presidential elector for New York in 1936 and delegate to the Democratic National Convention in 1944 during Roosevelt's campaign. (Courtesy of Susan Benton Schock.)

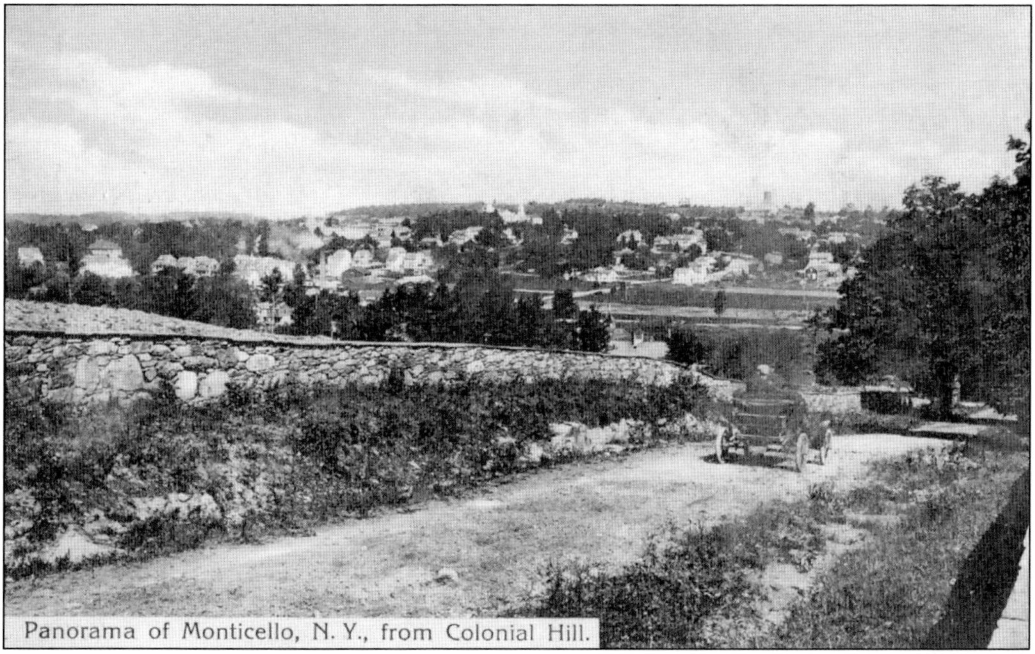

Pictured above is the mansion of Col. John O'Neil, built on Colonial Hill as seen from Colonial Hill Drive. Toward the bottom, the road approaches a meadow presently used for athletics and sometimes for commencement ceremonies. (Courtesy of Richard Benjamin Sr.)

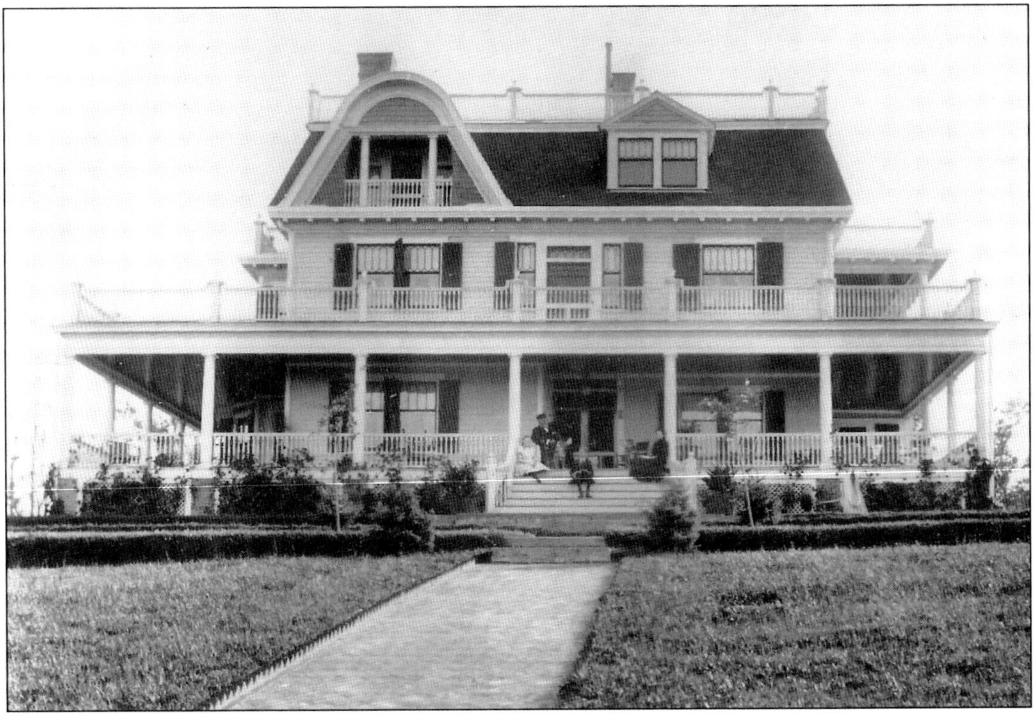

Here are two views of Col. John O'Neil's mansion on Colonial Hill. The view from the rear (below) shows the servants' entrance. In its later years, the mansion was used as a boardinghouse for tourists and summer guests. (Both, courtesy of Denise Connolly.)

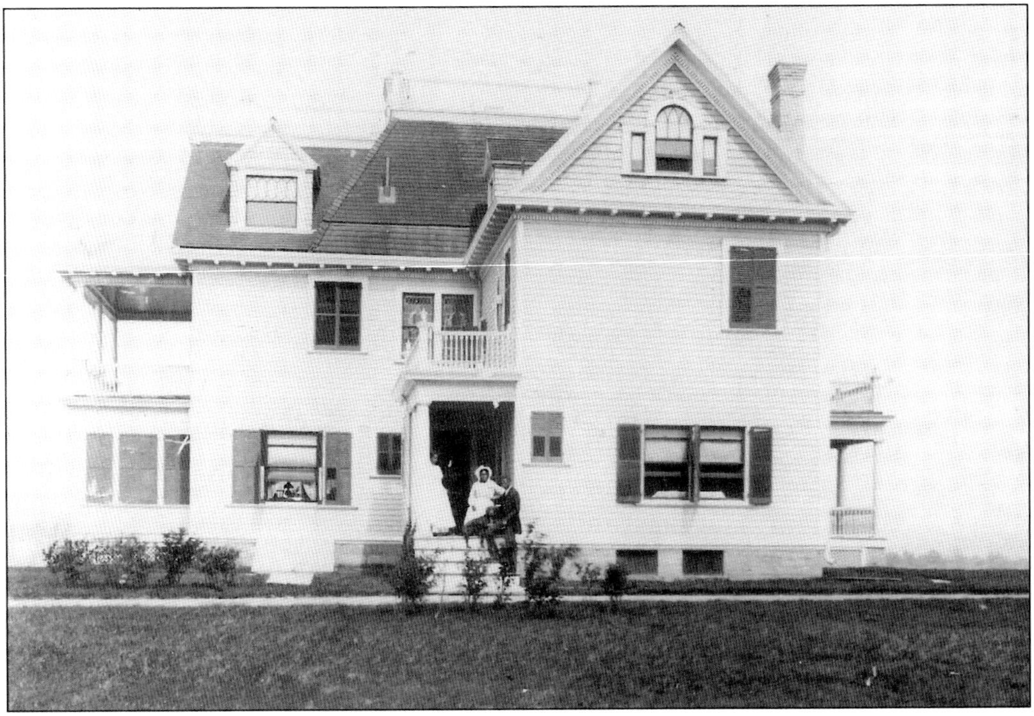

This photograph taken by Kenneth D. Niven shows some of his colleagues at New York Telephone Company installing new telephone lines in April 1930. On October 28, 1929, the Village of Monticello accepted $3,000 from New York Telephone Company for permission to lay underground electrical conductors, ducts, pipes, cables, wires, and manholes. The billboard on the left is for Wrigley's chewing gum. (Courtesy of Daniel K. Niven.)

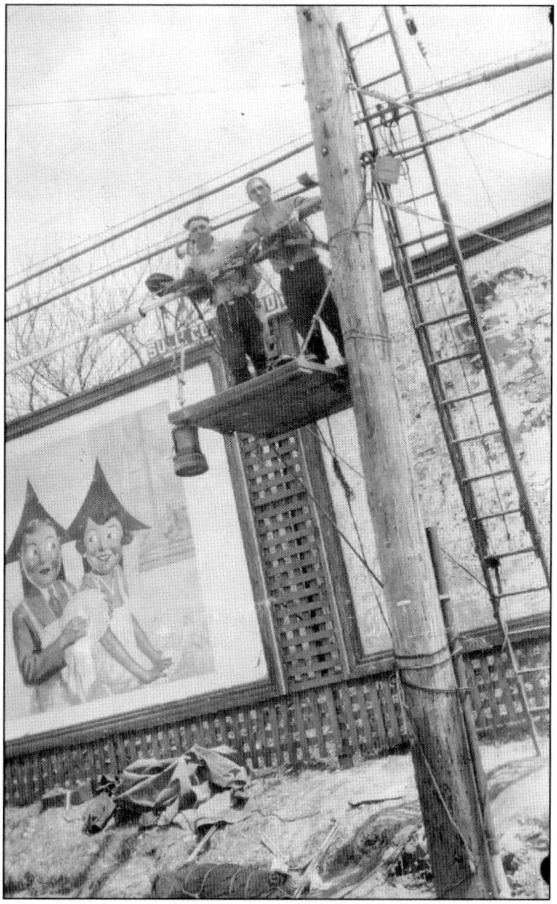

Pictured below is the original Van Etten Oil Company office, which was a shack on Saint John Street near the site of the present-day Van Etten Oil Company headquarters. In the 1920s, Richard Van Etten was a Texaco salesman. In 1944, he founded the Van Etten Oil Company. (Courtesy of Van Etten Oil Company.)

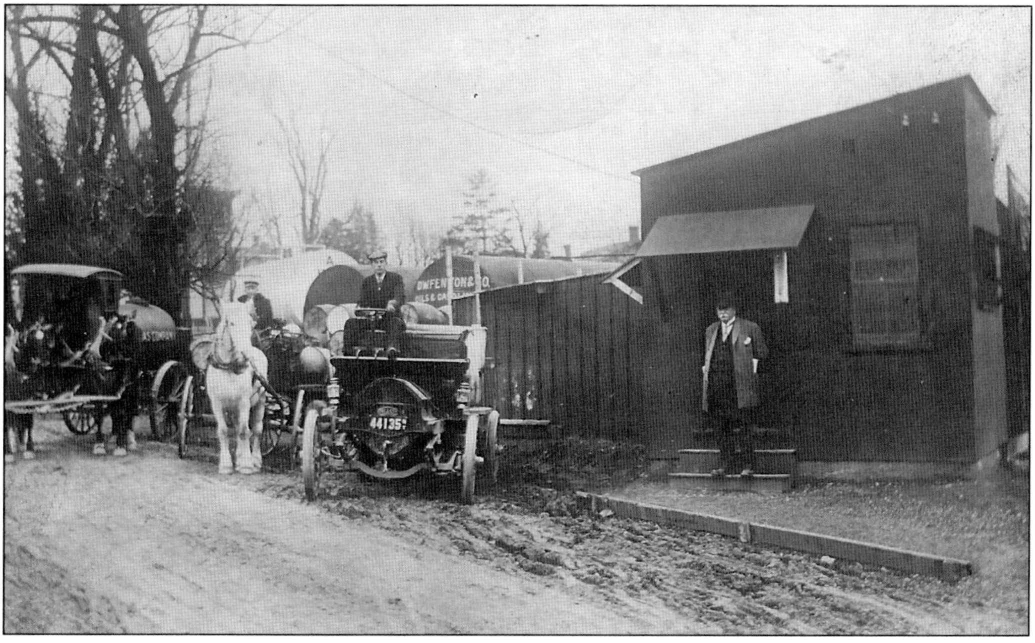

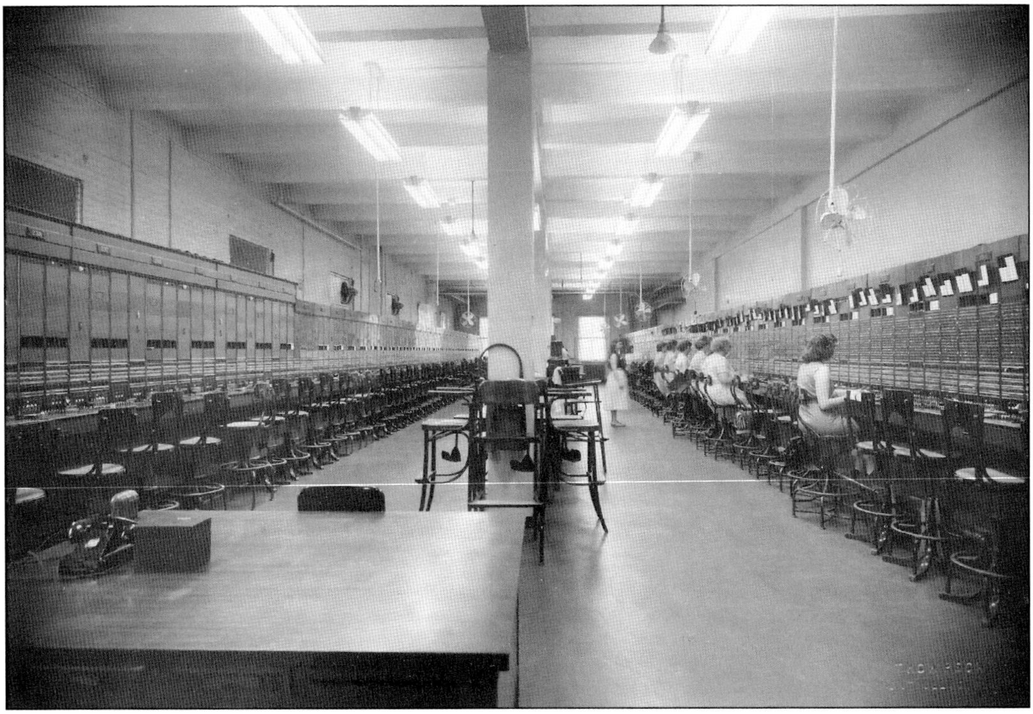

Built by the Monticello Telephone Company, this structure still stands on Saint John Street beside the former Monticello High School (later Monticello Middle School). In 1912, there were 192 telephones in Monticello. Three years later there were 316. All operators were female. Many were not local but came to Monticello for these jobs. The advertisement appearing below is from a 1959 Monticello High School yearbook published in 1959. (Courtesy of Susan Benton Schock.)

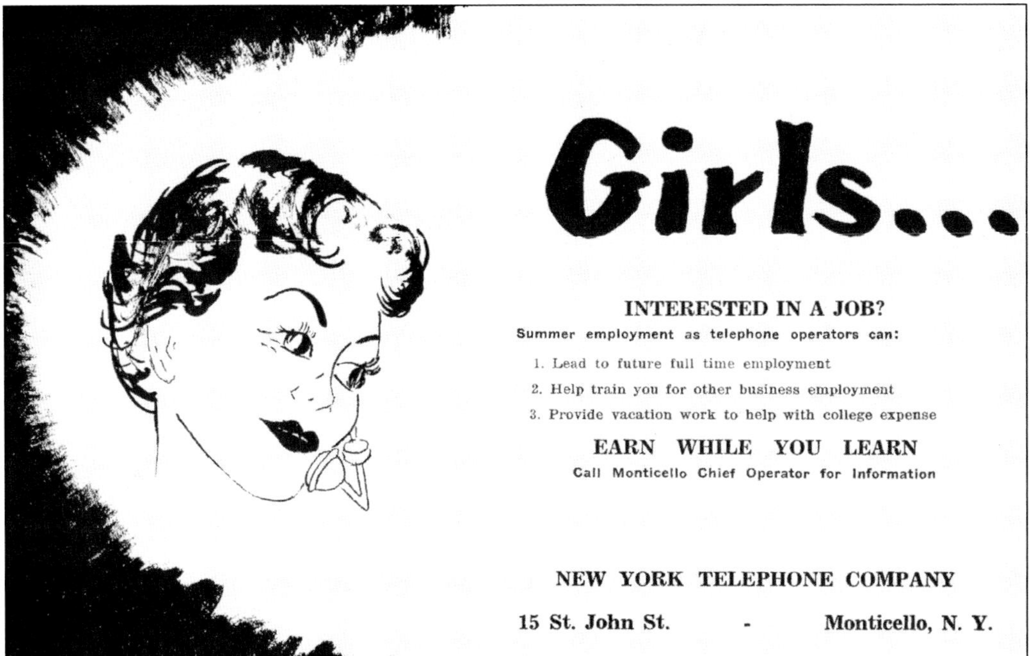

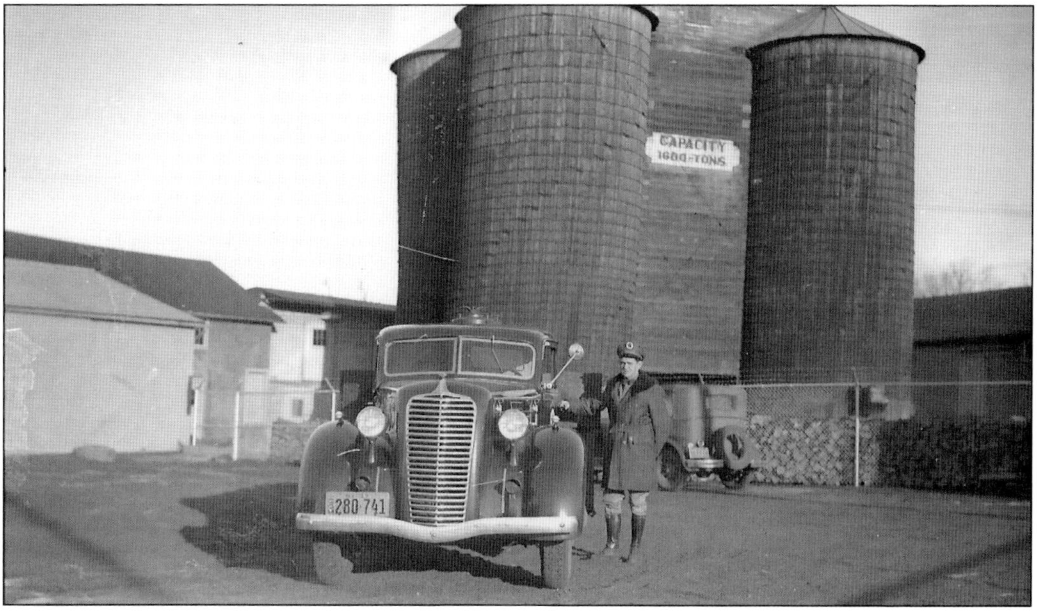

Parked beside the Callery and Rundle coal bins adjacent to the Monticello railroad depot, this 1947 Brockway truck was owned by the Van Etten Oil Company. Trains stopped just before the coal bins by the train station. In earlier years, Frank H. Osborn operated a coal and wood business near this location. (Courtesy of Van Etten Oil Company.)

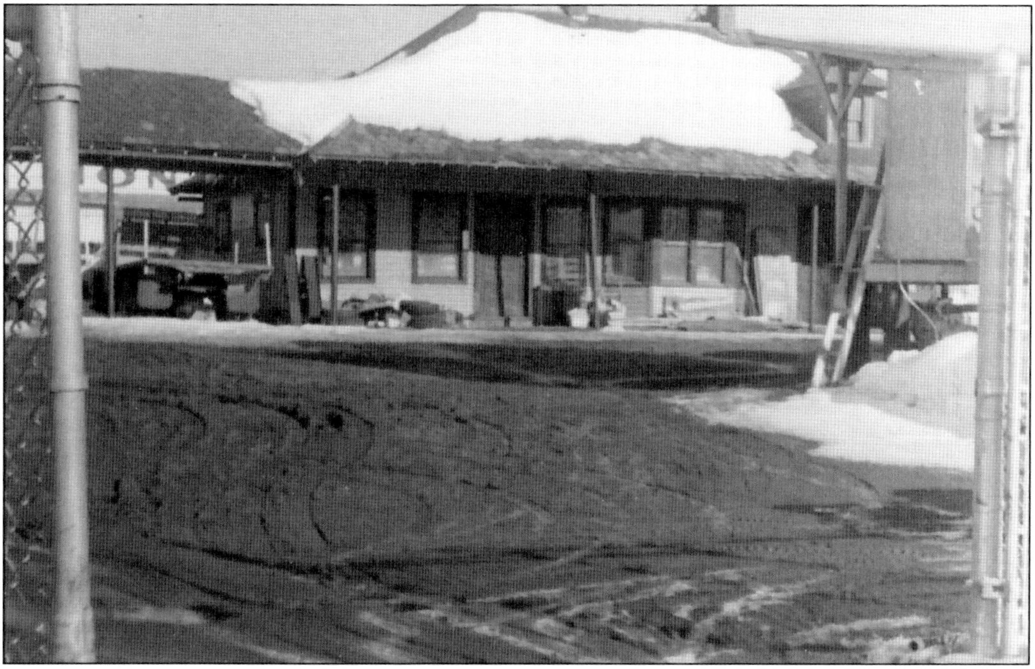

This building is owned by the Van Etten Oil Company, which erected a marker in cooperation with the O&W Railway Historical Society identifying the former station as the Catskill Mountain destination for sportsmen and vacationers from 1896 until the O&W halted operations March 29, 1957. The former depot, once a boon to the community, is now a warehouse and shop for repairing oil burners. (Courtesy of Van Etten Oil Company.)

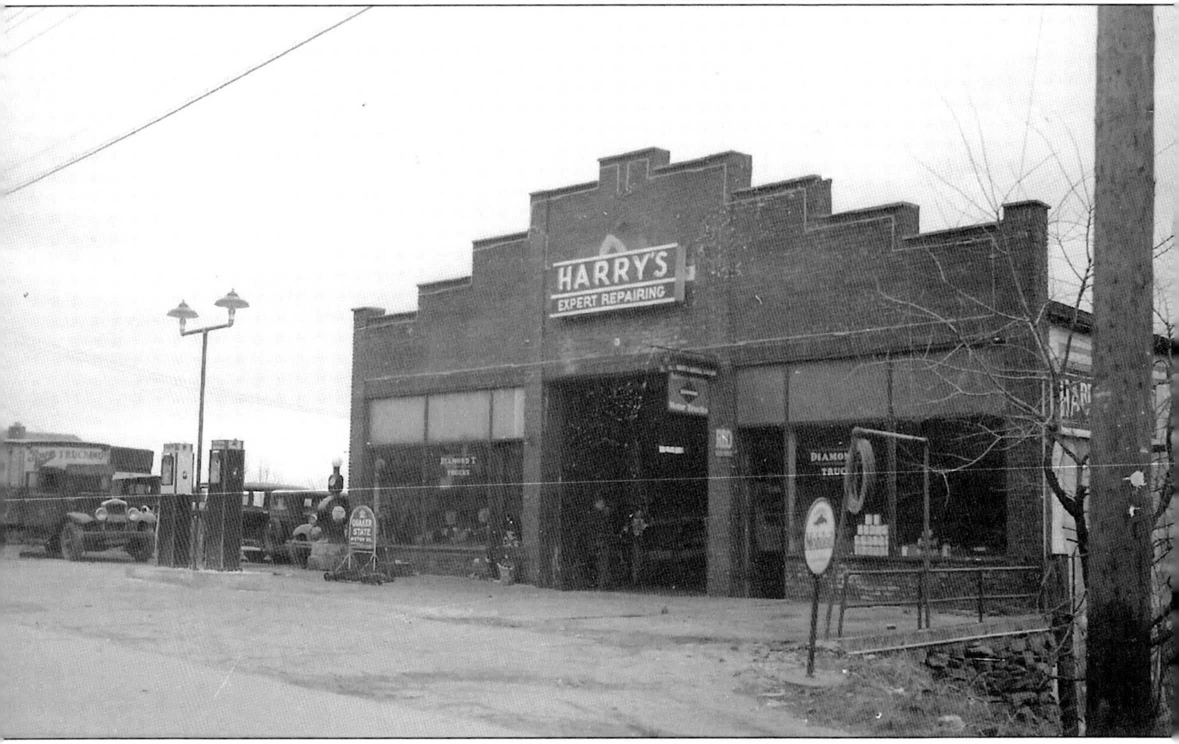

Harry's Expert Repair, located on the right side of what was called Toll Gate Hill (now Pleasant Street Extension), was owned by Harry Pashkow. A neighborhood and an entire street were obliterated by blasting when the clover leaf for exit 105 was constructed on the Route 17 bypass, allowing traffic to avoid driving through Monticello's downtown. (Courtesy of Van Etten Oil Company.)

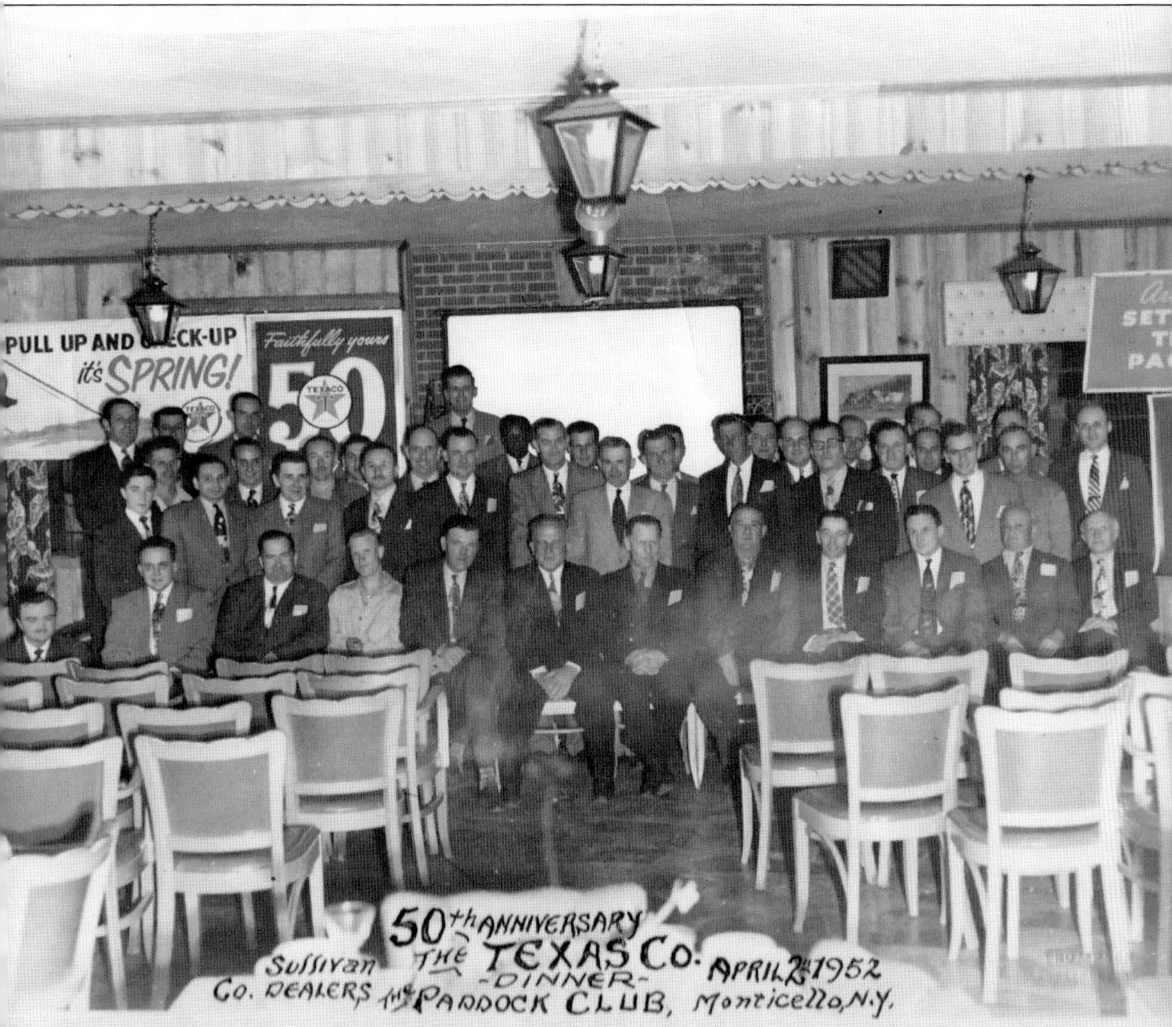

Pictured is the 50th anniversary of the Texas Company, Sullivan County dealers, April 2, 1952, at the Paddock Club on East Broadway across from the former Apollo shopping plaza. From left to right are (first row) John T. Evans Jr., Marvin Weiss, Thomas McDoal, Richard Stringer, Fred McClernon, Herbert Weiss, Emil Hindemith, Fred Gutekunst, Walter Theimer, Willart T. Sherman, Harry Levits, and Jacob Mowshowitz; (second row) Lee Kehley, Victor Weiss, John Murran, Ben Lewis, Larry Vantran, consignee Richard Van Etten, zone manager Paul B. Loy, Charles C. Klothe, Clifford Slater, John Baran, Allan W. Yuill Jr., Ernest Crispell Jr., Arthur Autz, and Charles Stachow; (third row) Earl Poley, Emerson Bossley, John Conway (father of Sullivan County historian John Conway), Bernard Haliczer, Harry Whipple, Sam Harden, Robert Bernhardt, John H. Morrison Jr., W. W. Wilsey, Elwood Baim, D. W. Purtell, Dan Simonson, J. J. Cummings, and state manager R. L. Saunders Jr.; (fourth row) Edwin Chellis, Richard Chellis, Richard Weigand, and Stephen Cross. (Howard Thompson photograph; courtesy of Van Etten Oil Company.)

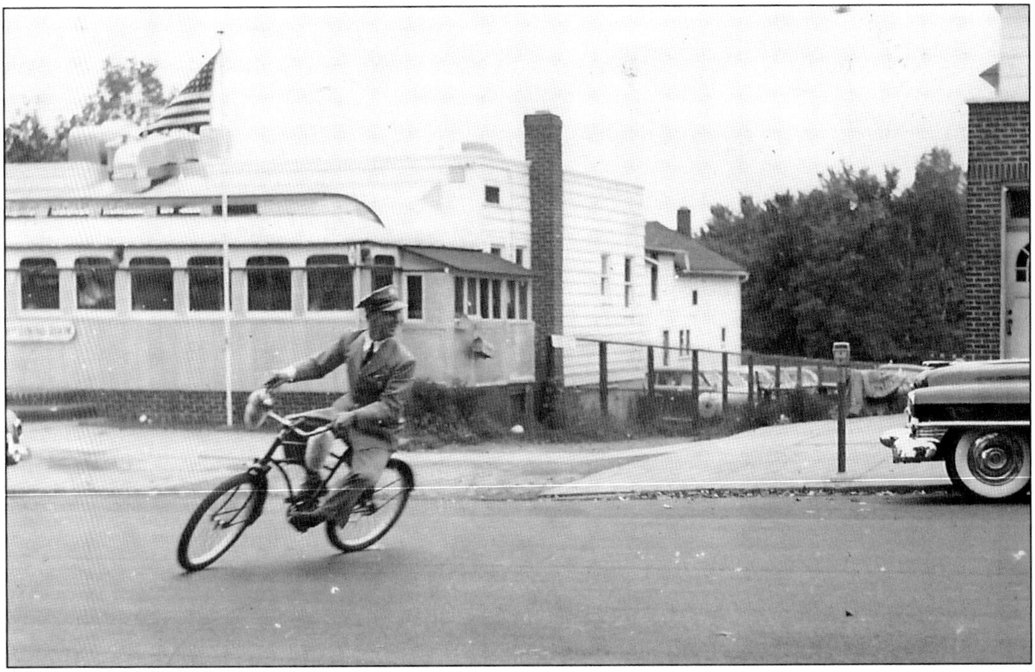

The Miss Monticello Diner has been a landmark on Monticello's main drag for two generations. The uniformed firefighter above playfully pedals a U-turn on a young girl's bicycle. The sign on the building says simply "Dining Room." (Courtesy of Monticello Fire Department.)

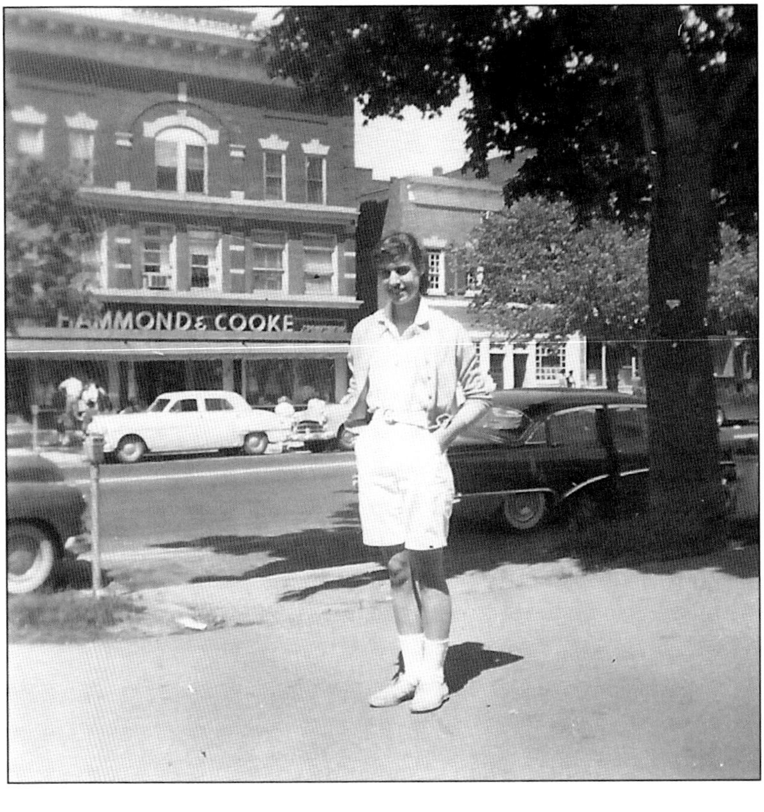

Susan Benton, daughter of *Republican Watchman* editor Alvin O. Benton, poses in white bobby socks on Broadway in 1954, across from Hammond and Cooke's department store. (Courtesy of Susan Benton Schock.)

Peter and Betty Ng stand at their parents' laundry in the Margolin building on Saint John Street in May 1958 (right), dressed for their First Communion. Parents Ng Yen and Yuen Sun Ying purchased the Sam Lee Laundry after he returned from serving in the army during World War II in 1943. (Courtesy of Peter Ng.)

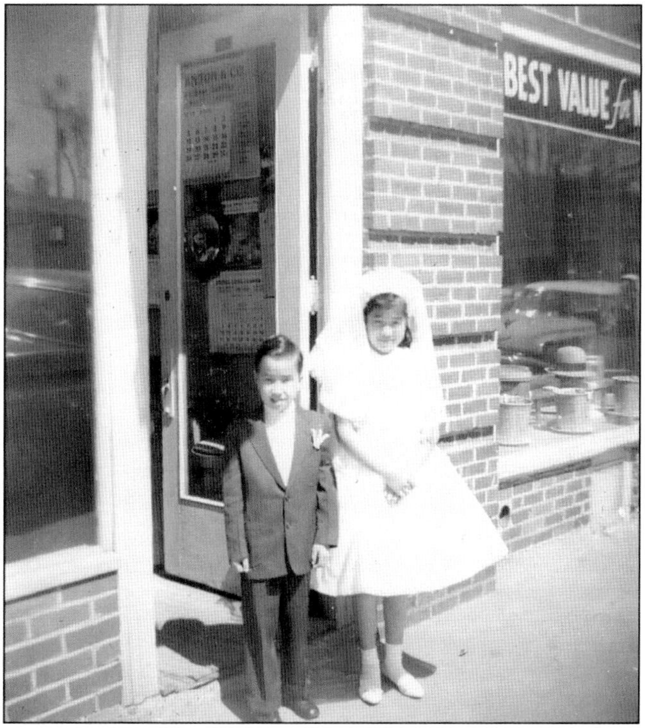

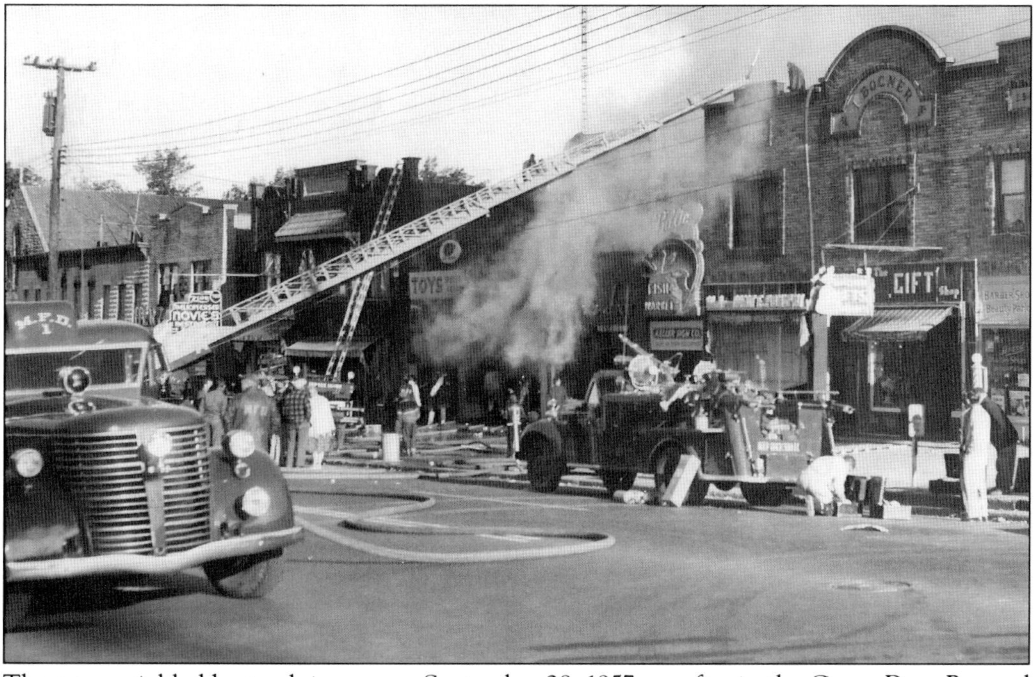

The new aerial ladder truck is seen on September 28, 1957, as a fire in the Green Door Bar and Grill at 294–296 Broadway (Bogner building) is extinguished. Shown are Sachus Candy Store, William Zank Clothing, and a gift shop in the Bogner building. Monticello's first paid fireman was hired in 1936. As of 1957, there were three paid firemen on duty 24 hours, with 86 active volunteers. (Courtesy of Monticello Fire Department.)

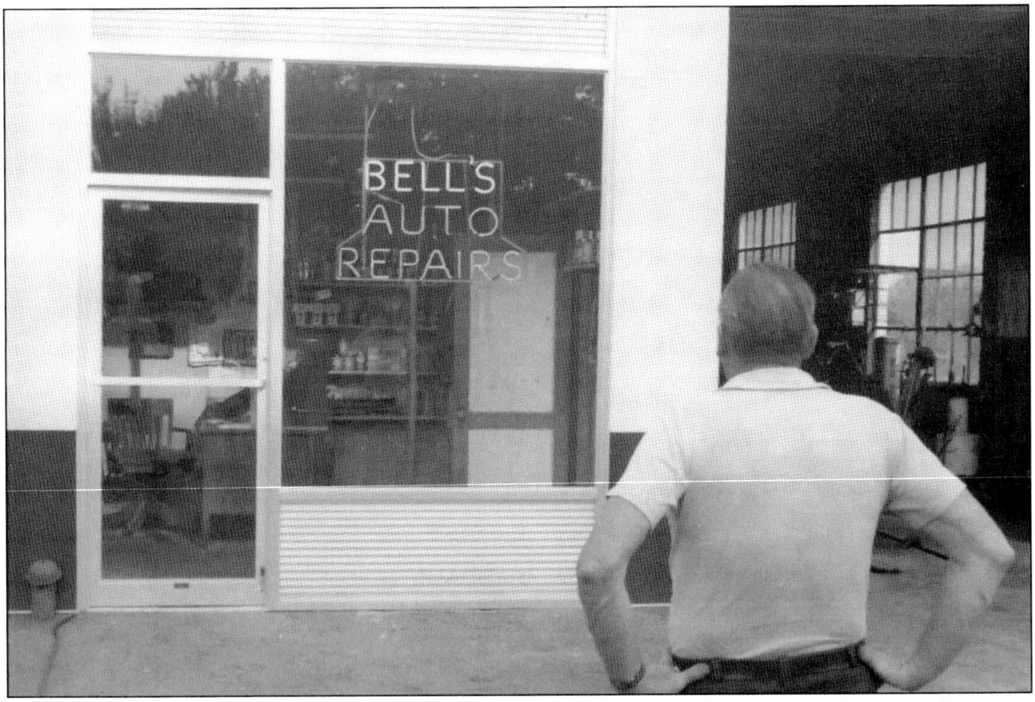

Bell's Garage was on Route 42 (Forestburgh Road,) where Plotkin's Liquor Store now stands, across the road from Evergreen Apartments. In the picture, admiring his flashing neon sign, is Wilbur Bell, the man who wore Texaco's silver star on his hat. His wife, Mildred, was an elementary school teacher in Monticello. (Courtesy of Van Etten Oil Company.)

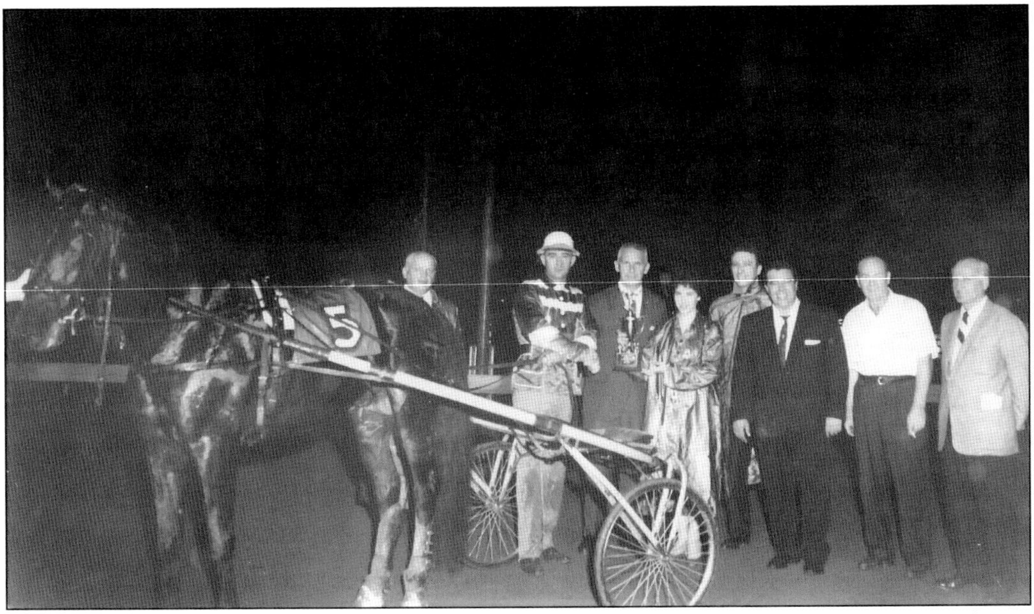

Monticello Raceway opened June 27, 1958, at a cost of $5 million. Seen in this image dated June 27, 1959, are Moe Kaplan of Broadway's Kaplan's Deli (in black suit and tie) with his daughter Susan Kaplan next to him. Manny Bogner of Bogner Seitel Lumber Company and automobile dealer Arthur Glick are in the back. (Courtesy of Susan Benton Schock.)

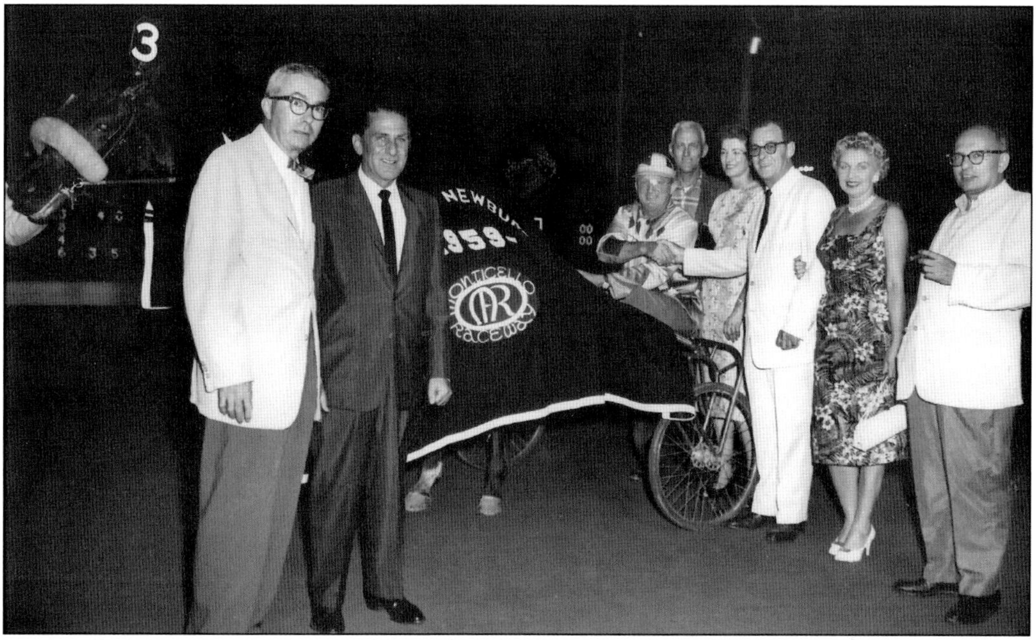

Monticello Raceway rose out of a former huckleberry patch known as Wolf's Corners northwest of the village. Track director and Broadway department store owner Don Hammond is pictured at left standing next to Sidney Sussman, owner of the former Windsor Hotel in South Fallsburg. At right is Frank Devlin, president of the track. The horse's blanket says 1959, the racetrack's second year in business. (Courtesy of Susan Benton Schock.)

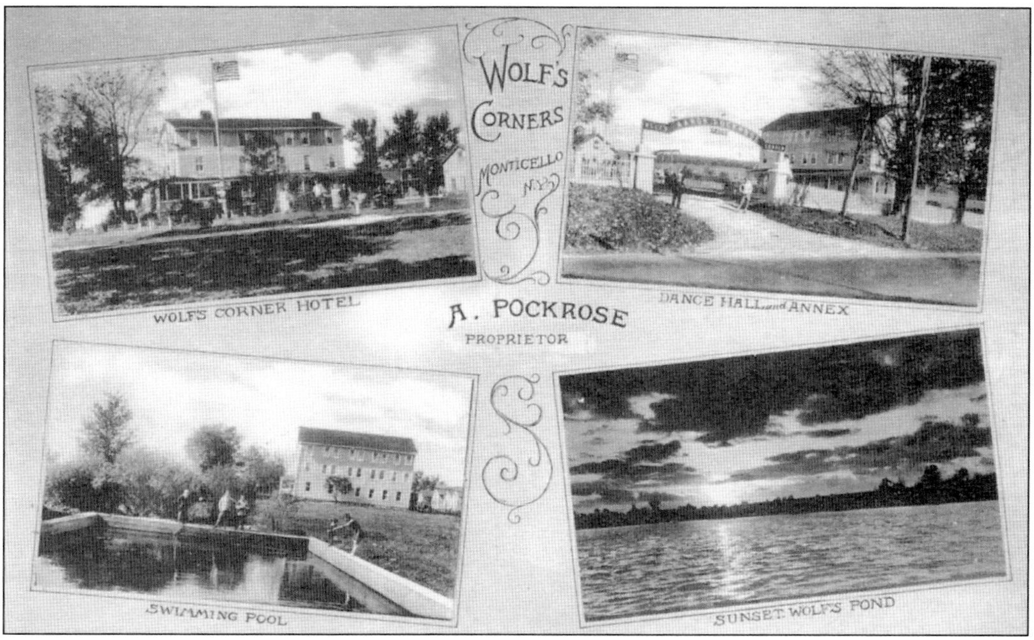

This old postcard advertises Wolf's Corners Hotel, which was previously located on the premises of the present-day Monticello Raceway and owned by Abraham Pockrose. At 275 acres, the farm was a well-equipped boardinghouse catering to city visitors. Wolf's Corners is described in period newspapers as being "on the Maplewood road." (Courtesy of Richard Benjamin.)

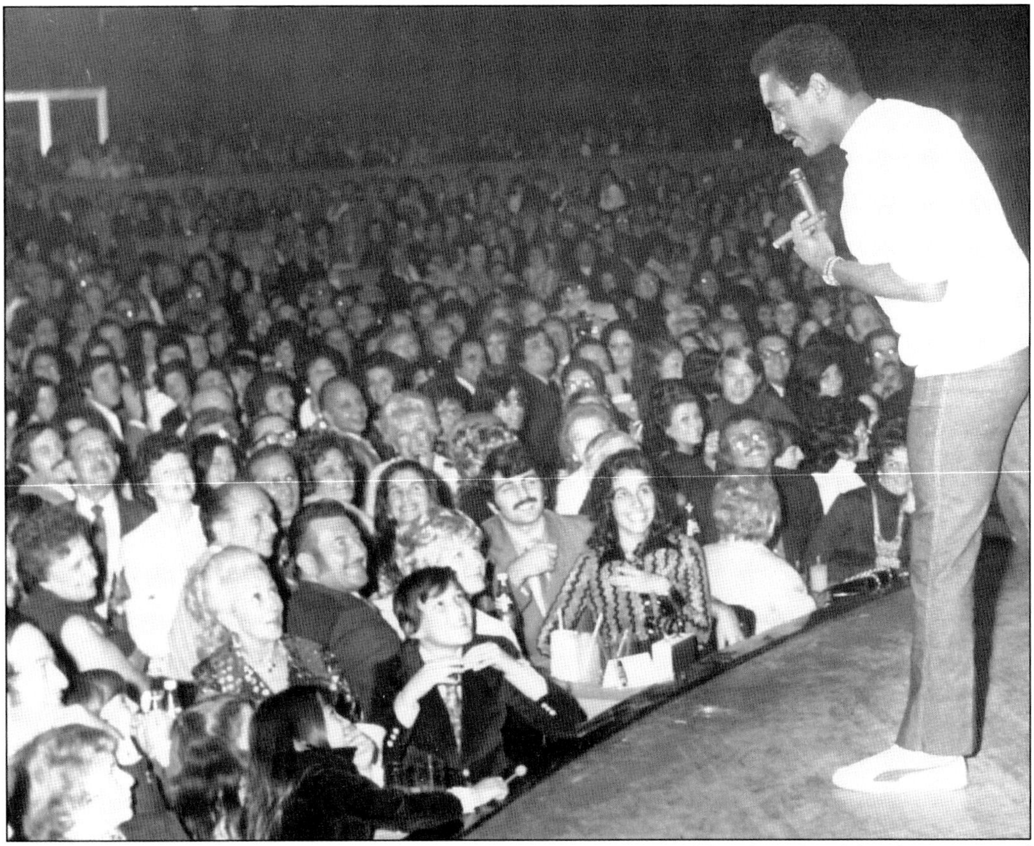

In and around Monticello, boardinghouses evolved into grand landmarks, like the Concord Resort Hotel 2 miles from village limits. Comedian Bill Cosby, above, and countless other entertainers packed the house all summer, year after year. In the front row (striped shirt) is Terry Nargizian and Monticello carpet wholesaler (and later village manager) Raymond Nargizian (with mustache), who were invited to the show by Concord owners George and Sharon Parker. (Courtesy of Cappelli Associates.)

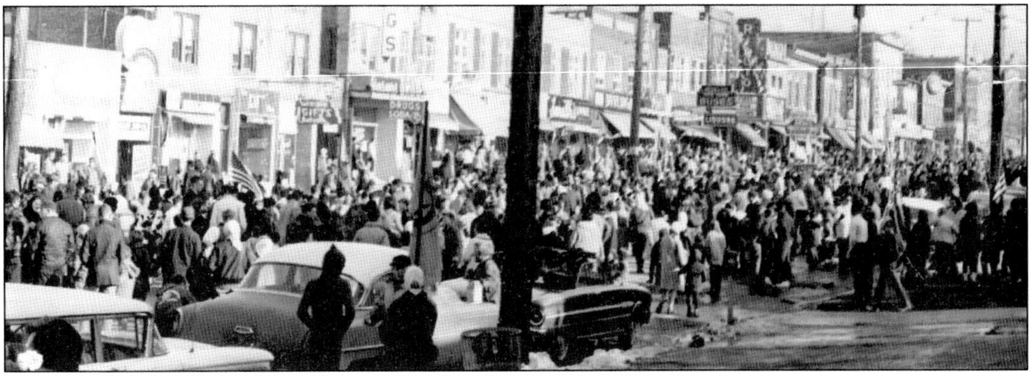

Above is a photograph of a holiday retail promotional. Santa Claus dropped Ping-Pong balls from a helicopter. Prizes given for specially marked balls brought a crushing crowd, each person hoping to at least win a free soda at Woolworth's fountain. The event was sponsored by the Monticello Chamber of Commerce, of which the photographer, Samuel Greene, was president. (Courtesy of Sylvia Greene.)

Four

CELEBRATIONS AND PUBLIC EVENTS

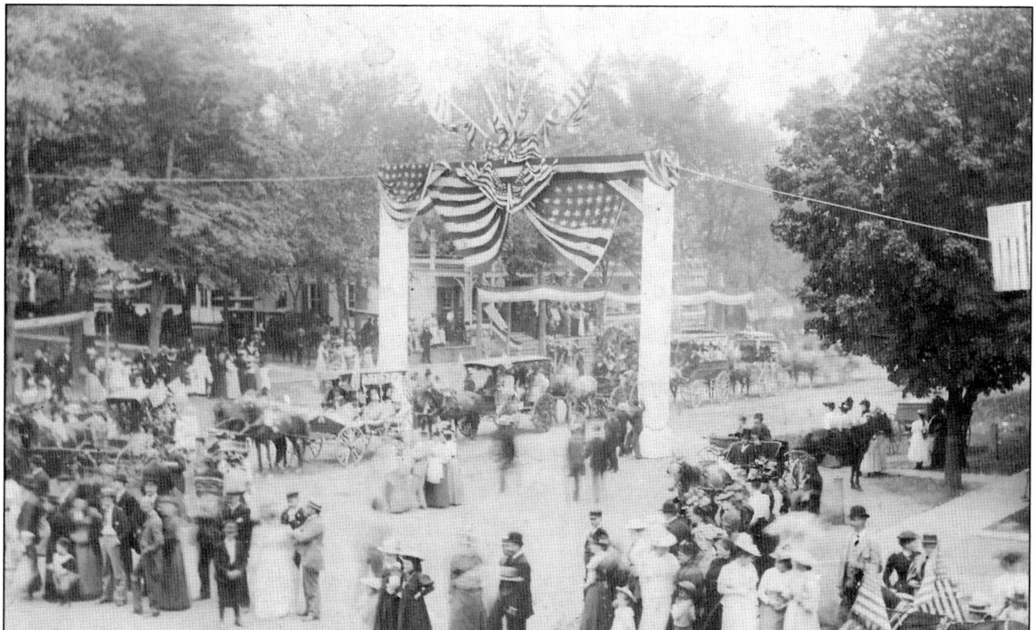

"Come, let us sit upon the Village Green / Was fairer lovelier Sylvan Grove e'er seen?" wrote A. C. Butts in 1898. This annual coaching day parade was photographed from the Rockwell Hotel balcony, showing Monticello's 1904 centennial. Judge Arthur C. Butts spoke. Arlington House was recognized for the best decorated one-horse wagon. The Towner family's wagon took second place, Frank Osborn third. Zilla Towner took second place for girls on horseback. (Courtesy of William Horton.)

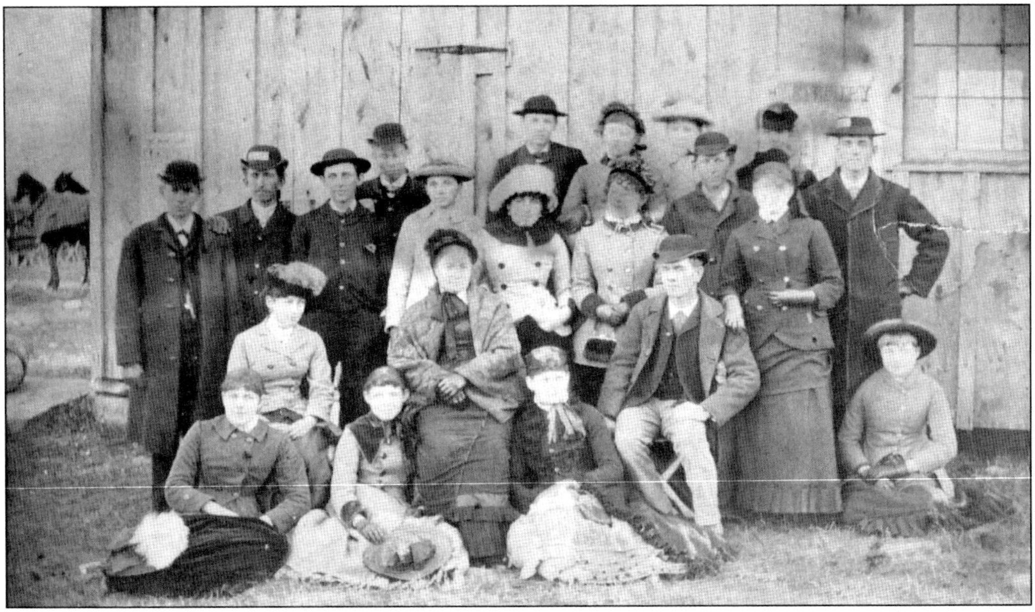

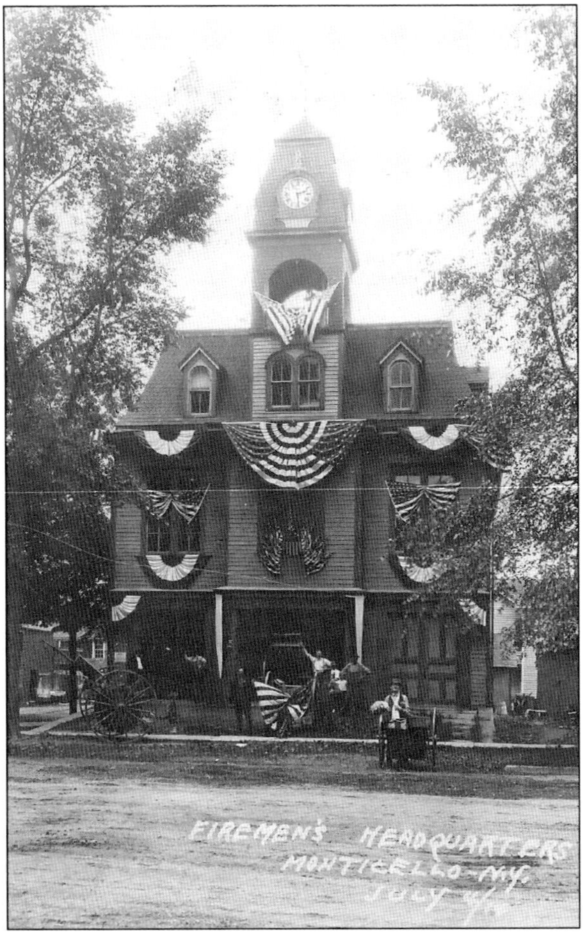

The local military service history *Something to Cherish*, privately printed after World War II, included a number of historical photographs like the one above. That work says that the image above was taken at the old fairgrounds on the hill. Andrew McCullough (standing third from the left with the flat hat), born May 1865, was 18 years old. Frank Osborn, born March 1863, was described by some who knew him as a "gay blade" at the age of 20 (standing at far right with the ticket in his hat). (Courtesy of William Horton.)

For the Fourth of July parade in 1914 at the municipal offices and fire hall on Broadway at Prince Street, government buildings and private businesses put care into decorating their premises with flags and banners to set the mood for the festivities. The clock on the tower says it is 2:30 p.m. By then, the parade had ended, and the firemen were putting their trucks away. (Courtesy of Monticello Fire Department.)

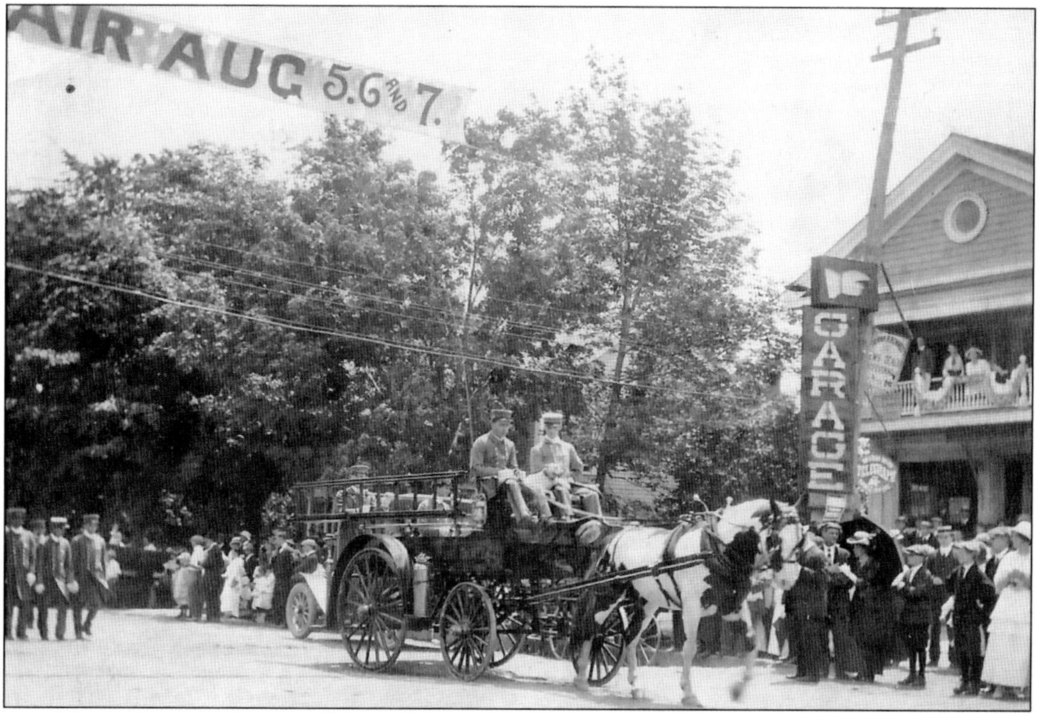

"Masonic Fair—Aug 5, 6 and 7," announces the banner at the corner of Broadway and Bank Street during the July 4, 1914, firemen's parade. The fair and parade were annual fund-raisers for the Masons, who were paying for their newly rebuilt temple from the proceeds. Repayment of the $11,000 reconstruction mortgage was celebrated in October 1951 with a mortgage-burning ceremony. (Courtesy of Monticello Fire Department.)

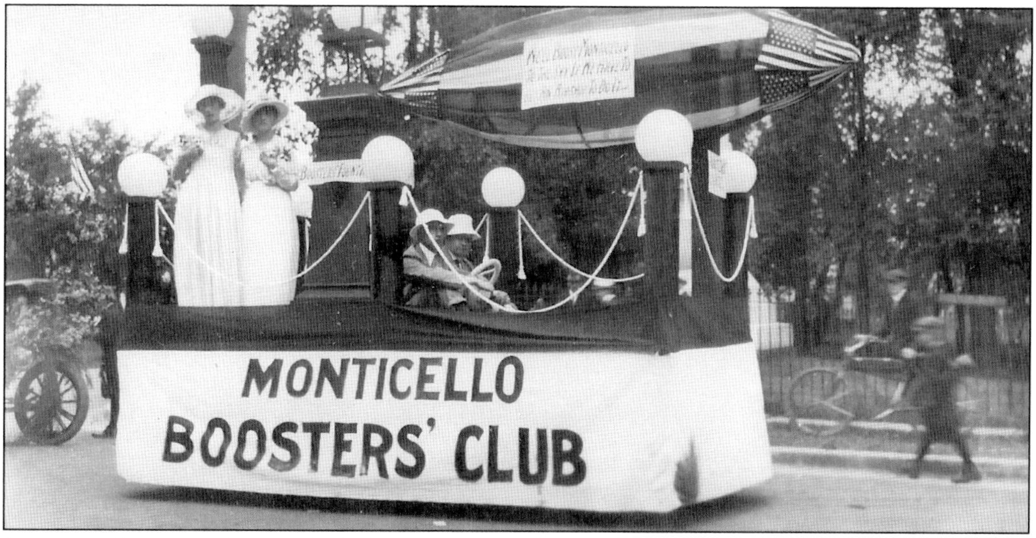

First prize for originality in the July 4, 1916, parade went to the Monticello Boosters Club. John V. Taylor and Edward Connell rigged up an automobile to represent the Monticello Boosters' Club. On it was the Boosters' fountain and the Boosters' decorative lights, like those that adorned Broadway. In the rear of the car were Florence McNeely and Josephine Buckley, becomingly dressed for the occasion. (Courtesy of Richard Benjamin Sr.)

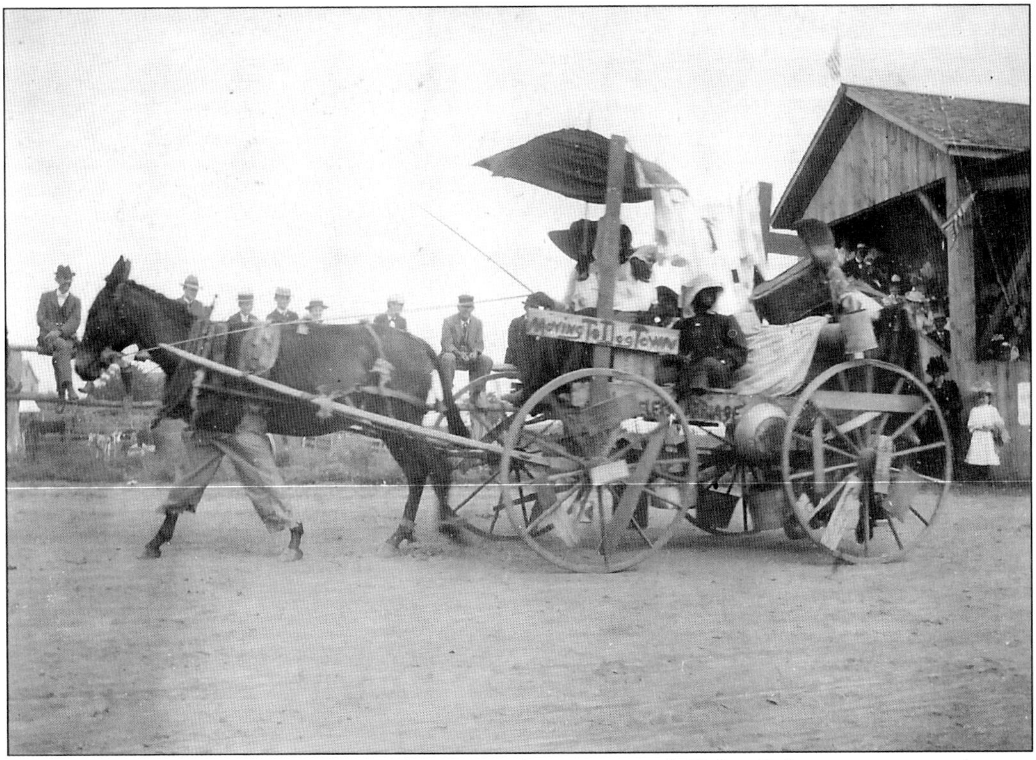

Of the above pictured float, the *Republican Watchman* reported, "John Osborn won second prize. His display was a wagon filled with dilapidate household effects, chicken coops, etc. . . . On top of the wagon was a sign bearing the words 'Moving to Dogtown.' Although the latter was more burlesque, in the opinion of the judges a steer hitched to a wagon was more of a novelty than a mule hitched the same way." The coaching day parade in September 1899 was attended by nearly 6,000 people—more than double Monticello's population at that time. (Courtesy of William Horton.)

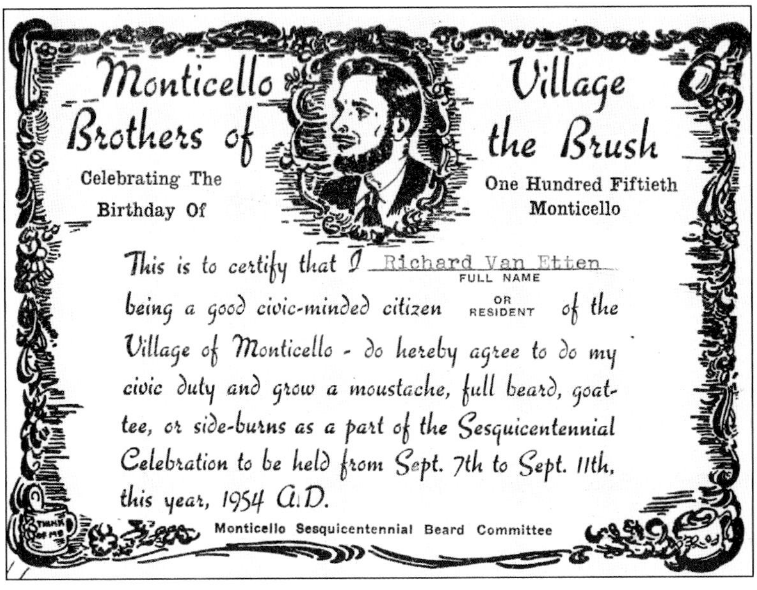
Monticello Village
Brothers of the Brush
Celebrating The One Hundred Fiftieth Birthday Of Monticello

This is to certify that I Richard Van Etten (FULL NAME) being a good civic-minded citizen OR RESIDENT of the Village of Monticello - do hereby agree to do my civic duty and grow a moustache, full beard, goat-tee, or side-burns as a part of the Sesquicentennial Celebration to be held from Sept. 7th to Sept. 11th, this year, 1954 A.D.

Monticello Sesquicentennial Beard Committee

Monticello's 150th birthday party was a huge event. Reportedly, nearly everyone in town took an active part in making it happen. Certificates of participation in the "Brothers of the Brush" promotional, like the one shown at left issued to Richard Van Etten, were given to men to document that they had gone without shaving. (Courtesy of Van Etten Oil Company.)

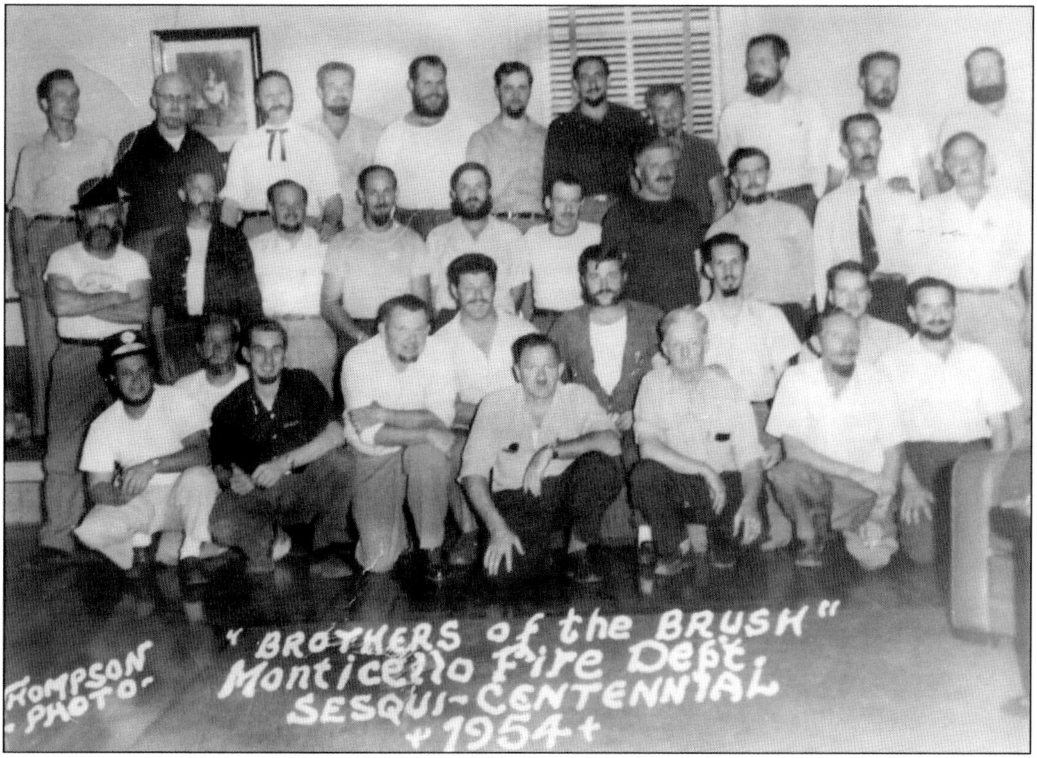

As described in the certificate of participation, for this group of men part of celebrating 150 years of community life meant growing facial hair in the style of old settlers—or at least how they imagined them to have been. Many women in the village were said to have been relieved when this aspect of the celebration ended. (Courtesy of Van Etten Oil Company.)

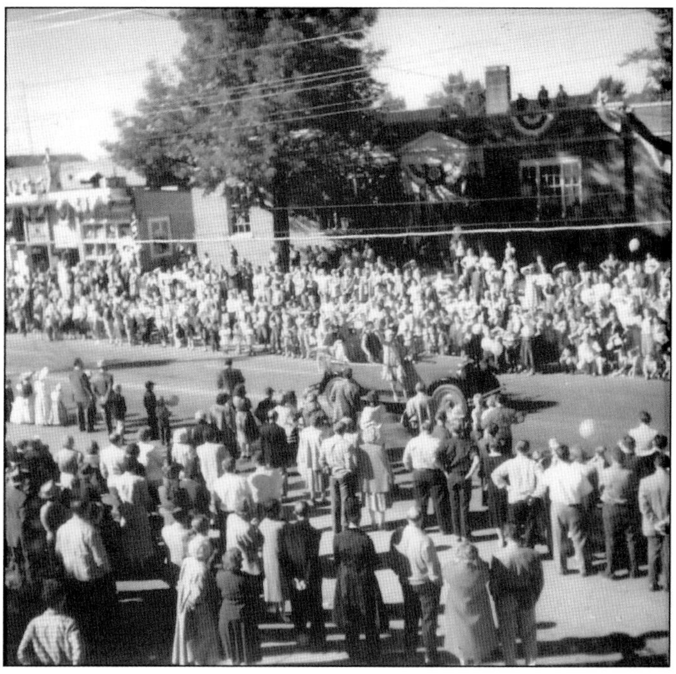

Monticello's mile-long Broadway is seen during the sesquicentennial parade in September 1954 with buildings festooned in patriotic style. It has been the site of many colorful parades featuring fire departments, fraternities, county fair committees, community groups, and countless costumed residents. (Courtesy of Monticello Post Office.)

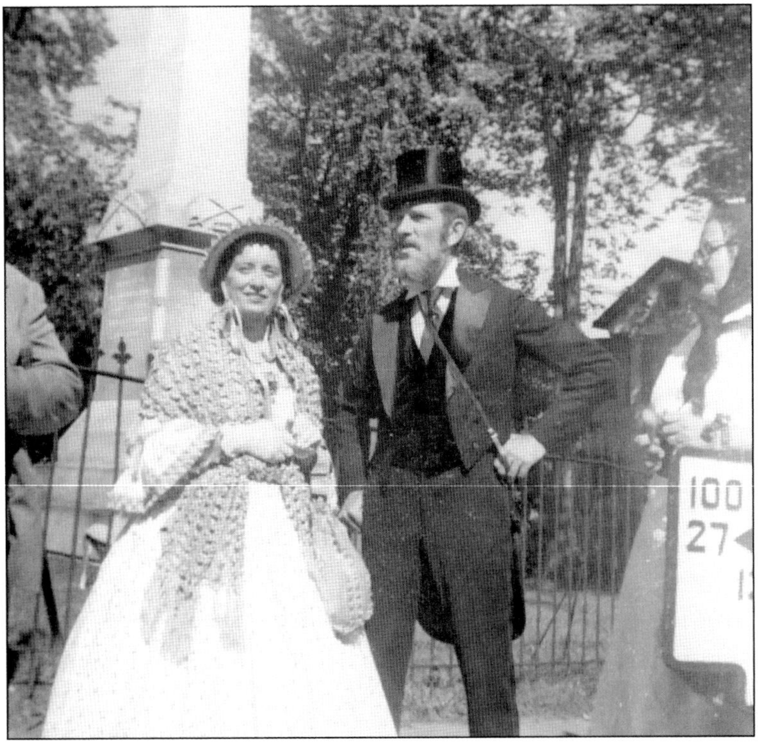

The *Soldiers and Sailors Monument*'s original location was at the corner of Jefferson Street when the village's sesquicentennial was celebrated in 1954. Kenneth D. Niven and Norma Niven pose in costume during the event marking the 150th anniversary of the village's settlement. (Courtesy of Daniel K. Niven.)

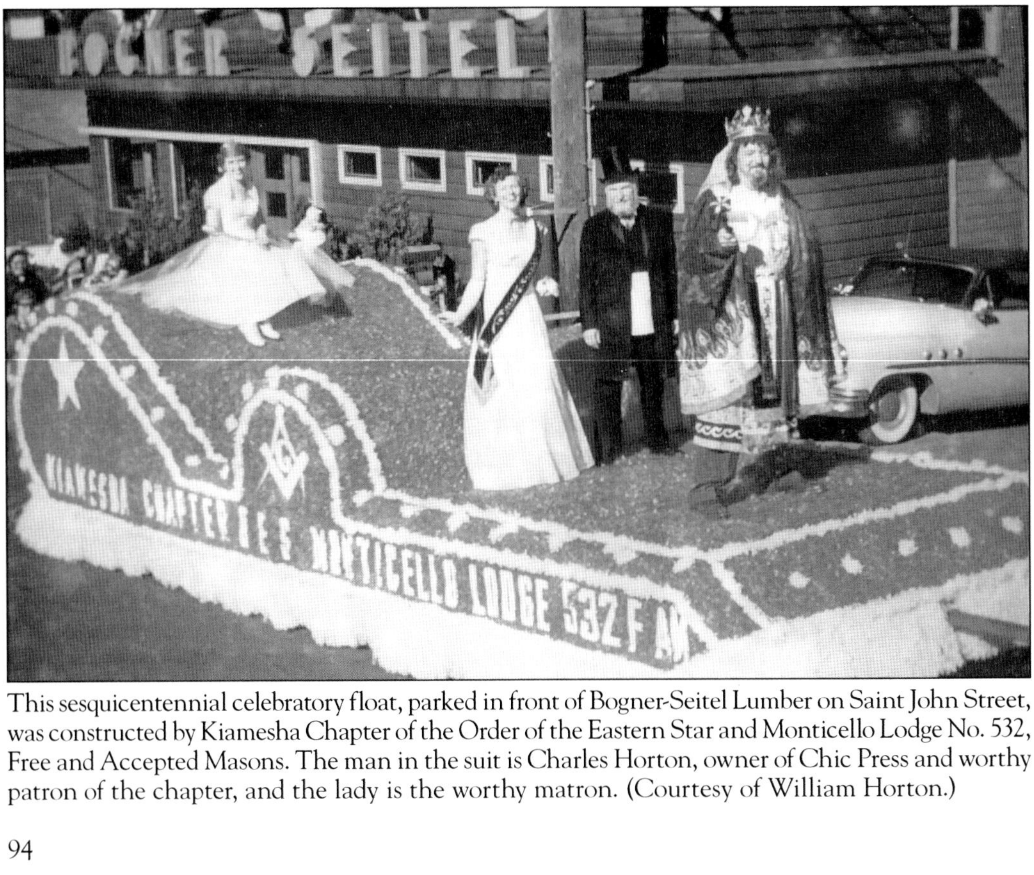

This sesquicentennial celebratory float, parked in front of Bogner-Seitel Lumber on Saint John Street, was constructed by Kiamesha Chapter of the Order of the Eastern Star and Monticello Lodge No. 532, Free and Accepted Masons. The man in the suit is Charles Horton, owner of Chic Press and worthy patron of the chapter, and the lady is the worthy matron. (Courtesy of William Horton.)

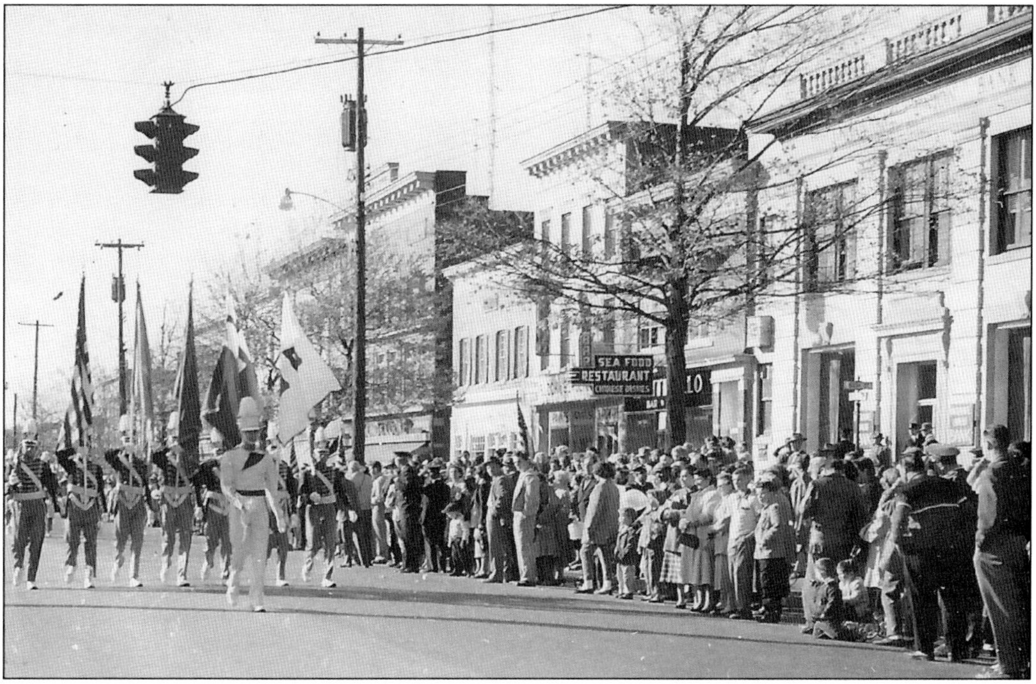

These photographs are of the Sullivan County Firemen's Field Day parade held on October 12, 1957. Above, throngs of onlookers line Broadway's curb near the corner of Bank Street as the Monticello High School honor guard passes in front of the former National Union Bank (now Key Bank). Below is a group of youth and senior citizens on a "music through life" float, with groups designated for teenage, mature, and golden years. The float is passing in front of D'Ari Pharmacy in the Margolin building (later the site of the Rhulen Insurance Company building and now a vacant lot) at the corner of Broadway and Saint John Street. (Courtesy of Monticello Fire Department.)

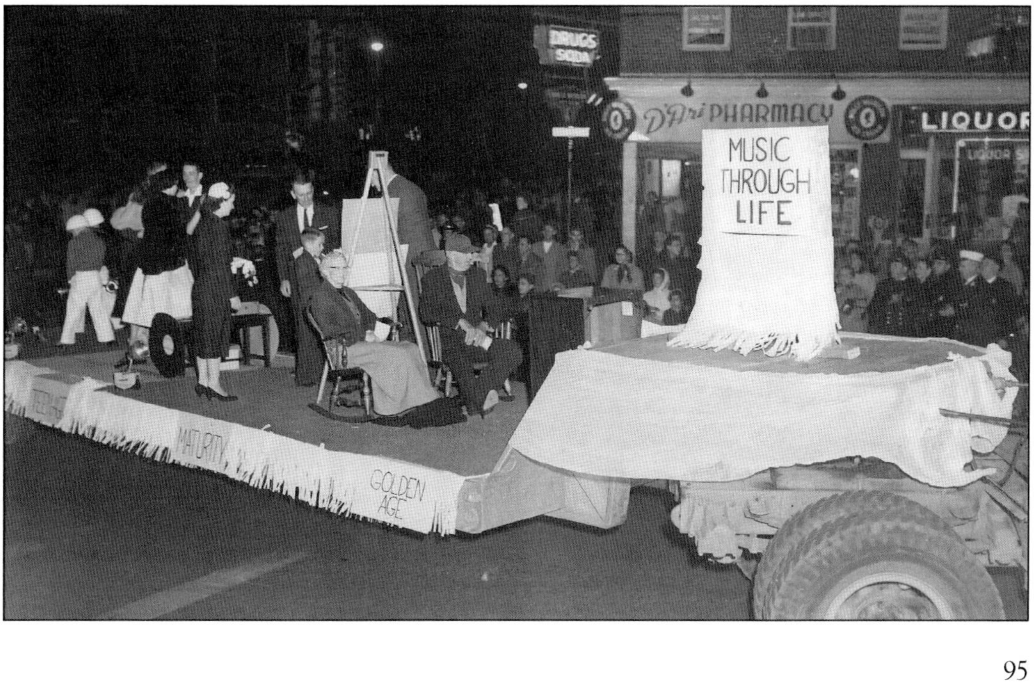

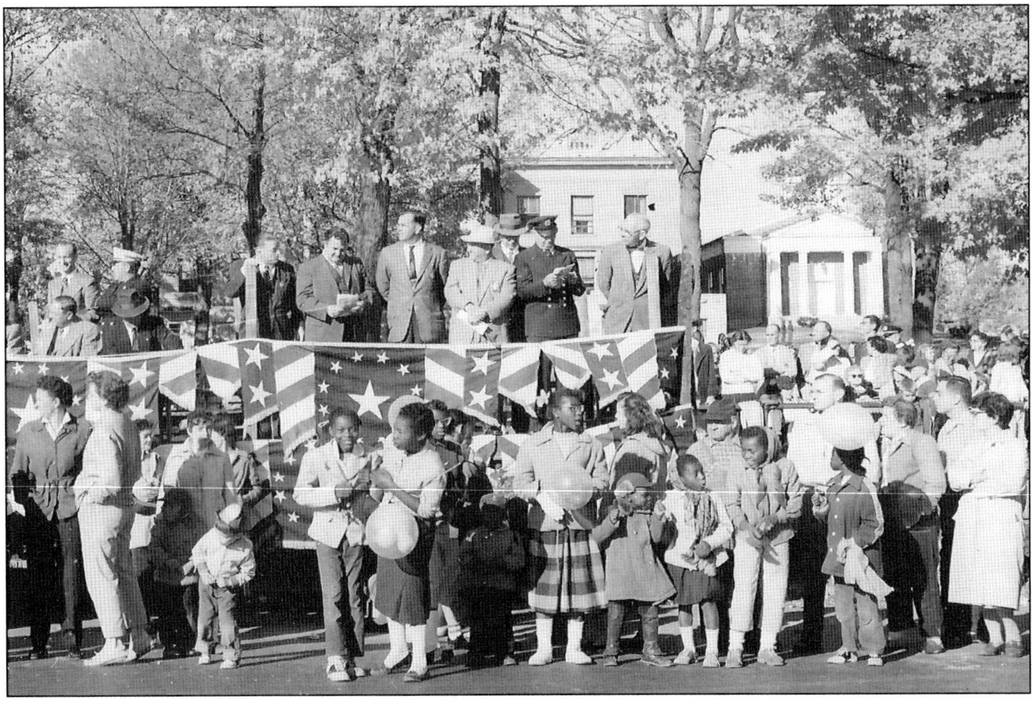

These photographs were also taken on Columbus Day 1957. Above, on the reviewing stand in front of the courthouse stood Sullivan County Court judge Lawrence H. Cooke and Monticello police chief Jack Sharoff (in uniform.) The children in front of the stand are members of the McCoy family. Pictured below at the same parade, several blocks west on Broadway, police officers Herbert Anton (right) and Julius Hocker stand in front of the post office across the street from the old town hall and firehouse. (Both, courtesy of Monticello Fire Department.)

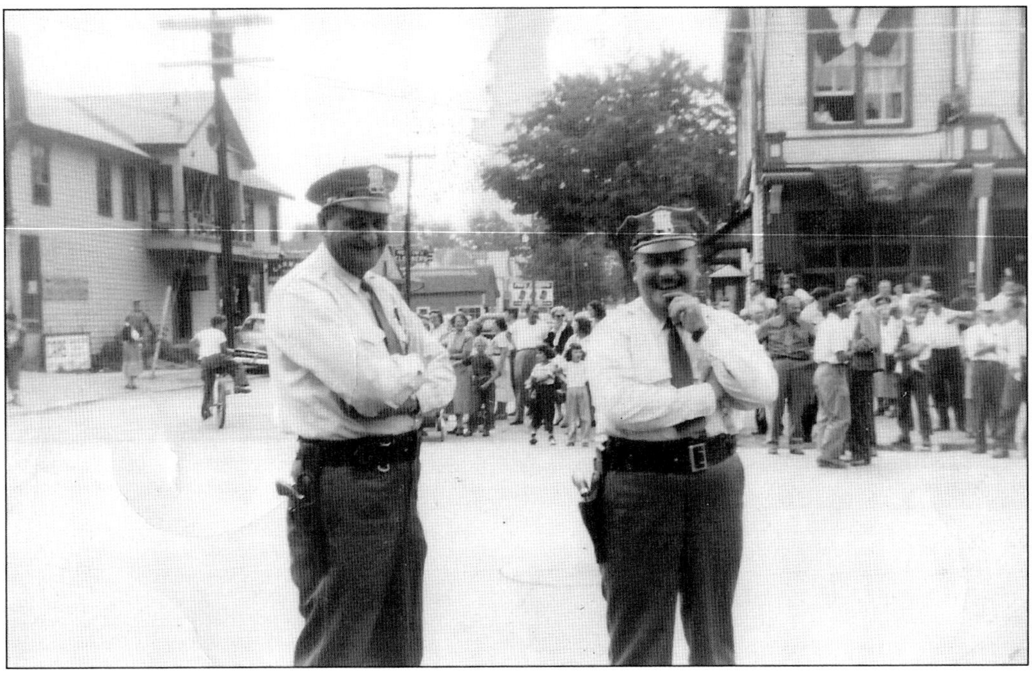

Five

WAR AND PEACE

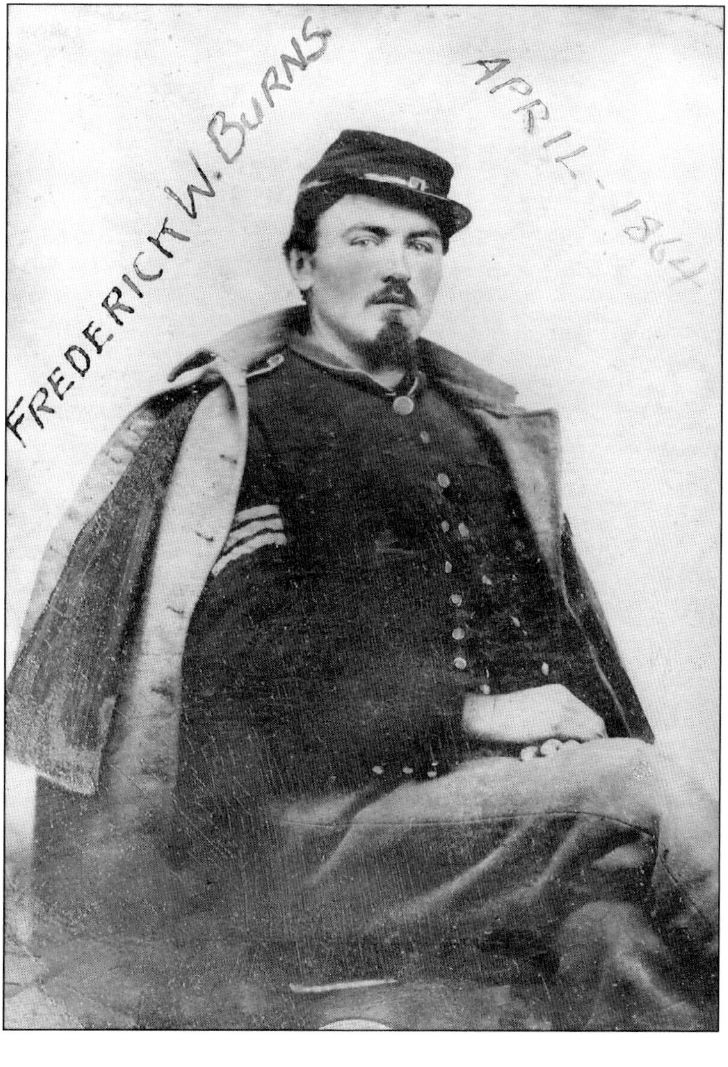

At right is Frederick W. Burns, born January 1835, a blacksmith who came to Monticello from Oakland Valley. He joined the Monticello Freemasons on March 19, 1864, and this photograph, taken one month later, hung in the lodge for decades. Quartermaster of Company A, 143rd Regiment, he was wounded at the battle of Peach Tree Ridge in Georgia on July 20, 1864. He died July 5, 1919, in Forestburgh, New York. (Courtesy of Monticello Lodge No. 532.)

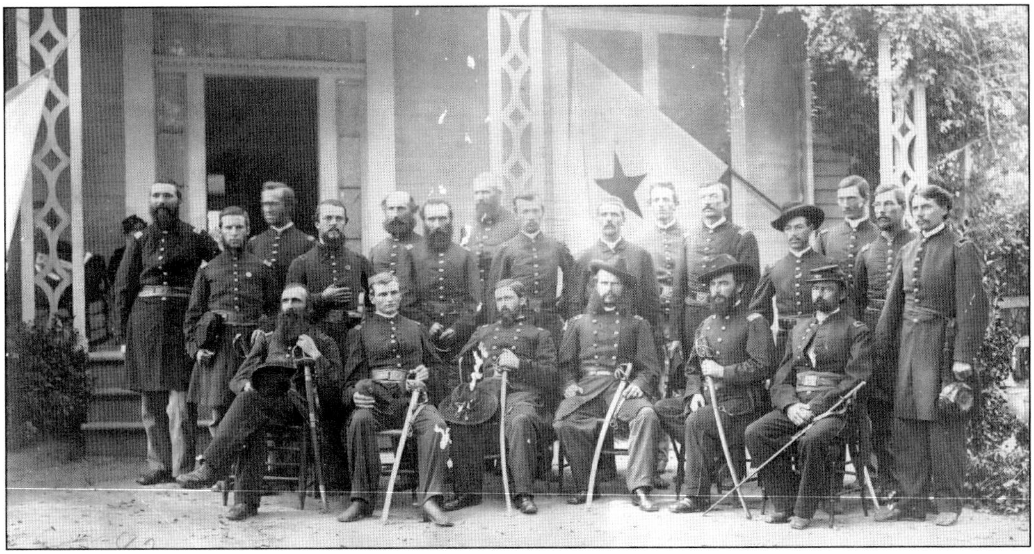

Pictured are officers from the 143rd New York Infantry after the capture of Atlanta in July 1864. From left to right are (first row) Capt. Harrison Marvin, Adj. Renssalaer Hammond, Lt. Col. Hezekiah Watkins, Col. Horace Boughton, Maj. John Higgins, Q. M. Edward C. Howard, and assistant surgeon William H. Stuart; (second row) Lt. Peter E. Palen, Lt. Isaac Jellif, Capt. Edward H. Pinney, Capt. George H. Decker, Lt. DeWitt Apgar, Lt. Wallace Hill, surgeon David Matthews, Capt. William R. Bennett, and Lt. Charles A. Smith; (third row) Capt. Lewis W. Stanton, Capt. William T. George, Lt. Dwight Divine, Capt. John F. Anderson, Lt. George Young, Lt. Richard M. J. Hardenbergh, and Capt. Benjamin Reynolds. (Above, courtesy of New York State Military Museum; below, courtesy of Monticello Lodge No. 532.)

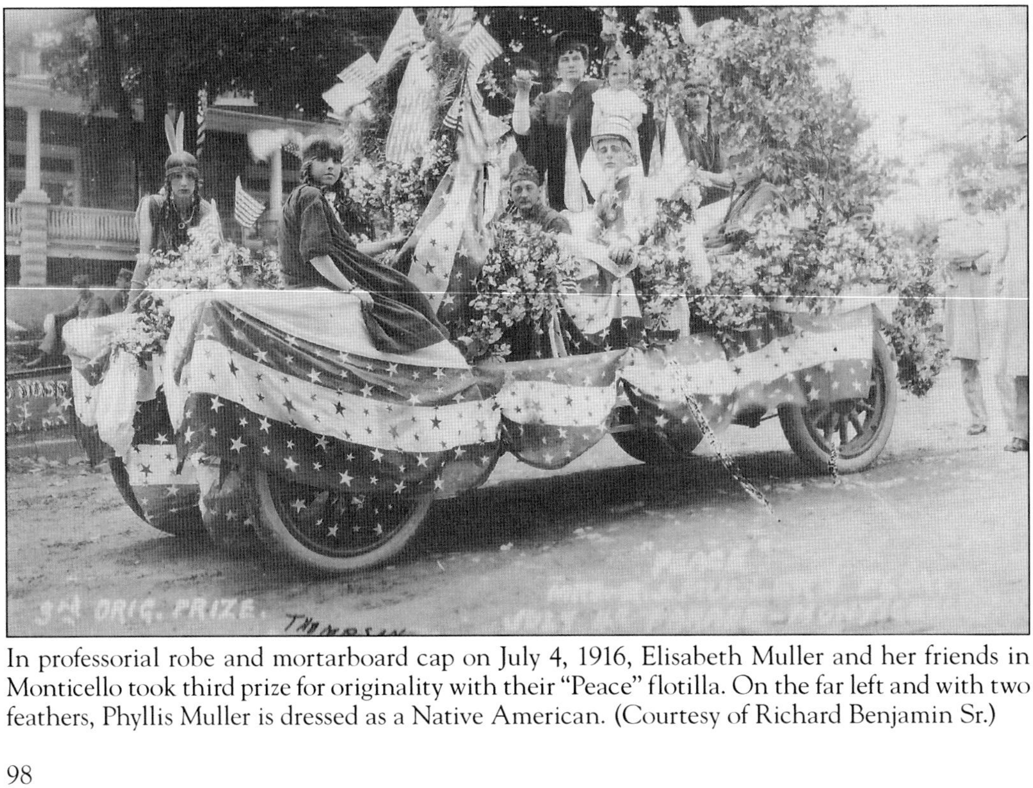

In professorial robe and mortarboard cap on July 4, 1916, Elisabeth Muller and her friends in Monticello took third prize for originality with their "Peace" flotilla. On the far left and with two feathers, Phyllis Muller is dressed as a Native American. (Courtesy of Richard Benjamin Sr.)

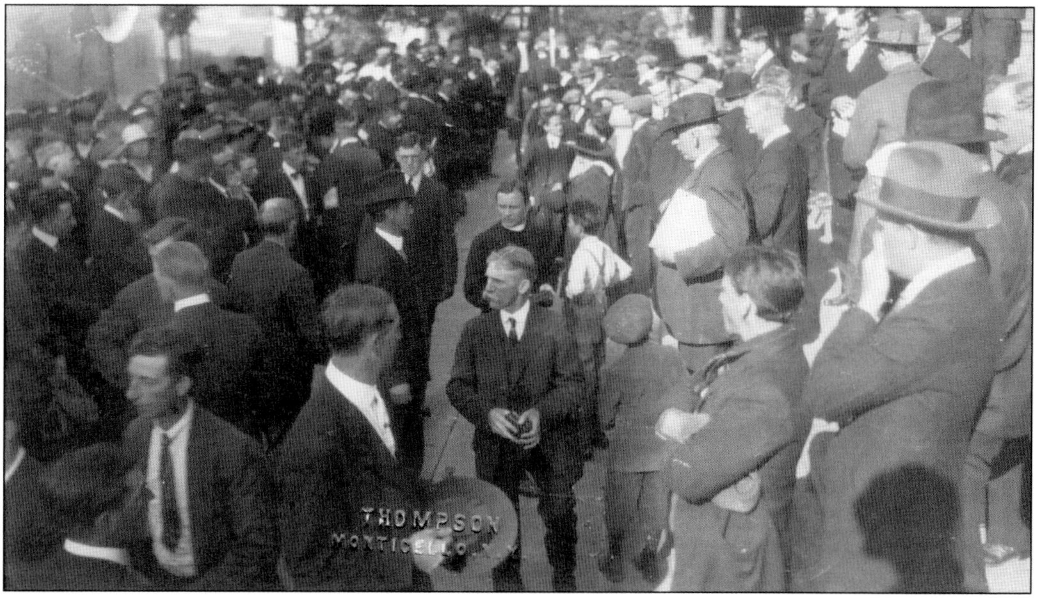

Presbyterian elder Kenneth D. L. Niven distributed New Testaments to draftees five months after the United States entered the war. Sheriff Elmer Winner is shown carrying a portfolio. The bearded man at his right is Presbyterian minister Rev. Hugh Russell Fraser. This undated picture may have been taken September 28, 1917, when a large crowd of "first draftees" and families assembled on the courthouse lawn. (Courtesy of Daniel K. Niven.)

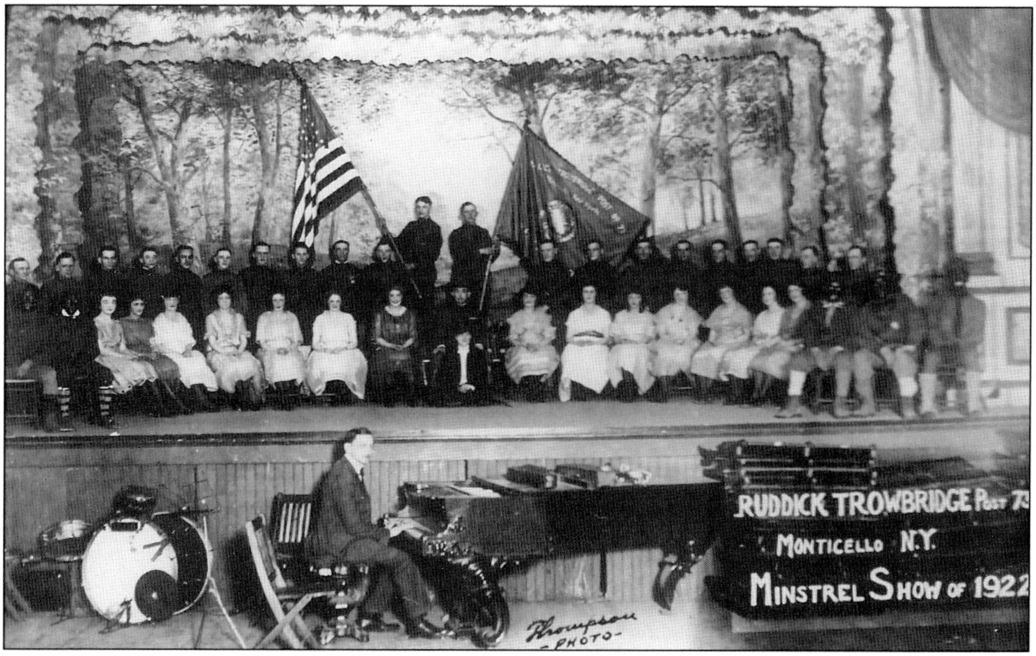

Pictured here is a minstrel show in the Lyceum Theater, which was owned and managed by Jennie Niven Guimond and her husband, Louis Guimond. Included among the performers were Jane Branigan, Nellie Toomey, Lucy Scmidt, Douglas Hill, James Mahoney, and Emiliano Gonzalez. Leon Barnum is holding the flag of Ruddick Trowbridge Post No. 73, American Legion. (Courtesy of Monticello Fire Department.)

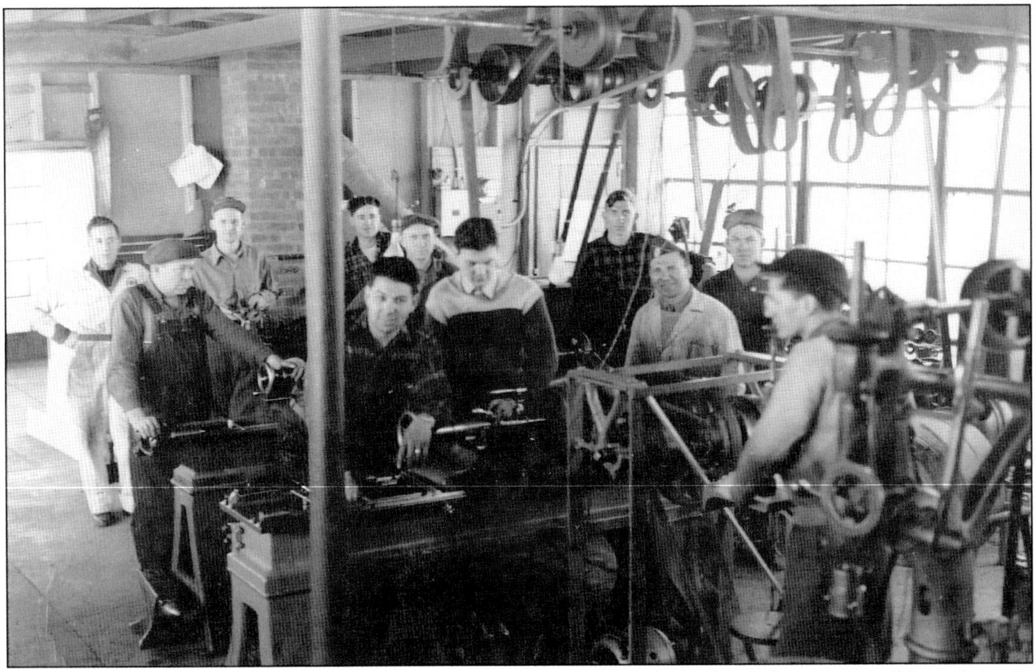

Pictured at the Wells' Defense School at 176 East Broadway (which no longer stands) on March 11, 1942, from left to right are (first row) Paul Blacker, Charley "Wings" Everett, John Huggler Jr., and Charles Wells; (second row) Herb Bowers, Ted Simenitzky, Emil Wells (teacher), Gene Smith, Bill Borman, Fred Daucher, a Mr. Sacks, and Norman Plotkin. After this training, Wells and Huggler went to Ohio to work as machinists at a defense plant during World War II. (Courtesy of Ruth Huggler.)

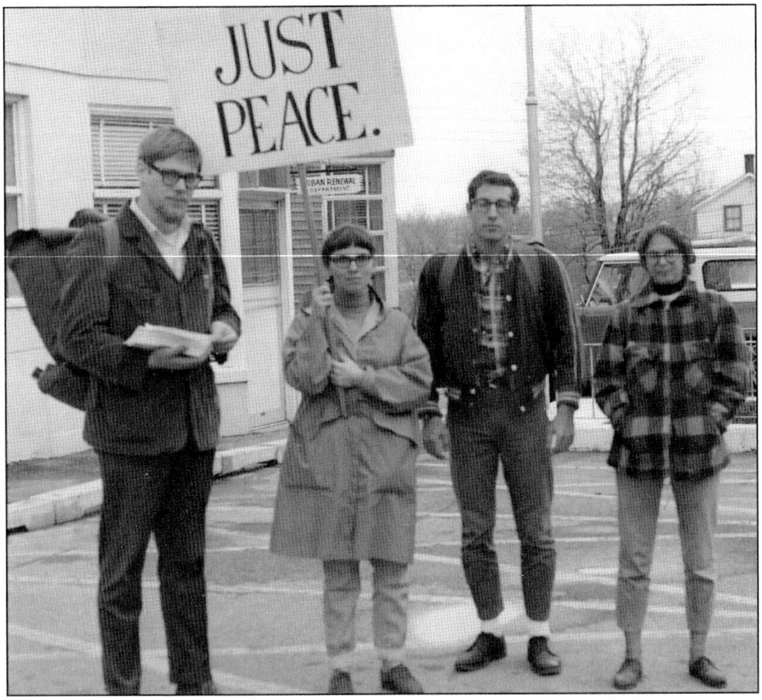

On May 6, 1967, Sara Meredith, Gilbert Meredith, Carol Kornfield of Manhattan, and David Martin of Queens leafleted an antique car parade on Broadway in Monticello with a plain sheet urging, "Try peace—If you don't like it you can always go back to war." The out-of-town protesters stayed at the Capri Motel with plans to go to Ellenville the next day, a witness told Monticello police. (Courtesy of Village of Monticello.)

Six

Government and Municipal Services

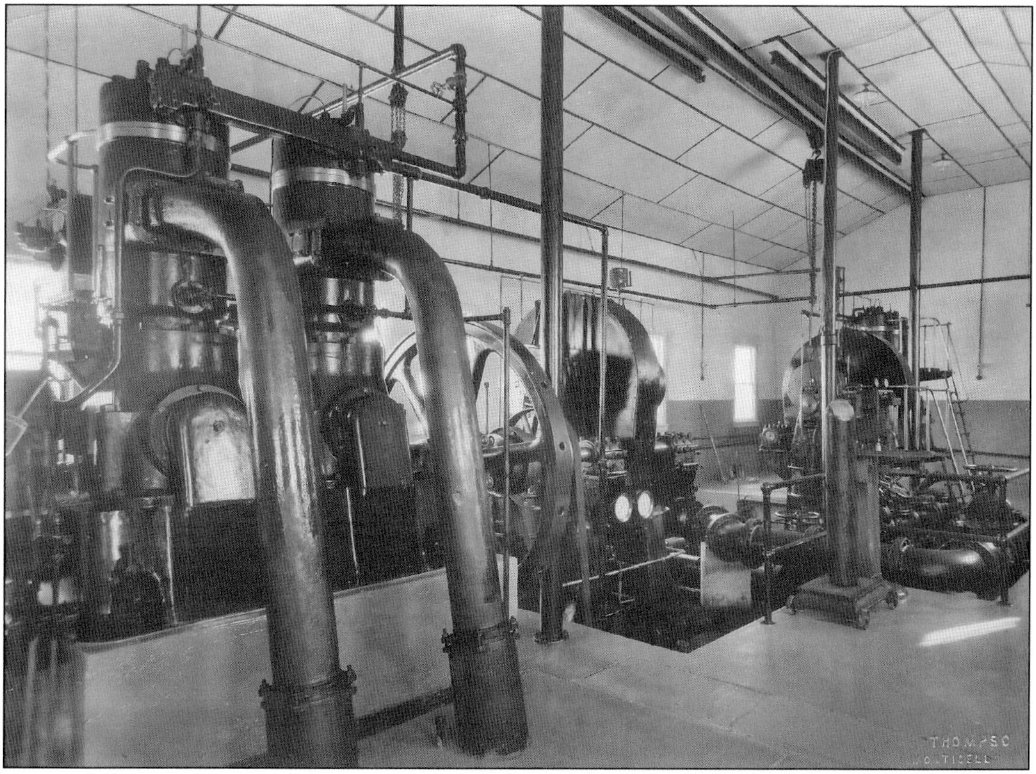

Pictured above is Monticello's pump station at Kiamesha Lake. In 1895, David Avery, president of the village board of trustees, fought for a new water system. Some trustees were opposed. His plan involved a driven well from which water would be pumped and stored in a large standpipe. But test bores were unsuccessful. This led to cost overruns and then to a cutback in the system. (Courtesy of Monticello Water Department.)

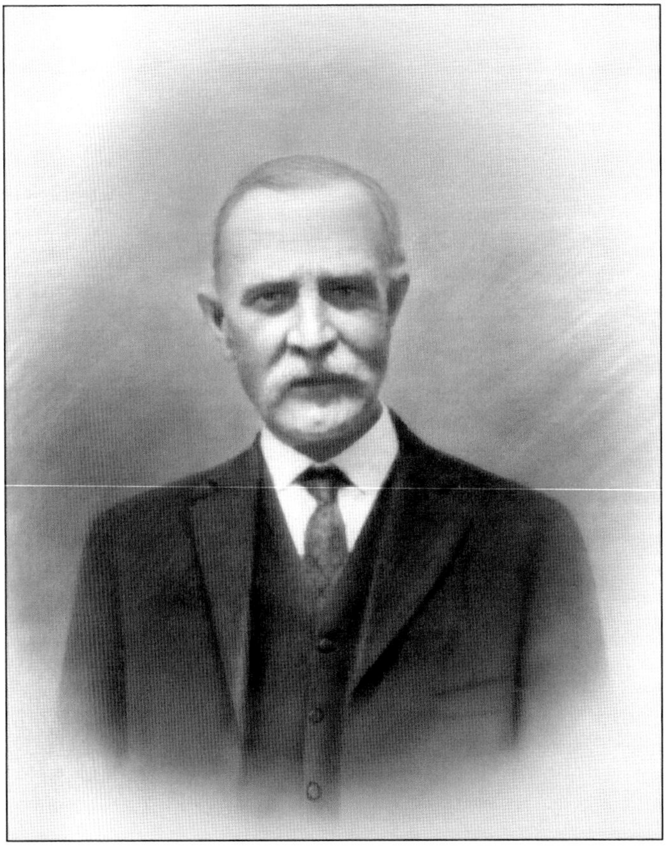

Robert McNickle (see page 73) was born in Ireland in 1854 to an English mother and an Irish father. In 1880, he was a laborer at the Monticello tannery, where he worked his way up to become superintendent of 60 men. He was supervisor of the Town of Thompson in 1892, on the village board, was village clerk, and was president of the local board of health when the water supply system was constructed. (Courtesy of Monticello Lodge No. 532.)

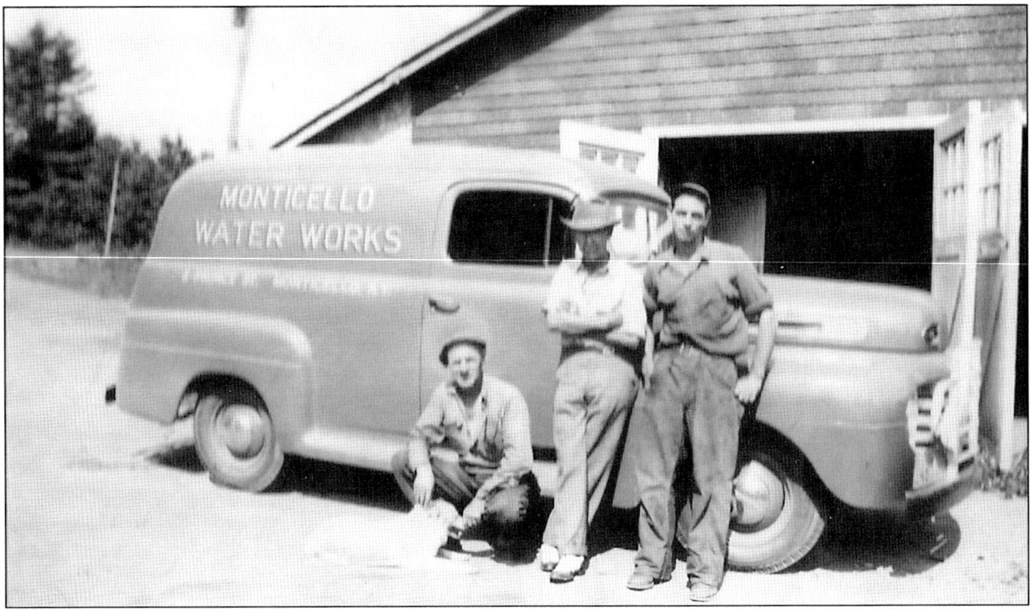

Pictured around 1950 is a storage garage behind the old town hall and firehouse on Prince Street. In front of a van used by the Village of Monticello Water Works are department supervisor Victor Decker (at right) and two coworkers. (Courtesy of Monticello Water Department.)

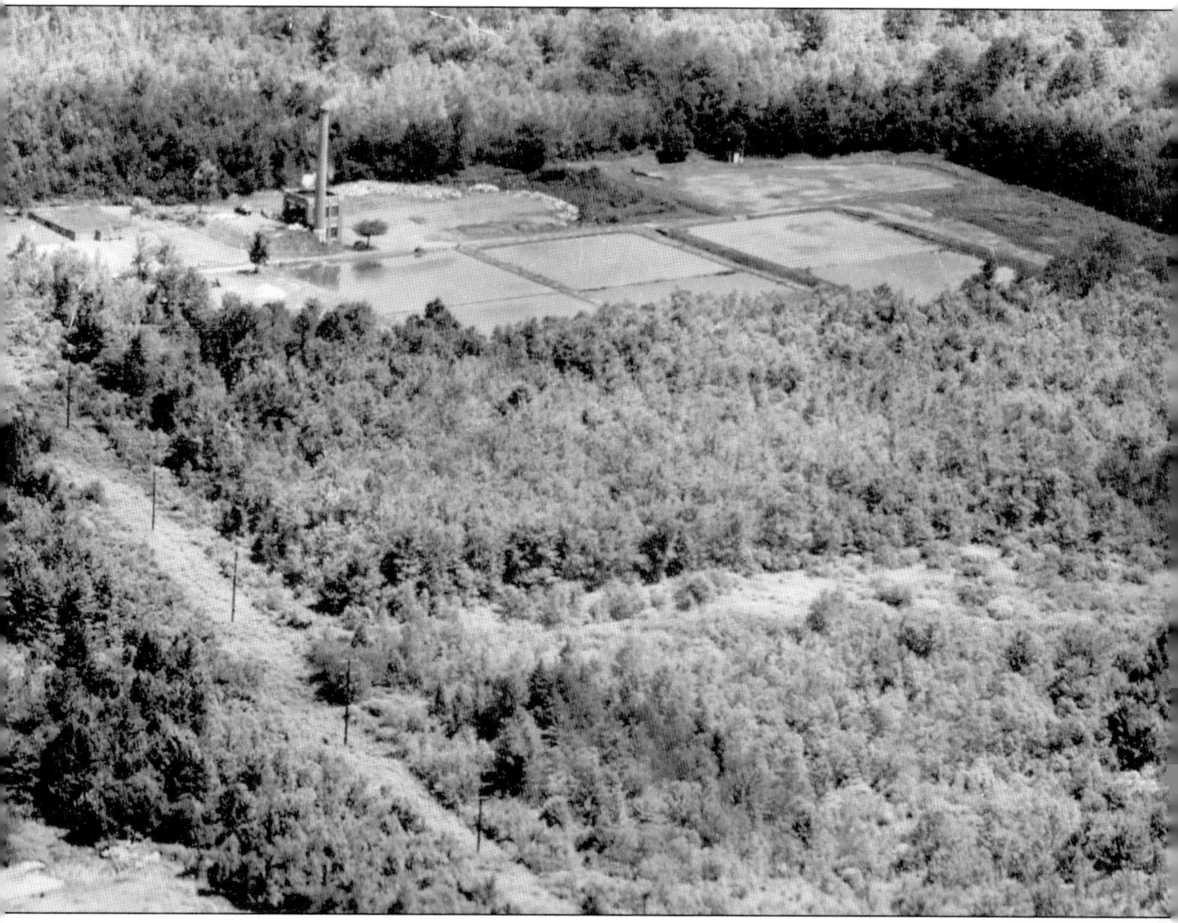

Pictured here is an early photograph of the Monticello sewer plant on Waverly Avenue. The sediment basins have been replaced by a more modern plant. The incinerator still stands but is no longer used. The Monticello election of March 1918—the first election in which local women voted—carried a proposition on the ballot to raise $1,000 for a new sewer plant. Only 60 votes were cast, of which 36 favored raising the money, 20 were against, and four were blank. The village board included Edward Martin Sr. (president), Isaac O. Smith (trustee), William F. Miller (treasurer), and Fred Carpenter (tax collector). "Now that the election is over, for the good of the village every man, woman, and child should do his level best to make the new administration a success. Wrangling over petty differences don't [sic] get a village anywhere," the editor of the *Republican Watchman* counseled. New York was one of the first states to recognize a woman's right to vote, in 1917. (Courtesy of Monticello Sewer Department.)

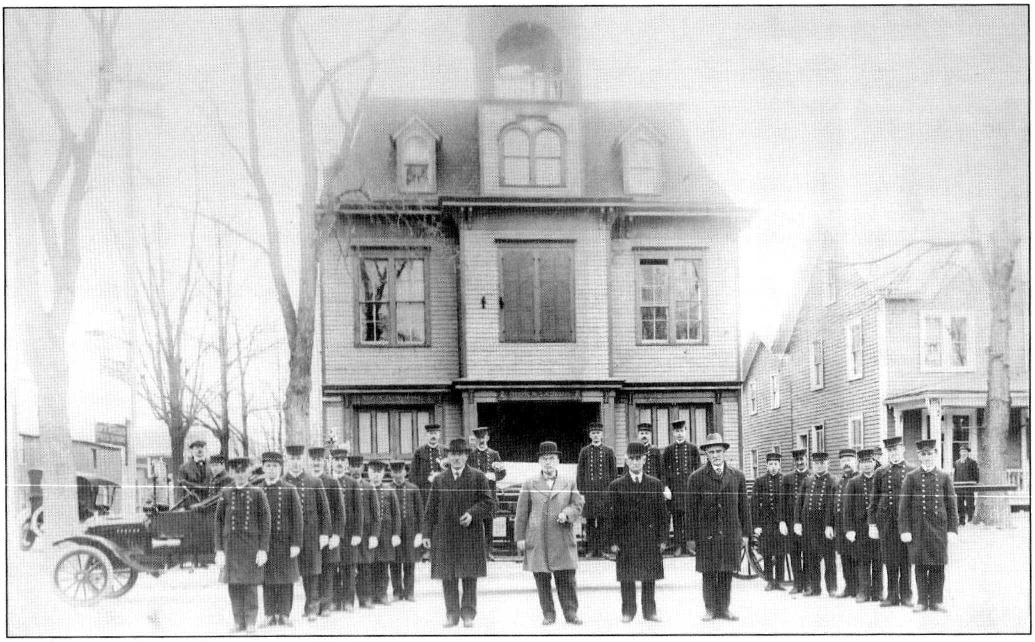

Rescue Hook and Ladder Company No. 2 is pictured here in 1905. Standing in front from left to right are William Nelson (village board trustee), Edwin Martin (village board president), Isaac O. Smith (village board trustee), and Robert McNickle (village board clerk). On the truck from left to right are George Goble, Roscoe Branch, Augustus Ross, Augustus Findley, Floyd Pelton, Fred Stratton, and Frank Armstrong. In the left line from front to back are Jerome Armstrong, John Mearns, John Mold, John Ross, Maurice Whipple, Charles Royce, John Lyons, and Charles Norris. In the right line from front to back are Paul Cuddeback, Charles Ebinger, John Jenkins, Walter Smith, Harry Mold, William Parish, and Delmont Race. (Courtesy of Monticello Fire Department.)

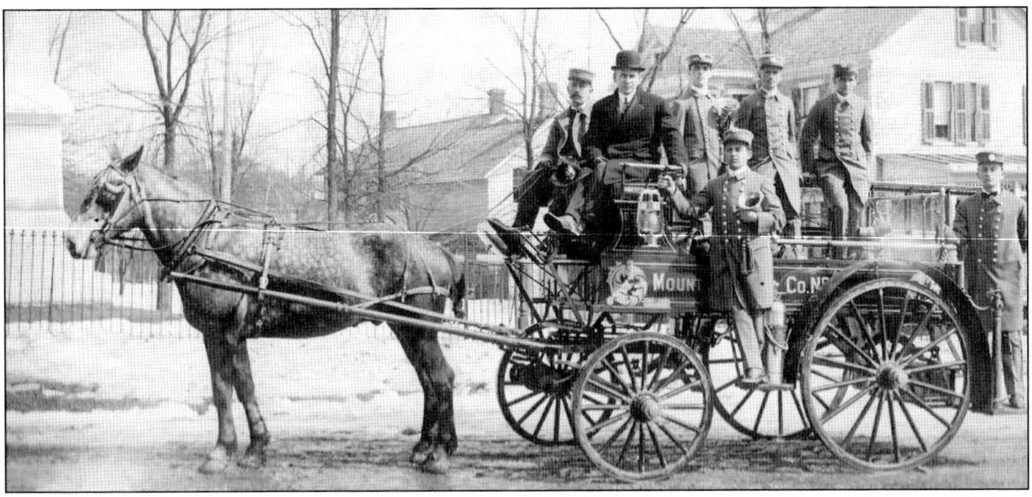

Seen here is the Mountain Hose Company No. 1 truck (1904–1914) at the *Soldiers and Sailors Monument* at its old location on the corner of Broadway and Jefferson Street. Pictured are Monticello ice dealer Holbert Liliholt, Main Street department store owner John J. Burns, office clerk Archibald C. Niven, pharmacist Robert S. York, shoe store owner Fred H. Carpenter, chemist Samuel Sprague, and postal worker Archibald C. Carey. (Howard Thompson photograph; courtesy of Monticello Fire Department.)

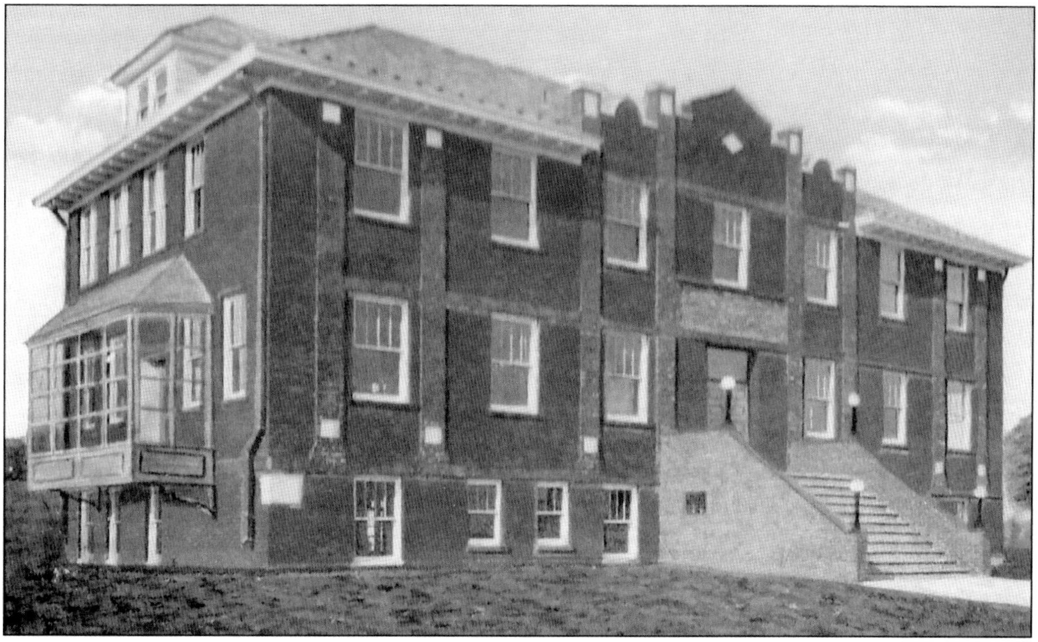

In 1921, a group of Monticello women organized the Hebrew Ladies Society. Their primary objective was establishment of a hospital. They reorganized on January 9, 1923, as the Hebrew Hospital Association, this time including men. Ground-breaking for a hospital on Landfield Hill took place on April 16, 1923. On June 14, 1925, the new hospital was dedicated. In 1931, a residence for nurses was built on the site. A separate hospital operated at 17 Hamilton Avenue. They merged with Liberty Maimonides Hospital during the mid-1960s to form one modern, centrally located hospital to serve the needs of all of Sullivan County. (Above, courtesy of Catskill Regional Medical Center; below, courtesy of Richard Benjamin Sr.)

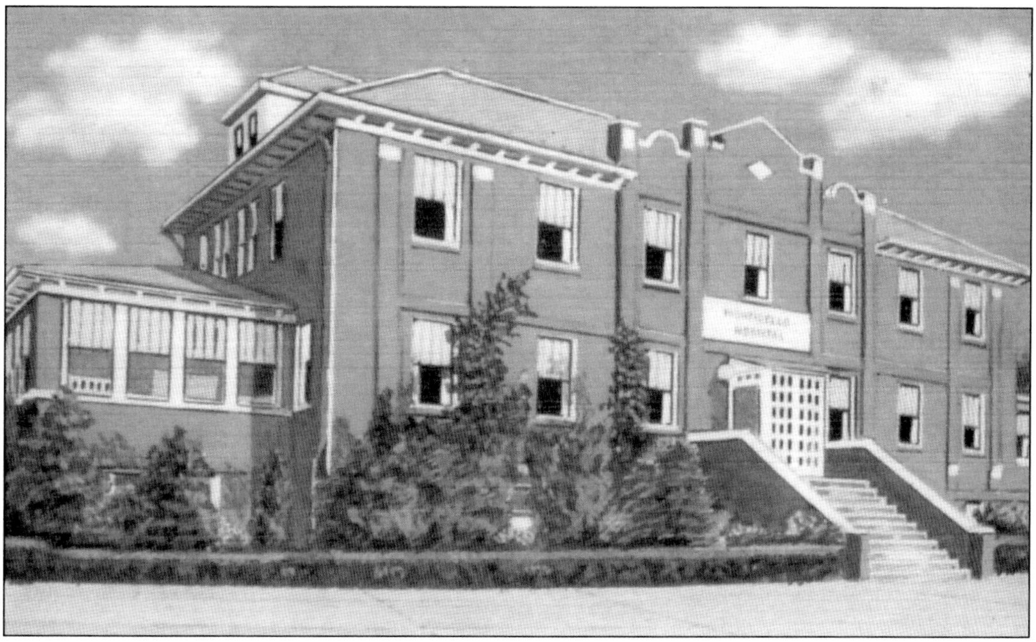

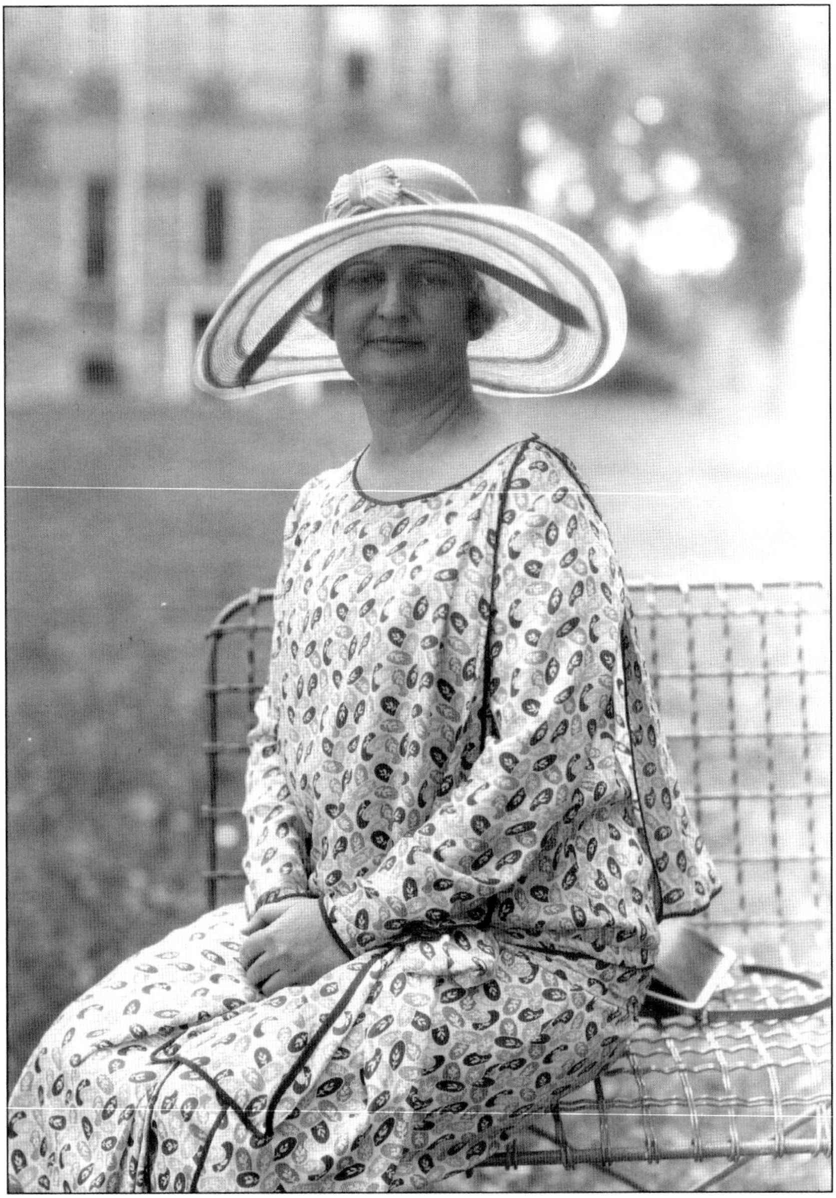

Maude Sheridan (pictured here in 1928) was the doomed love of the namesake of Monticello's public library, Tusten, New York, artist Ethelbert B. Crawford. The son of a railroad tycoon, Crawford was reportedly decorated for bravery after risking his life to rescue passengers after a flash flood in June 1914 at the Baddengorm Burn by Carrbridge, Scotland, which caused five deaths when a train plunged into floodwaters. Sheltered by an overprotective mother all of his life, Crawford and his mother visited Colorado Springs to display his art. There he met and fell in love with Sheridan. When his mother refused to bless their wedding, Crawford shot himself in the heart. Heartbroken, Sheridan made a career with Colorado Agricultural College Extension Service. After his suicide, Crawford's mother left an endowment for the construction of a library in Monticello, providing her son's paintings remain on permanent display. For more on this story, or to see Crawford's paintings, visit the Crawford Library. No photographs are known to exist of Crawford. (Courtesy of Colorado State University Library.)

The namesake of the law library in the Sullivan County Courthouse, Hamilton Odell (1834–1922) was the son of Lyman and Mary Scott Niven Odell and a nephew of Gen. A. C. Niven. In 1917, when Odell retired, he donated about 800 legal volumes. Upon his death, his colleagues wrote to the *New York Times*, "The passing from earth of this fine and beautiful spirit evoked only the briefest comment in the public journals of his home." (Courtesy of Daniel K. Niven.)

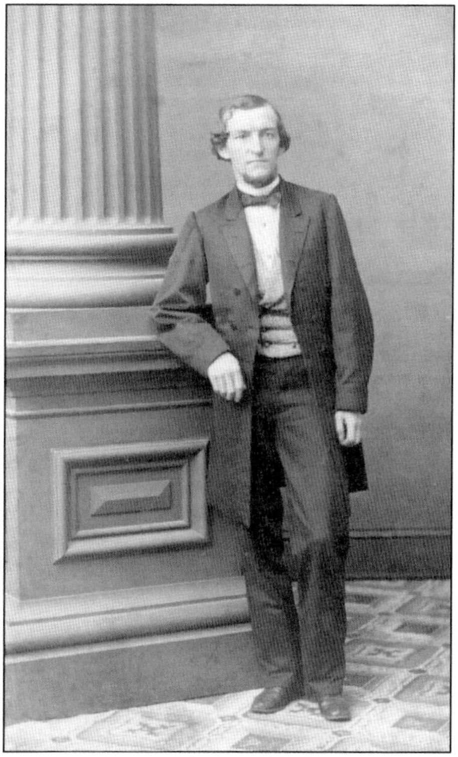

Fireman George Gregory Jr., dressed as Sparky the Fire Dog, distributed flyers announcing "Fire Destroys!" in front of Hammond and Cooke's department store (now 424 Broadway) on May 16, 1959. Sparky the dalmatian has been the mascot of the National Fire Protection Association since 1951. Why the lady is wearing sunglasses at night and who she might have been remain a mystery. (Courtesy of Monticello Fire Department.)

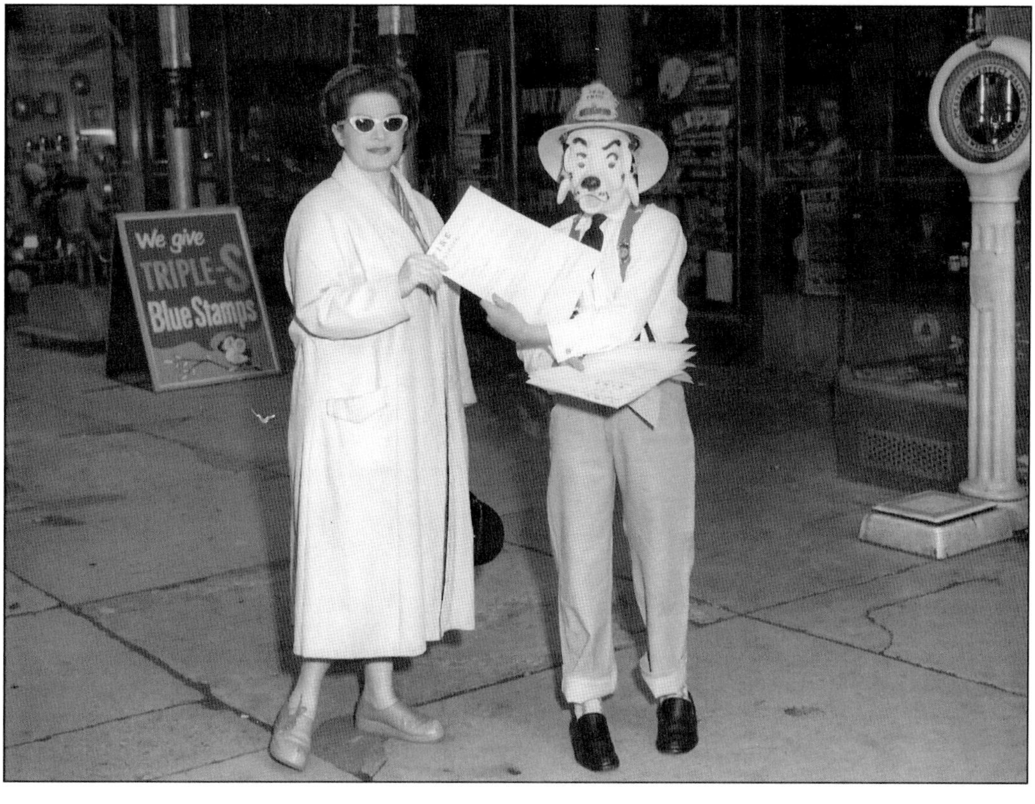

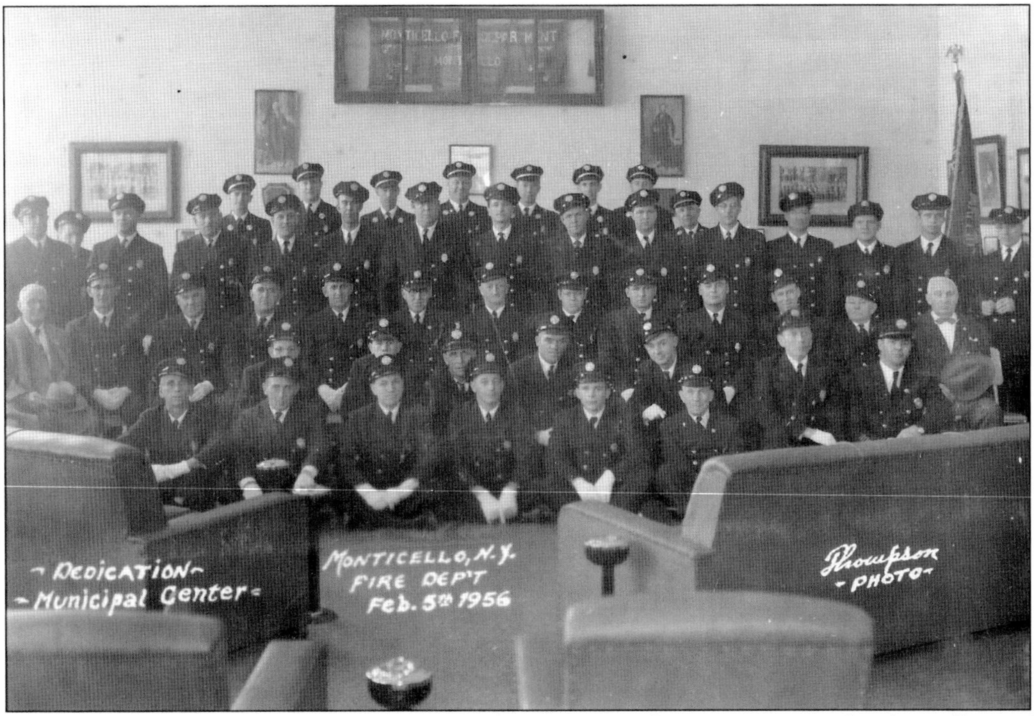

Above, volunteers and paid firefighters stood at attention facing inspection by the Village of Monticello Board of Trustees for the first time in the new fire hall at the municipal complex located at 2 Pleasant Street, near the corner of Broadway. Below, inspecting officials on May 19, 1957, included Mayor Donald Block; trustees Donald Pelton, Abe Rosenberg, and Foster Little; and village manager Thomas Belmont. Trustee Reynolds resigned from office on August 1, 1957, and trustee Joseph Block was appointed to fill the vacancy. (Richard Milburn photographs; both, courtesy of Monticello Fire Department.)

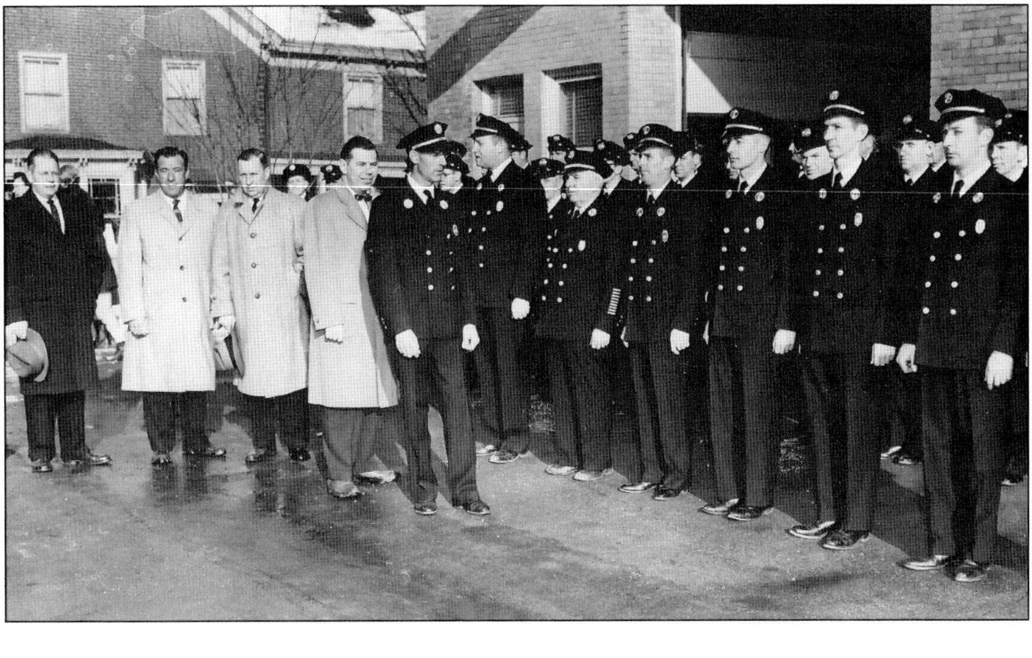

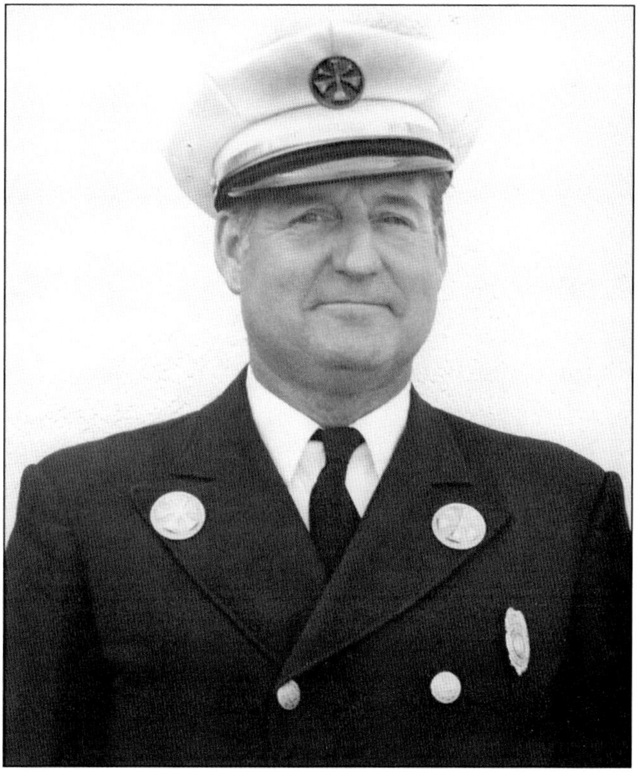

Henry Stratton (November 2, 1914–March 22, 1987) is pictured at right in dress uniform. He was chief of the Monticello Fire Department for the years 1961–1962 and 1967–1968. Below, in more casual attire, Stratton poses with a cigarette in humorous defiance of the "No Smoking" sign behind him at the Van Etten Oil Company plant on Saint John Street. (Both, courtesy of Van Etten Oil Company.)

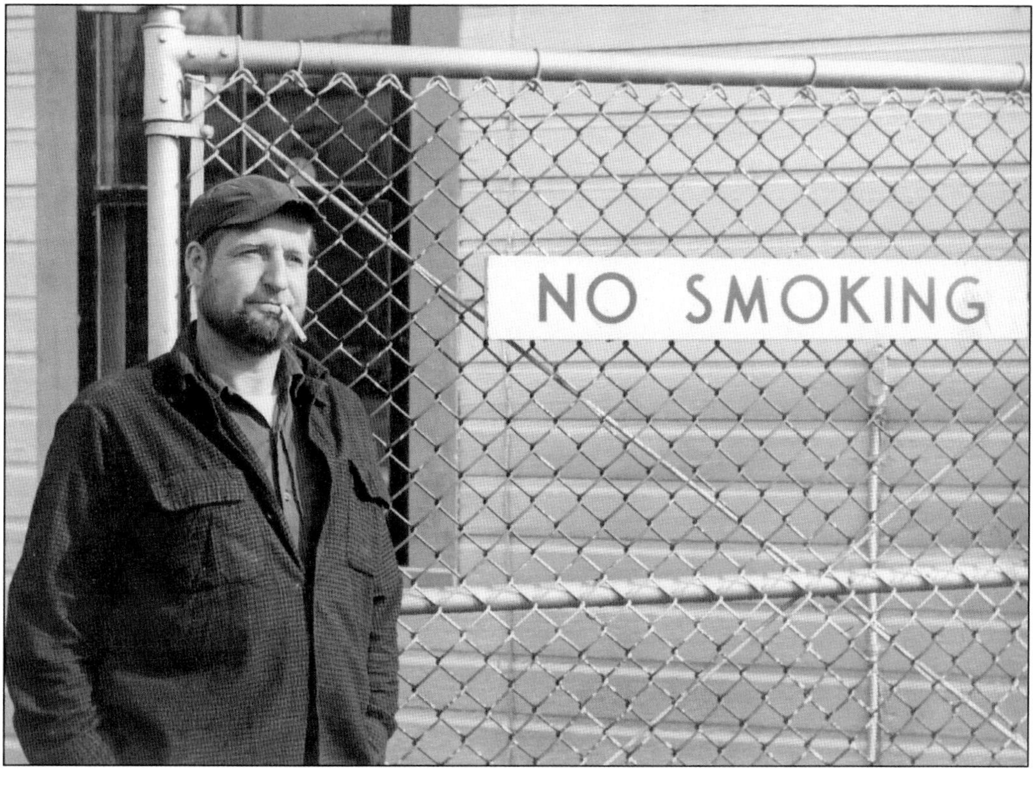

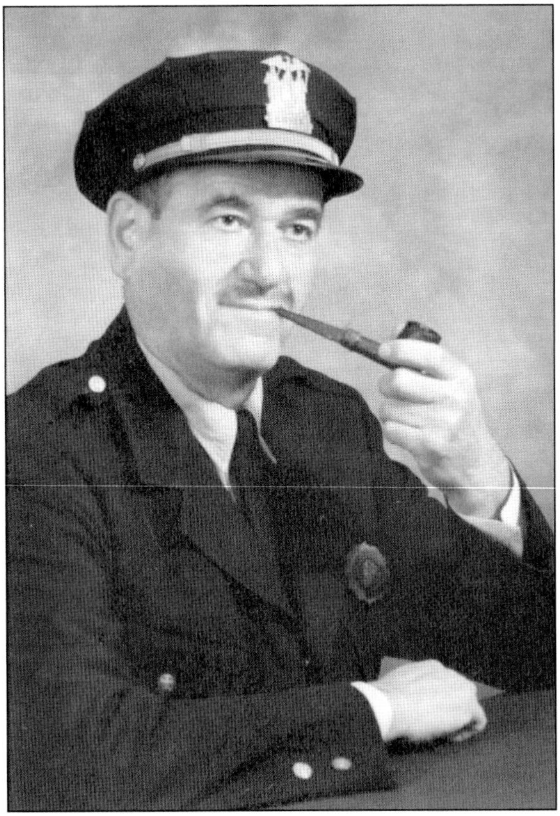

Jacob "Jack" Sharoff (1912–1988) was Monticello's police chief for 30 years. He served on the village board and later on the Thompson town board. "I remember him when the police station was in the middle of Broadway, across from the post office. He would patrol the streets all night when everyone was sleeping, going through parking lots, making sure everyone was safe," a longtime friend recalled. Pictured below is Sgt. Howard Morgan, Monticello's first African American police officer. (Above, courtesy of Roslyn Sharoff; below, courtesy of Village of Monticello Police Department.)

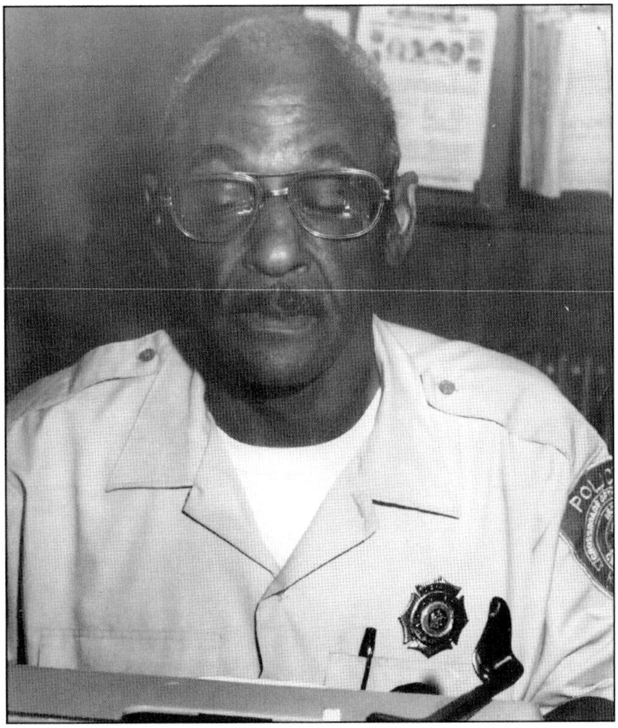

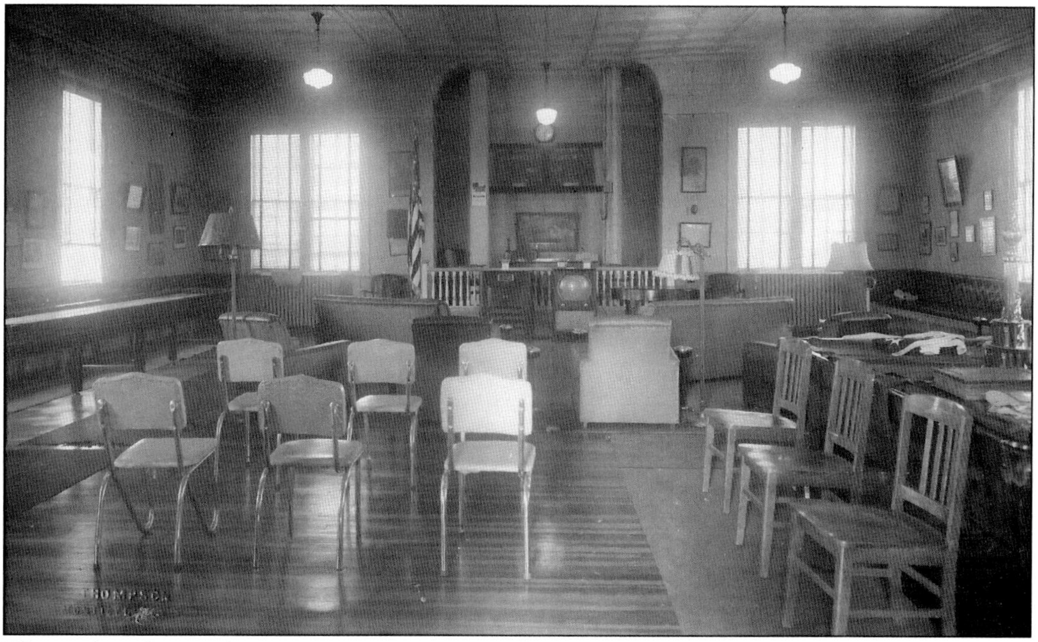

The mid- to late 1950s was a prosperous time for Monticello. The municipality changed to a council-manager form of government. Monticello Racetrack opened for the first time, and the regional hotel industry was booming. Monticello was expanding at a faster rate than ever before. It is not surprising that in a time of such expansion it would be decided Monticello needed a new municipal center to replace the rustic old town hall at the corner of Prince Street and Broadway. The interior of the old town hall and firemen's headquarters is shown above, around 1955. The building, now known as Village Hall, at 2 Pleasant Street, was dedicated January 8, 1956. (Above, courtesy of Village of Monticello; below, courtesy of Monticello Fire Department.)

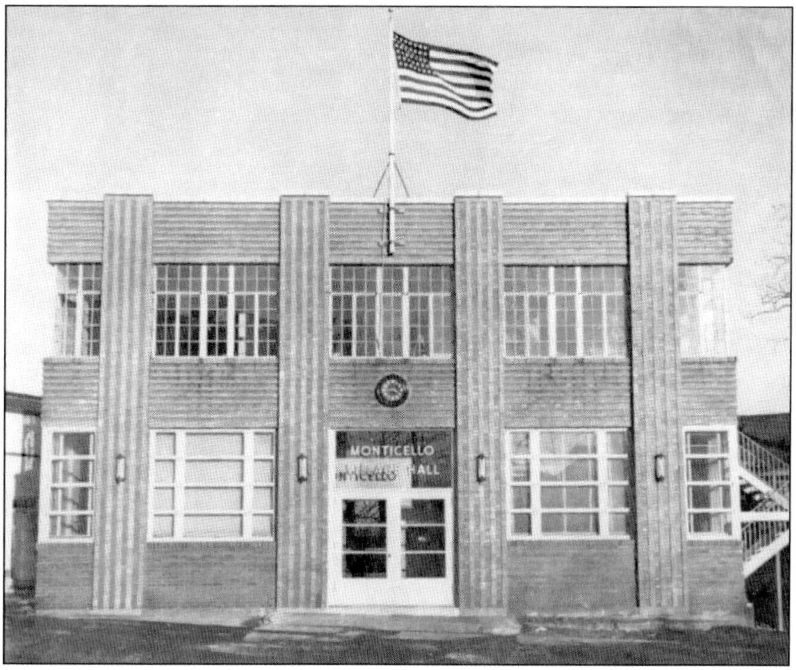

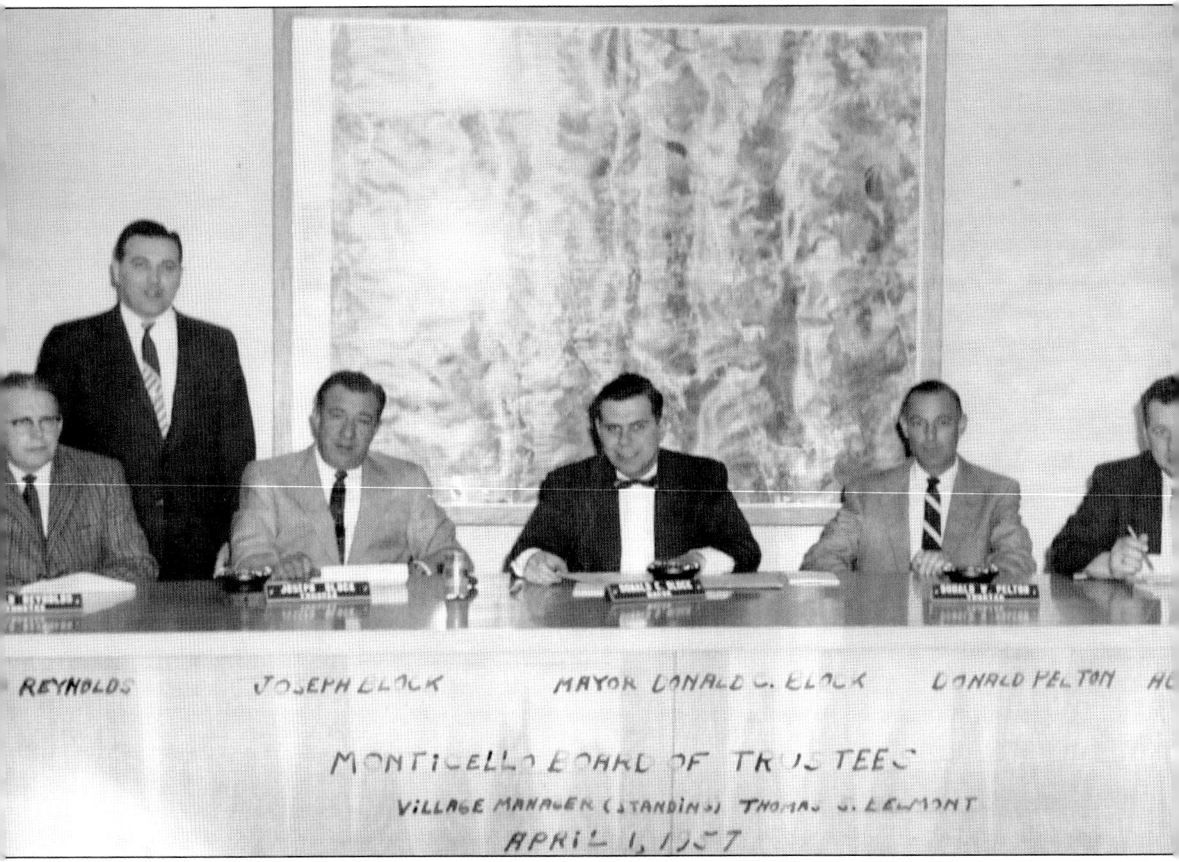

This photograph was taken at the organizational meeting of the village board of trustees with Monticello's first village manager. Seated from left to right are trustee Harold Reynolds, trustee Joseph Block, Mayor Donald C. Block, trustee Donald Pelton, and trustee Abe Rosenberg. Standing is Thomas Belmont, the first village manager of the village of Monticello to be hired after the adoption of the 1954 referendum. In the election of March 18, 1954, the ballot carried this referendum: "Shall the Government of the Village of Monticello, New York, be conducted under the Village Manager Plan, as provided for in Article Fifteen A of the Village Law of the State of New York?" The vote was 492 in favor, 206 opposed. This modern form of government provides for the board of trustees to appoint and oversee a professional manager who is the chief executive officer of the village and serves at the pleasure of the board. The board is comprised of the mayor and four trustees, each with one equal vote, and determines policies that the manager carries out. The referendum refers specifically to Article 15A of the old village law, not the revised statute adopted in 1973, so the old law still governs Monticello's form of government. (Courtesy of the Village of Monticello.)

Seven

Community Organizations, Churches, and Schools

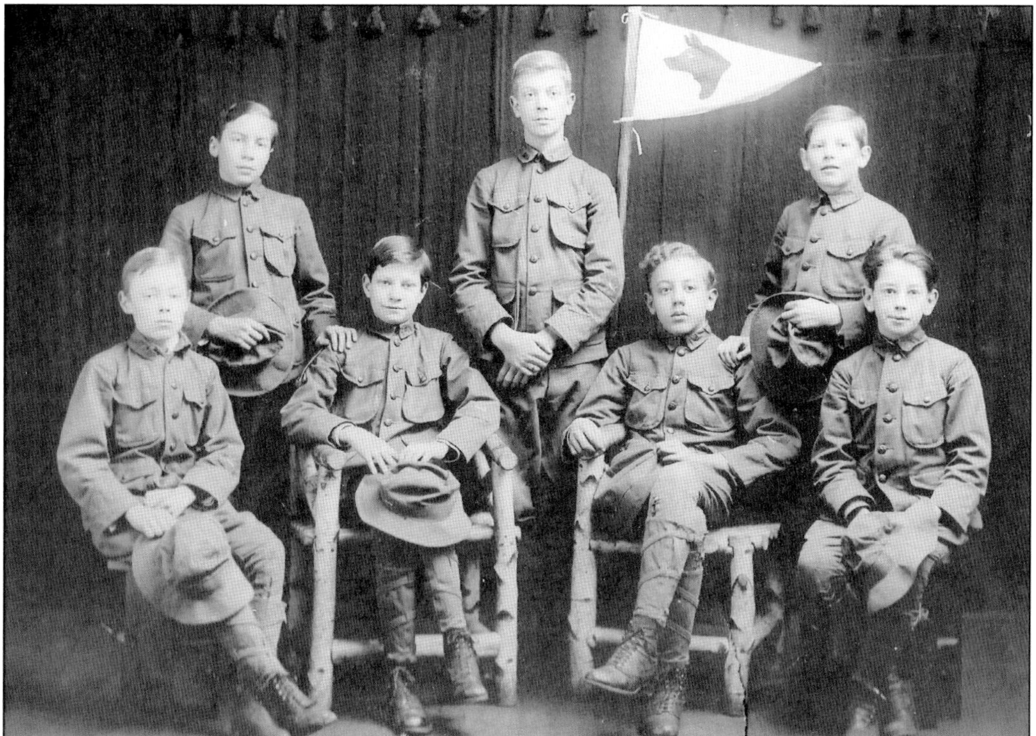

Pictured on December 25, 1913, is the "Wolf Patrol," Boy Scout Troop 2 at the First Church of Monticello Presbyterian. Pictured from left to right are (first row) Howard Johnson, Malcolm Fraser, John Sloat, and Herbert Branch; (second row) Leander Durland, Harold Stechner, and Ernest Schroeder. (Courtesy of Sullivan County Historical Society.)

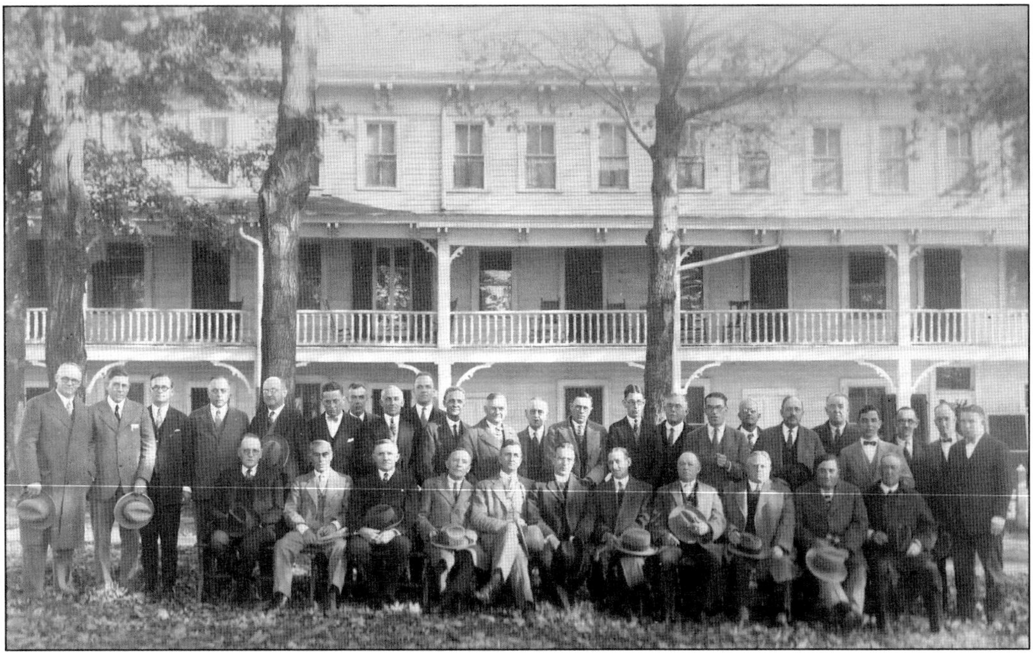

In 1927, the Monticello Rotary Club met on the village green for this photograph. From left to right are (first row) Dr. Ralph Breakey, Dr. Phil Krukin, Fred Crain, Henry Geber, Van Hornbeck, Father Richard Fitzgerald, Roscoe Branch, Matthew Ryan, Judge Ralph Smith, Chester A. Osborn, and Dr. Seth Osborn; (second row) Frederick Starck, John A. Cooke, Hyman Wahrhaftig, Alonzo Calkin, James Kelly, Ralph Kerr, J. Terwilliger, J. Stanton Ennis, Harry Miller, Jack Hess, Arthur Kyle, Leon Q. Brools, Roy Barton, Herbert Branch, A. M. Scriber, Sherwood Trowbridge, Edward LeFevre, Frederick Stratton, Bert Scriber, Isaac Cohen, Wesley G. Durland, Philander Avery, and Kennety Ross. (Courtesy of Richard Benjamin Sr.)

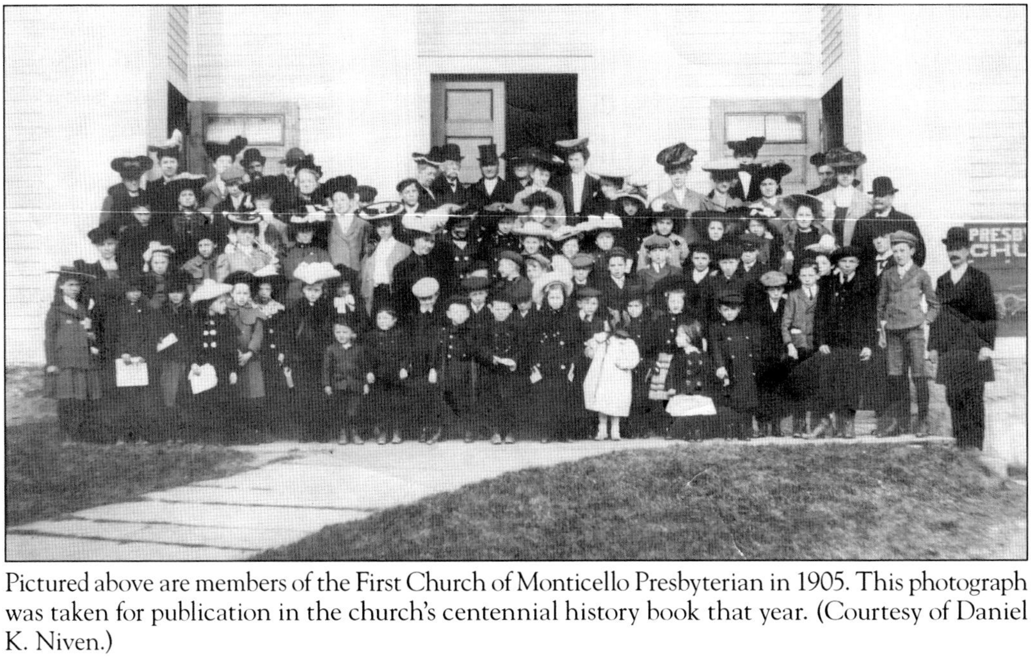

Pictured above are members of the First Church of Monticello Presbyterian in 1905. This photograph was taken for publication in the church's centennial history book that year. (Courtesy of Daniel K. Niven.)

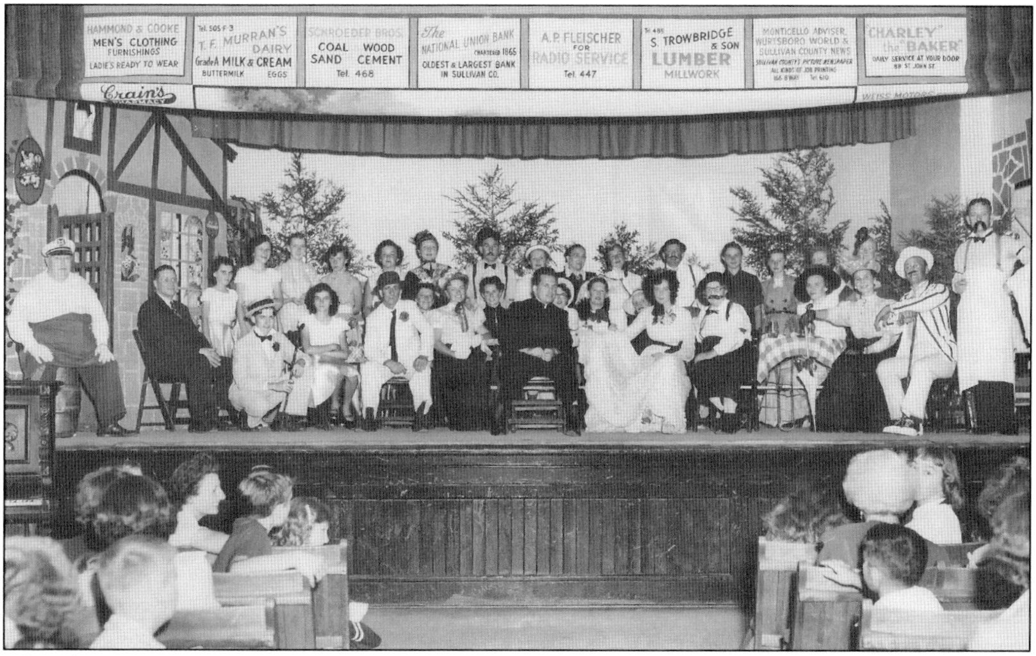

Churches are central to the social life of many communities. Such is true in Monticello. Pictured above is a musical presented by members of St. Peter's Roman Catholic Church. Seated onstage in black suit at the left is Judge Lawrence H. Cooke. Other cast members have not been identified. Billboard advertisements on the stage were sponsored by various Monticello businesses. (Courtesy of Susan Benton Schock.)

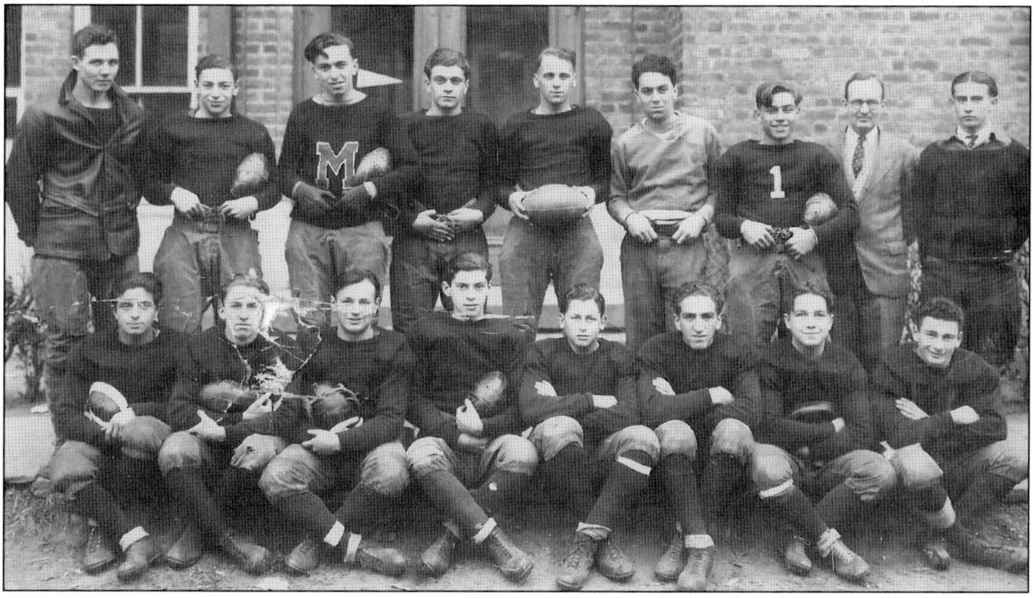

This is the Monticello High School football team in 1928–1929. Pictured from left to right are (first row) Sammy Raitan, Curtis Frank, Sammy Nemit, Norman Altman, Abraham Rosenberg, Moe Feingold, Conrad Perrins, and Harold Moscowitz; (second row) coach George Sexton, Robert Silberman, Nathan Feinberg, David Katz, Carl Schock, Agustave Newman, Isador Gordon, principal Kenneth Rutherford, and manager Emil Motl. (Courtesy of Robert Schock.)

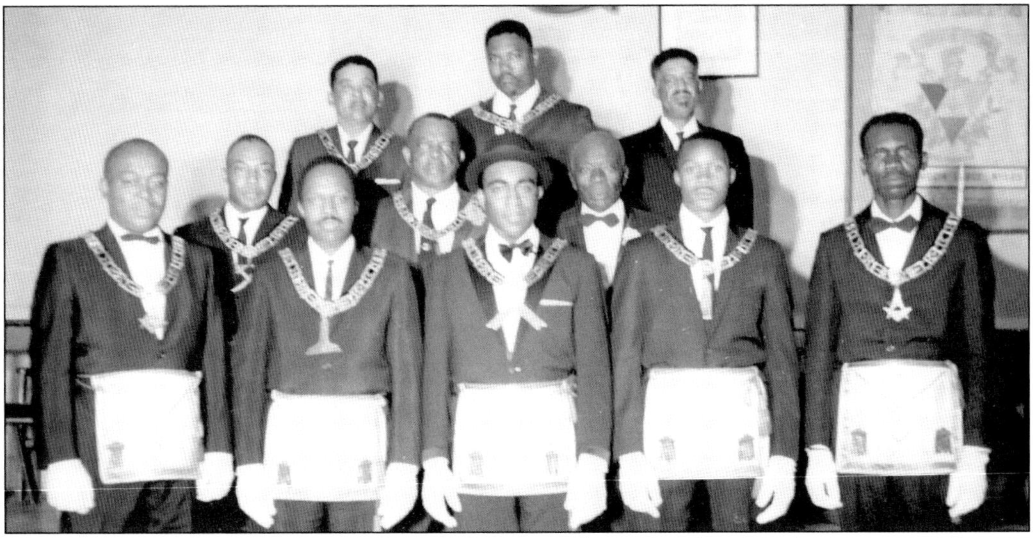

Pictured above is the charter line of officers and members of Bethany Lodge No. 101, AF&AM (Prince Hall Affiliate.) The lodge currently shares space with three other lodges in Liberty. Many members lived (and live) in Monticello. Pictured from left to right are (first row) George Dunn, Frank Wilson, Bazeley Elijah Perry, Curtis Ray Luster, and Horace McKinney; (second row) David Armstead, Leroy Green, and George Brooks; (third row) Jack Wallace, Albert Luster, and a Mr. Allen. Members below are, from left to right, James P. Luster, Richard Gilliard, Shelley Kimmon, Roosevelt Johnson, and Leo Davis. Prince Hall Masonry began when Prince Hall and 14 other free black men were initiated into Lodge No. 441, Irish Constitution, with the 38th Regiment of the British Army at Fort Independence, Boston Harbor, on March 6, 1775. Bethany Lodge's first worshipful master was Monticello resident Bazeley Perry in 1962. Later he cofounded Starlight Chapter No. 74, Order of the Eastern Star. (Courtesy of Bethany Lodge No. 101.)

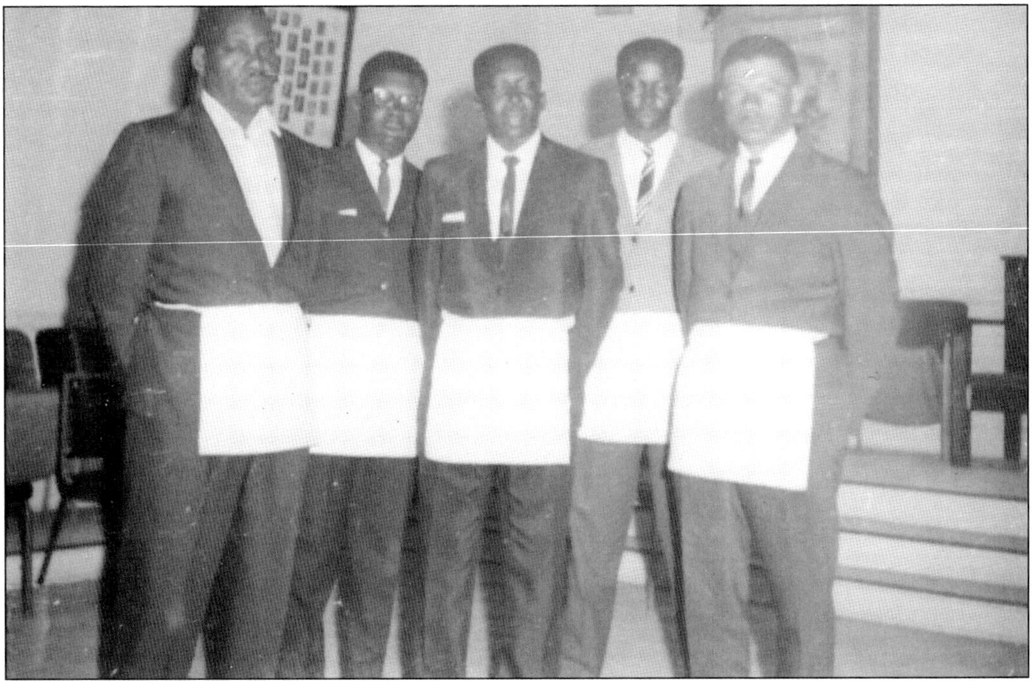

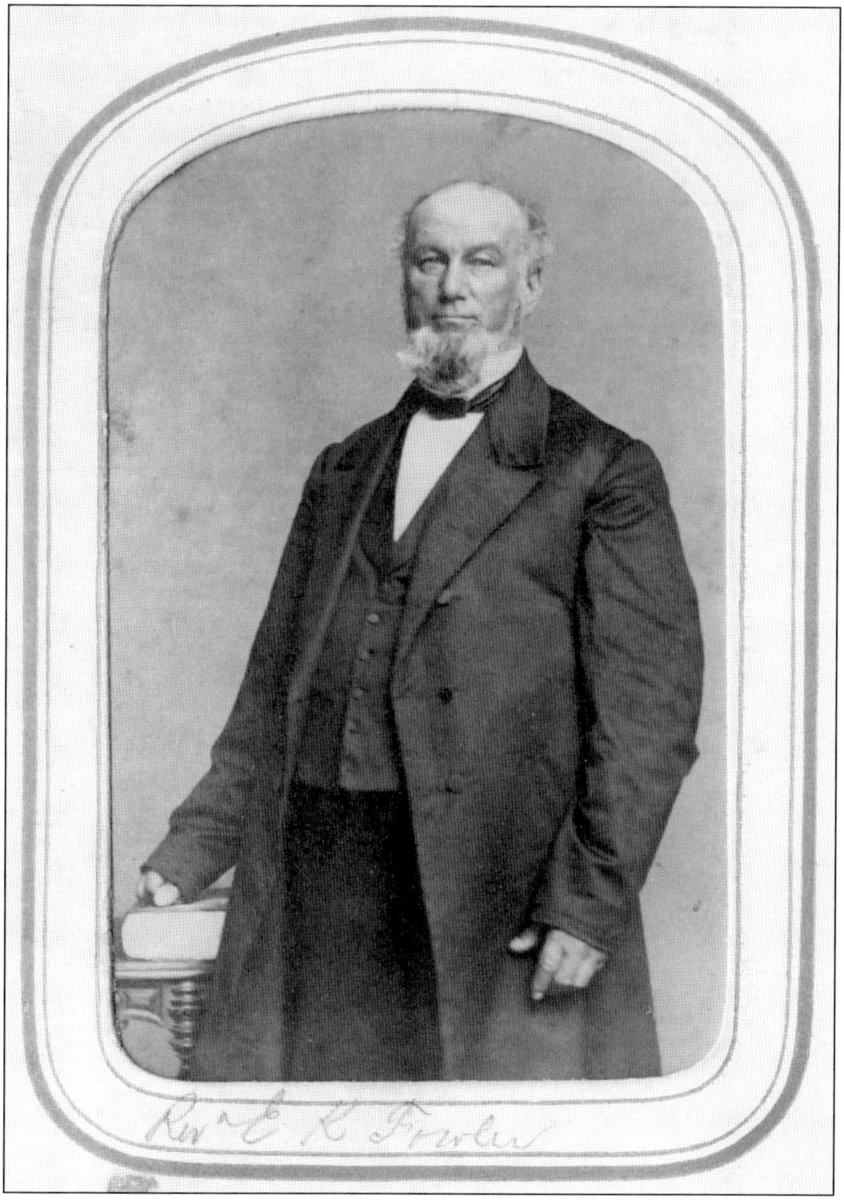

Rev. Edward Keaton Fowler of St. John's Episcopal parish is remembered as "an energetic and godly man" born in East Chester, New York, about 1799. When Reverend Fowler arrived, 11 communicants worshiped in the courthouse. St. John's history recalls of the reverend, "Some of his eccentricities, which must be told, faithfully to portray his character, cause us to smile. He was charitable in the extreme. He received his salary once a month, after which he would tour the county. All the beggars for miles around would lie in wait for him, and the result would be that, when he reached home, he would be well nigh penniless, and would receive a terrific scolding from his wife, who, though independently wealthy, was not interested in charitable work. They were afterwards separated, for her ambition would not stoop to remain longer in the woods. Fowler, with great consecration for his work, never sought a reconciliation, and in this he was staunchly upheld by his parishioners, who claimed that the only mistake he ever made was to marry his wife." (Courtesy of Daniel K. Niven.)

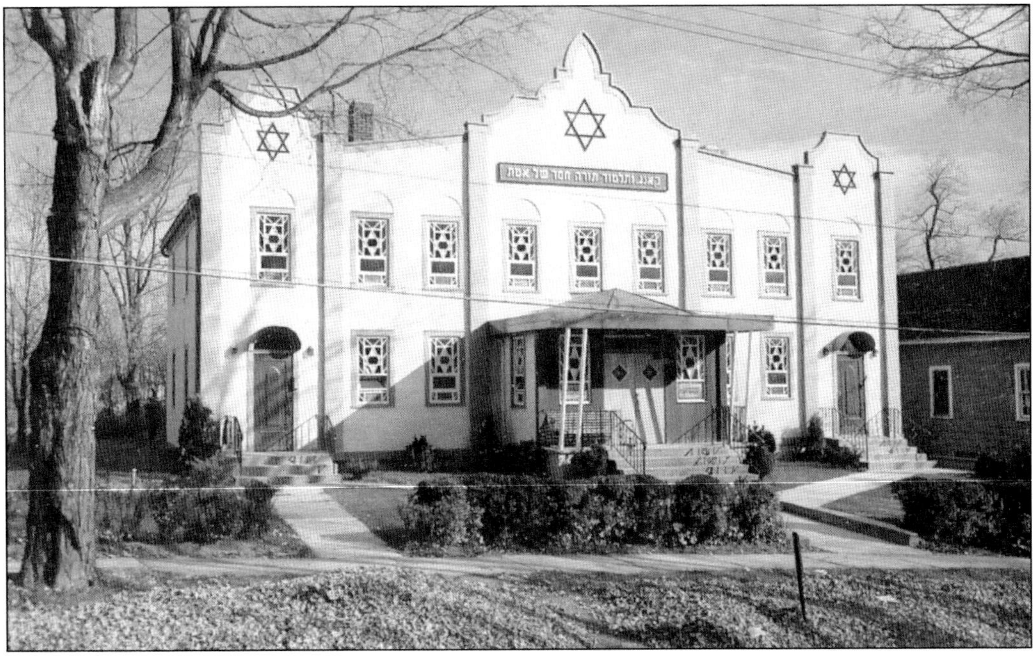

The house of worship pictured above was built by St. Peter's Roman Catholic Church in 1867 and was used for Catholic worship until 1899. It was a storage garage until it was bought by the Monticello Grange, who later sold it to Congregation Chesed Shel Emes for use as the Liberty Street Synagogue. In November 1963, this congregation merged with the Jewish General Aid Association and expanded the Landfield Avenue Synagogue (below, shown prior to expansion.) The basement of the Liberty Street building served during the 1990s as a soup kitchen operated by the Sullivan County Federation for the Homeless and the Salvation Army. It is now the spiritual home to the First Baptist Church of Monticello. (Both, courtesy of Richard Benjamin Sr.)

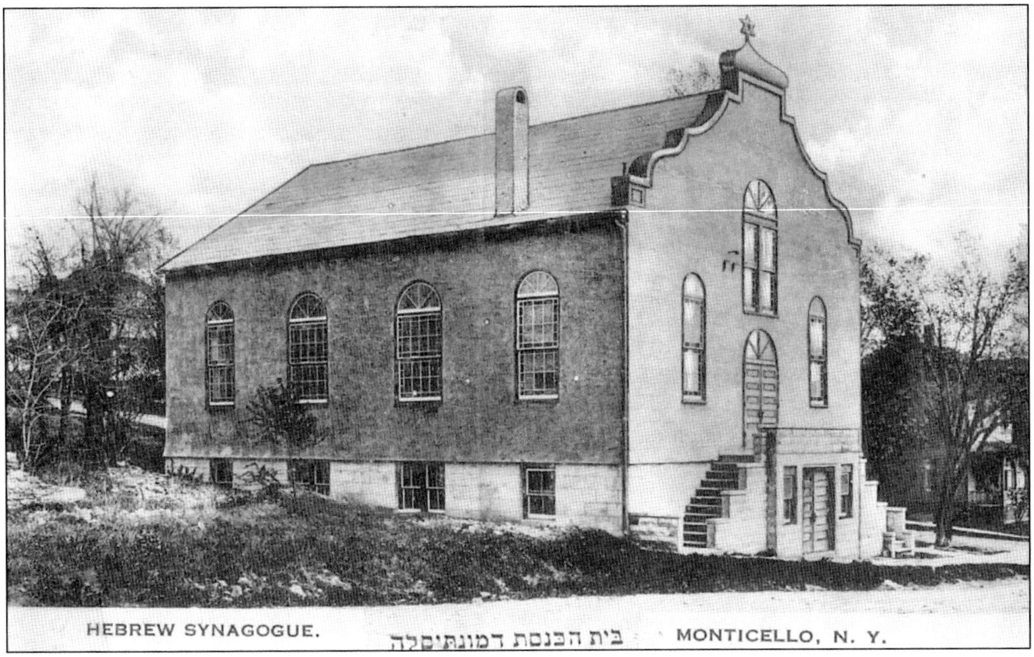

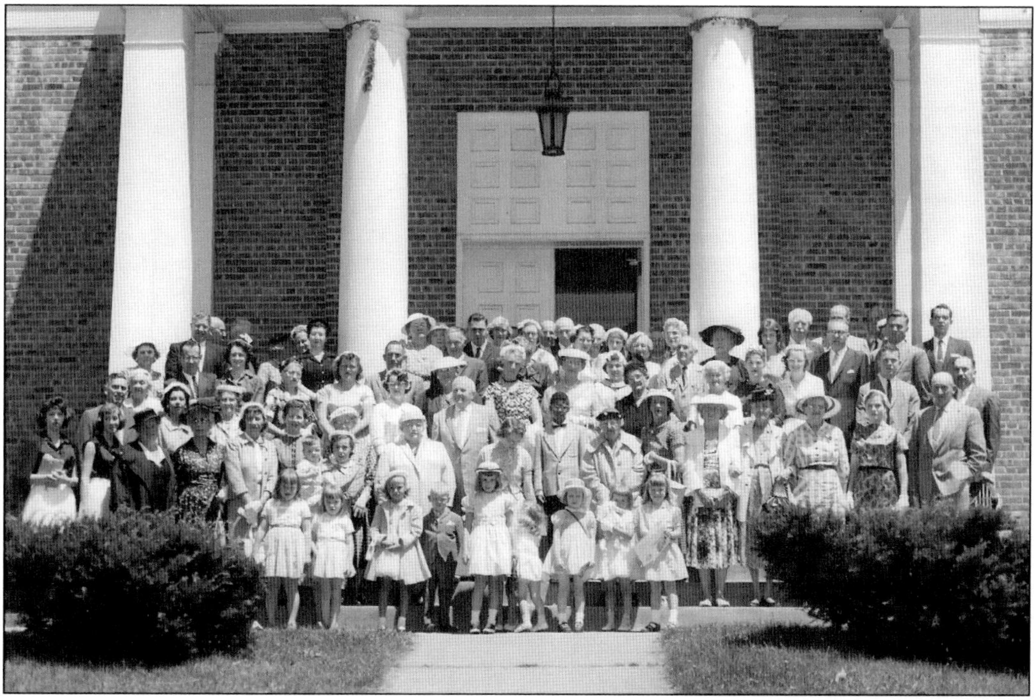

Members of the First Church of Monticello Presbyterian gathered on June 26, 1960, to commemorate 150 years. By 1807, Presbyterian clergy were supplied to Monticello by the Presbytery of the Hudson, meeting in the Exchange Hotel on Main Street. The September 5, 1810, formal organization was overseen by Rev. Daniel Hopkins of the General Assembly of the Presbyterian Church in the United States. (Courtesy of First Church of Monticello Presbyterian.)

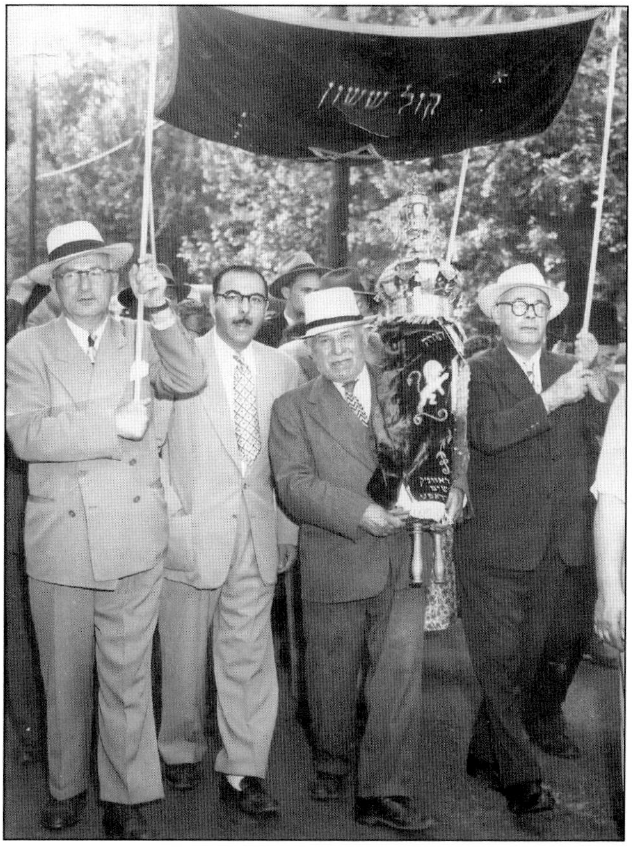

Pictured from left to right carrying a Torah through the streets of Monticello are a Mr. Wahrhaftig, Jacob Katz, Harry Raiten (with Torah), and Simon Weiner. The Torah is wrapped in a mantle embroidered emblematically with the lion of Judah, and the men are carrying a chuppah (marriage canopy), traditionally supported by four garlanded poles, and accompanied by followers. (Courtesy of Edythe Raiten)

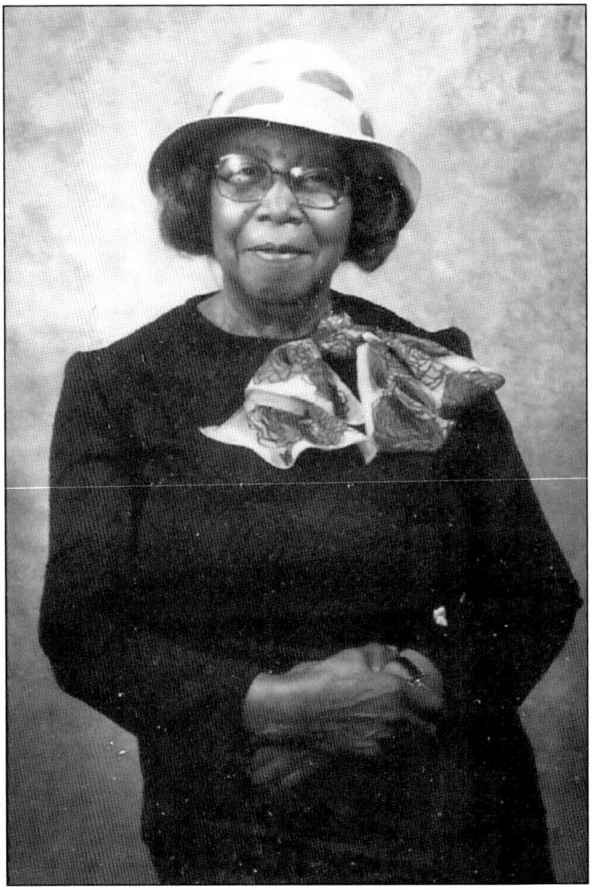

Martha Finn, pastor and founder of Bethlehem Temple, was born September 16, 1895, in Baton Rouge, Louisiana. After moving to Monticello in 1932, she sought to worship but found no church of like faith except a Pilgrim Holiness Church. She met Mary King (Hughes), who owned a boardinghouse and held services there, but soon they needed larger quarters. The church then met in a bungalow on Rock Ridge, but this too filled to capacity. They relocated to Smith Street, but neighbors said they made too much noise. "Mother Finn," as she was known, consulted the Lord, who she said told her to build a church. By 1938, she paid $100 for a lot on Fairground Road. The church, built by its members, was dedicated in 1939. Mother Finn lived to be 92, seeing great-great-grandchildren. She died in 1988, the first woman ever to serve on the board of directors of the Pentecostal Churches of the Apostolic Faith. (Courtesy of Dorothy McCoy.)

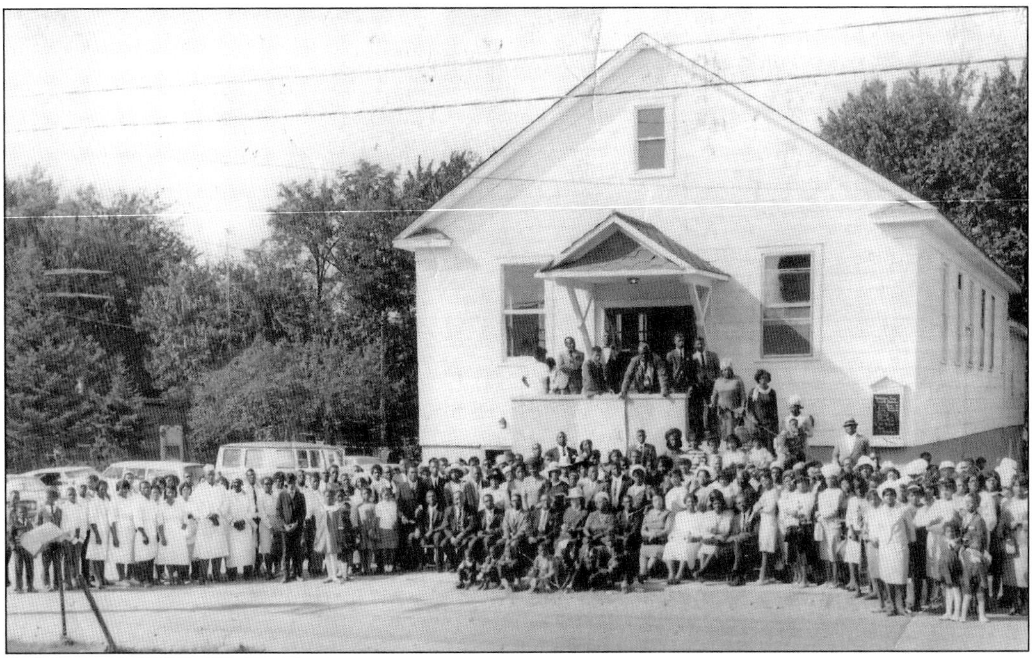

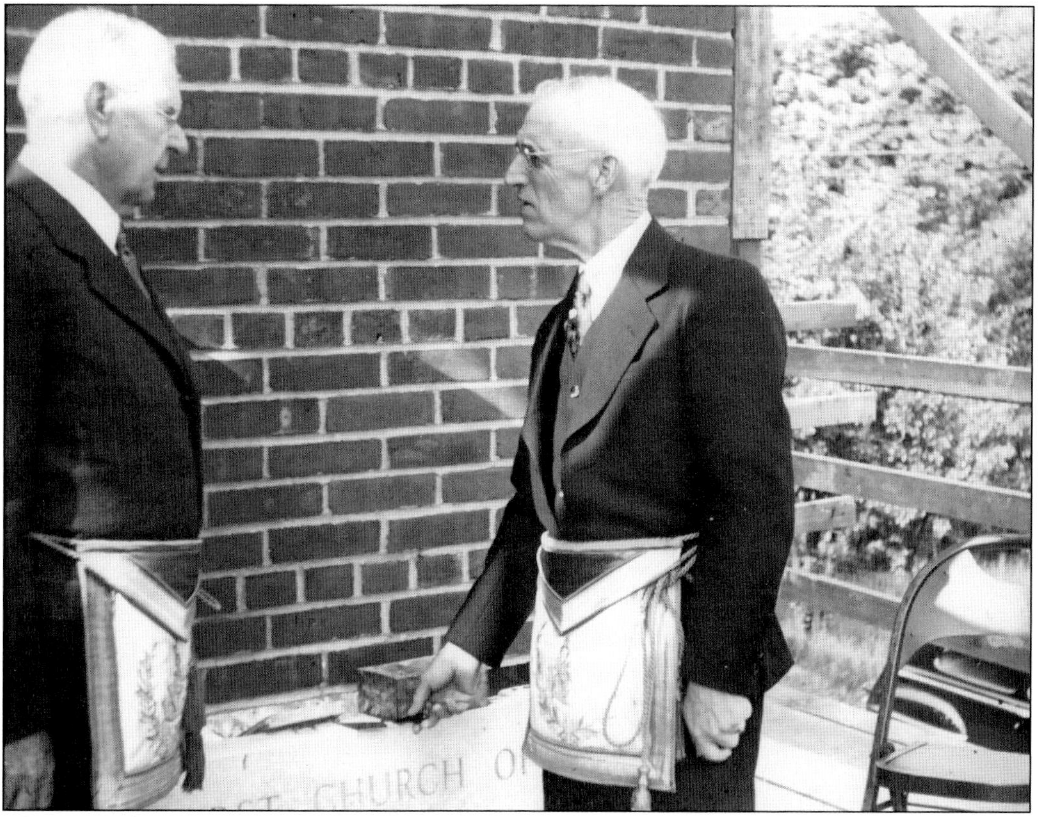

The original Presbyterian church burned January 13, 1844, was rebuilt, and burned again December 30, 1944. When the Masonic lodge burned down in 1909, the Presbyterian church invited the Masons to use their building for services. When the church burned in 1944, the Masons returned the favor, and services were held in the Masonic temple for three years. On June 15, 1947, a cornerstone was laid by District Deputy Grand Master Charles Burns (right) of the Sullivan-Delaware Masonic District (who in younger days was the first village president to assume the title mayor) and Emory Stalker (left) of the building committee. (Courtesy of the First Church of Monticello Presbyterian.)

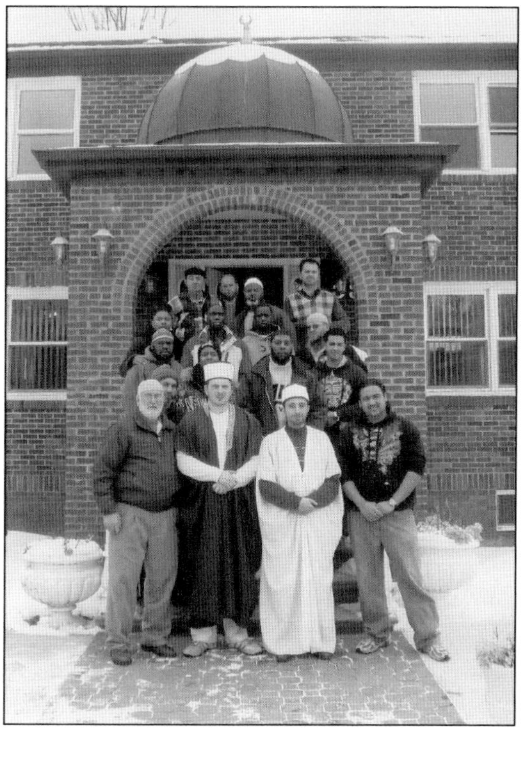

Leaders, members, and visitors at the Monticello Islamic Center at 33 Cottage Street, founded in 2004, posed for a photograph for this book. Executive board member Ibraham J. Makovic is at front left. (Courtesy of Monticello Islamic Center.)

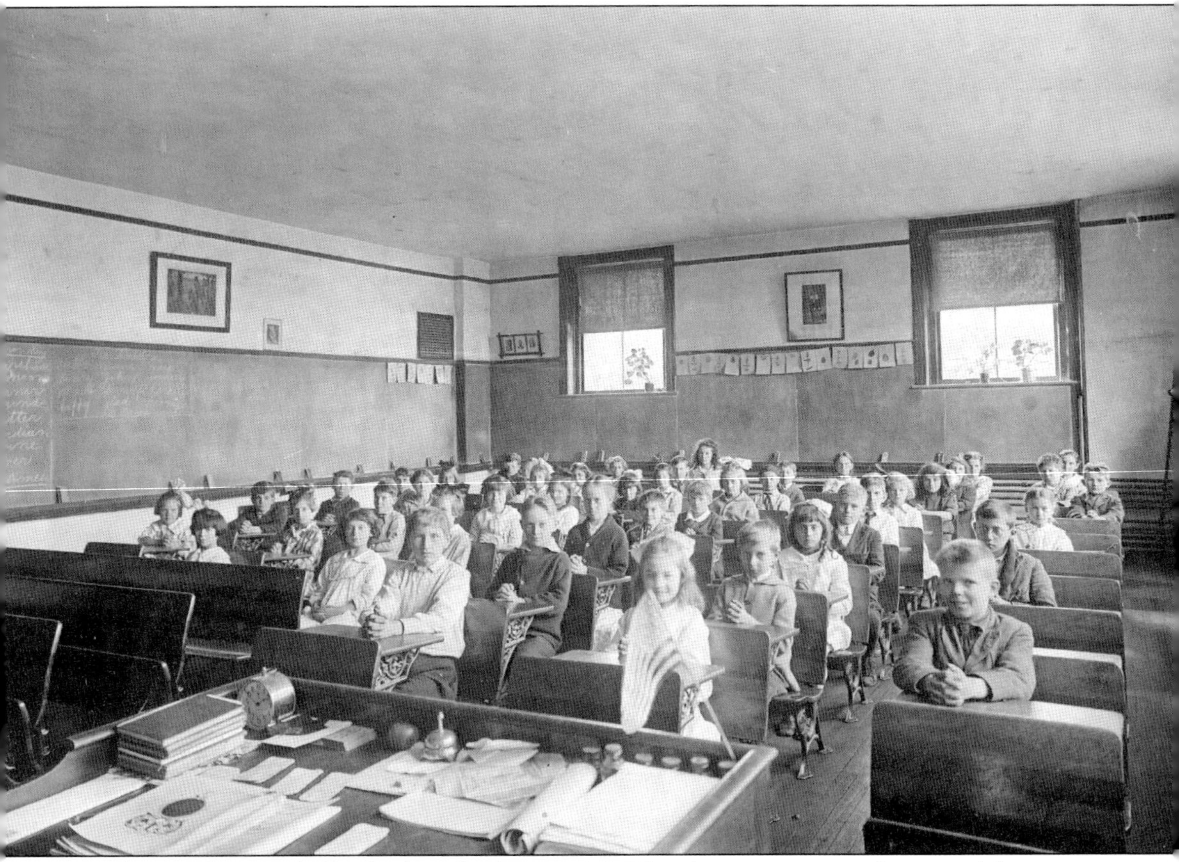

This is Lillie Marshall's third grade class in 1917. The classroom was in the rear of the grammar school facing the playground. From left to right are (first row from front of room to the back) Mary Bell, Ken Unkenholtz, unidentified, Wilton Lewis, unidentified, Leonard Robinson, and unidentified; (second row) Rebecca Hoffman, Ruth Thompson, Joseph Stackhouse, Madeline Hembdt, Catherine Hindley, unidentified, and unidentified; (third row) Gladys Reitt, unidentified, Janet Donaldson, Sadie Cohen, unidentified, unidentified, Thomas Branch, and ? Johnson; (fourth row) Ernest Lowerre, Stewart Thompson, unidentified, Charles Bennett, Richard Frank, Dolores LaTourette, unidentified, Abraham Marcus, and Margaret Johnson; (fifth row) Muriel Murray, Milton Armstrong, Ida Weiss, Eugene Carpenter, Kenneth D. Niven, Ada Taylor, Esther Goldstein, Rachel Katz, and ? Johnson; (sixth row) Edward Wyant, unidentified, Clare Brundoke, Albert Johnson, and Hyman Frank. (Courtesy of Daniel K. Niven.)

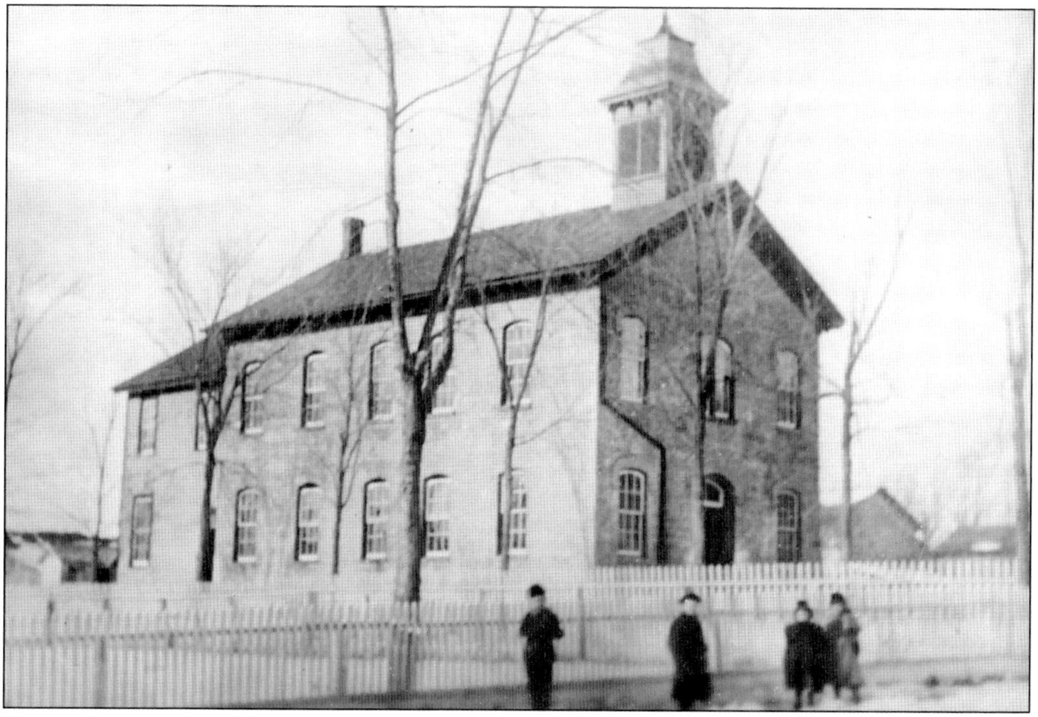

Pictured here is the old grammar school on St. John Street. James Eldridge Quinlan's *History of Sullivan County* notes, "In 1807 a school was opened in a log-house . . . on lands now owned by Henry R. Low, and west of the residence of Reuben B. Towner," which is approximately the same spot as the present school. (Courtesy of Sullivan County Historical Society.)

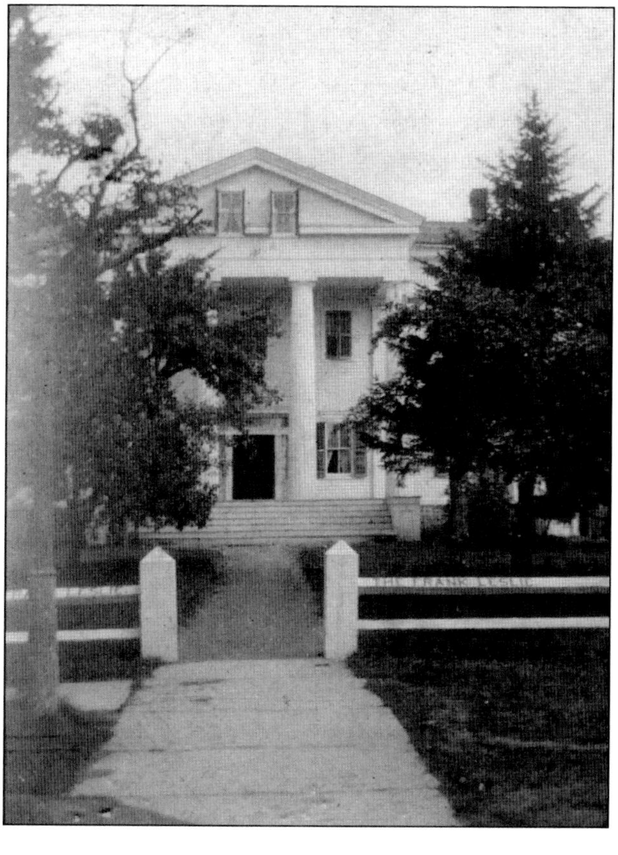

The Monticello Academy opened in the 1840s under the initial name of the Sullivan County Institute and was established by Henry R. Low. The academy continued under a special act of legislature and was subject to the visitation of the board of regents and the control of a board of trustees. The academy became the Frank Leslie Hotel, later known as the Feiner House. The property was eventually purchased by Sullivan County and dismantled. (Courtesy of Sullivan County Historical Society.)

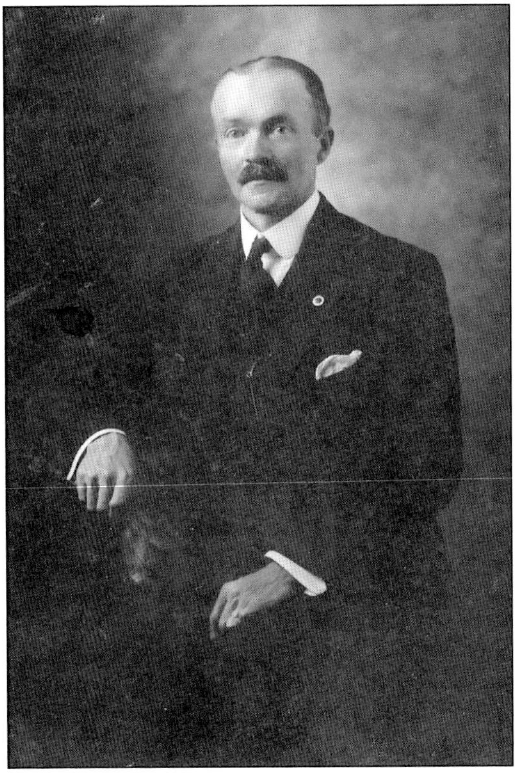

Fulton Street resident and local historian Edward F. Curley (1866–1938) is best remembered as the author of *Old Monticello* (1930), a series of stories and sketches published serially in the *Republican Watchman* (which he edited in the early 1930s) and then in book form. He directed Curley's Funeral Home and was a licensed funeral director since 1906. He ran the Curley (Victoria) Hotel until 1902, and later the Terrace restaurant on Pleasant Street. (Courtesy of Richard Benjamin Sr.)

William Galbraith "Bill" Smith (1920–1998) was Sullivan County historian from 1974 to 1992, village of Monticello historian from 1969 to 1992, regional president of the Municipal Historians of New York State, president of Sullivan County Historical Society, and vice president of County Historians Association of New York State. He was a member of the board of directors of the Frederick A. Cook Society and of the Catskill Entertainment Hall of Fame and Museum. In 1990 he received the Albert Core Distinguished Service Award for outstanding contributions to New York State history education. (Courtesy of Virginia Smith.)

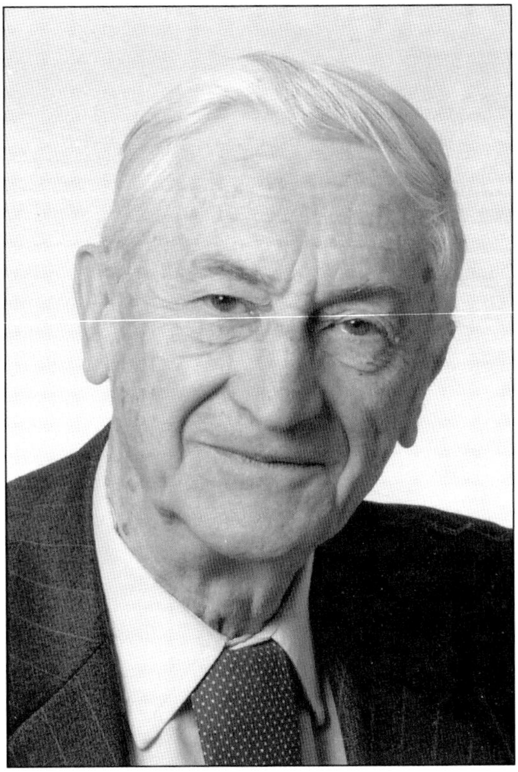

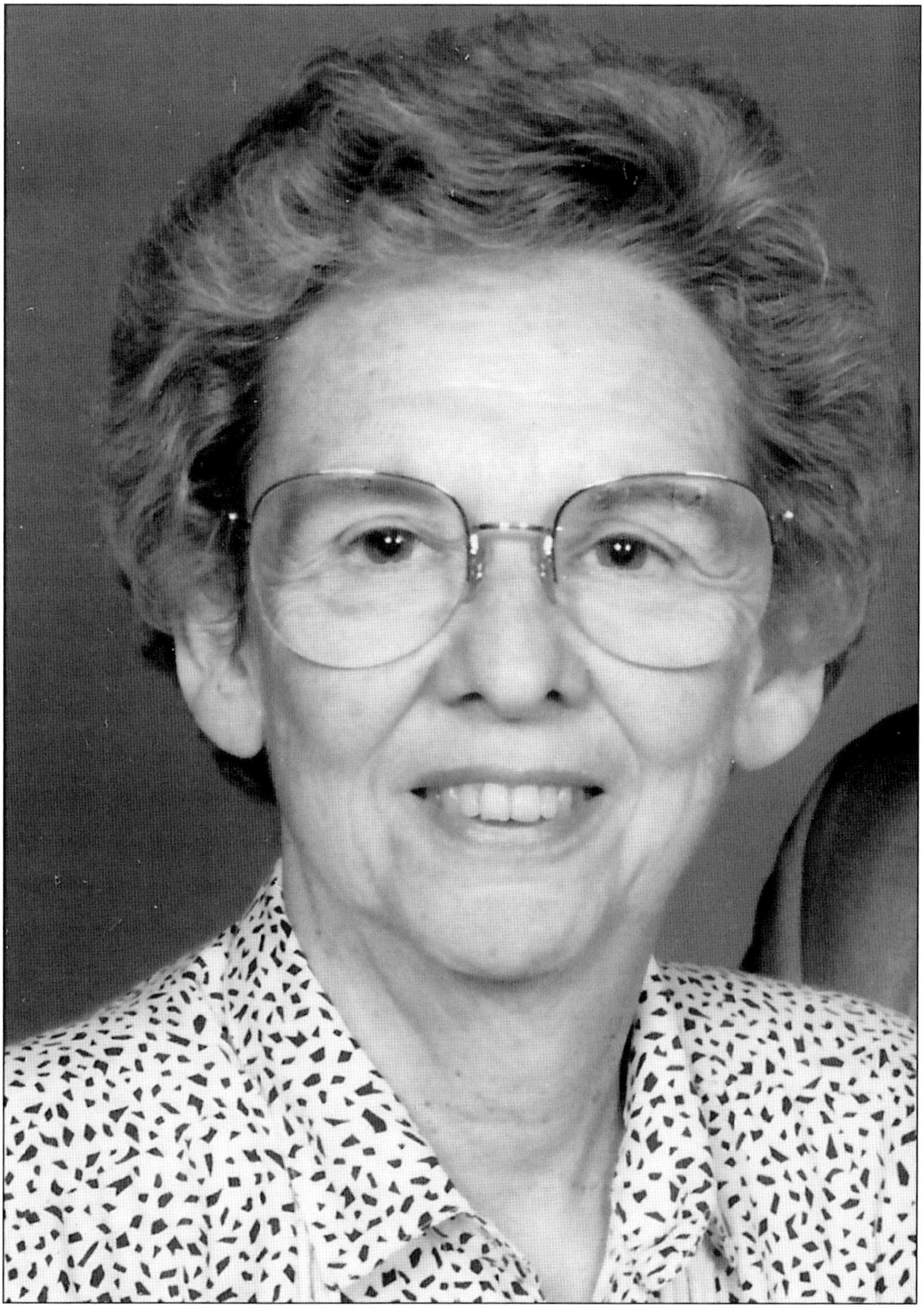

Marjory Durland Smith dedicated herself to teaching the community to value its heritage. She was historian for the town of Thompson for over 30 years and was president of the Municipal Historians Association of New York State, of the Hudson Valley Historians Association, and of the Sullivan County Historical Society. She was director and museum chairperson for Sullivan County Museum and chief census enumerator for the Monticello Central School District for many years. (Courtesy of Virginia Smith.)

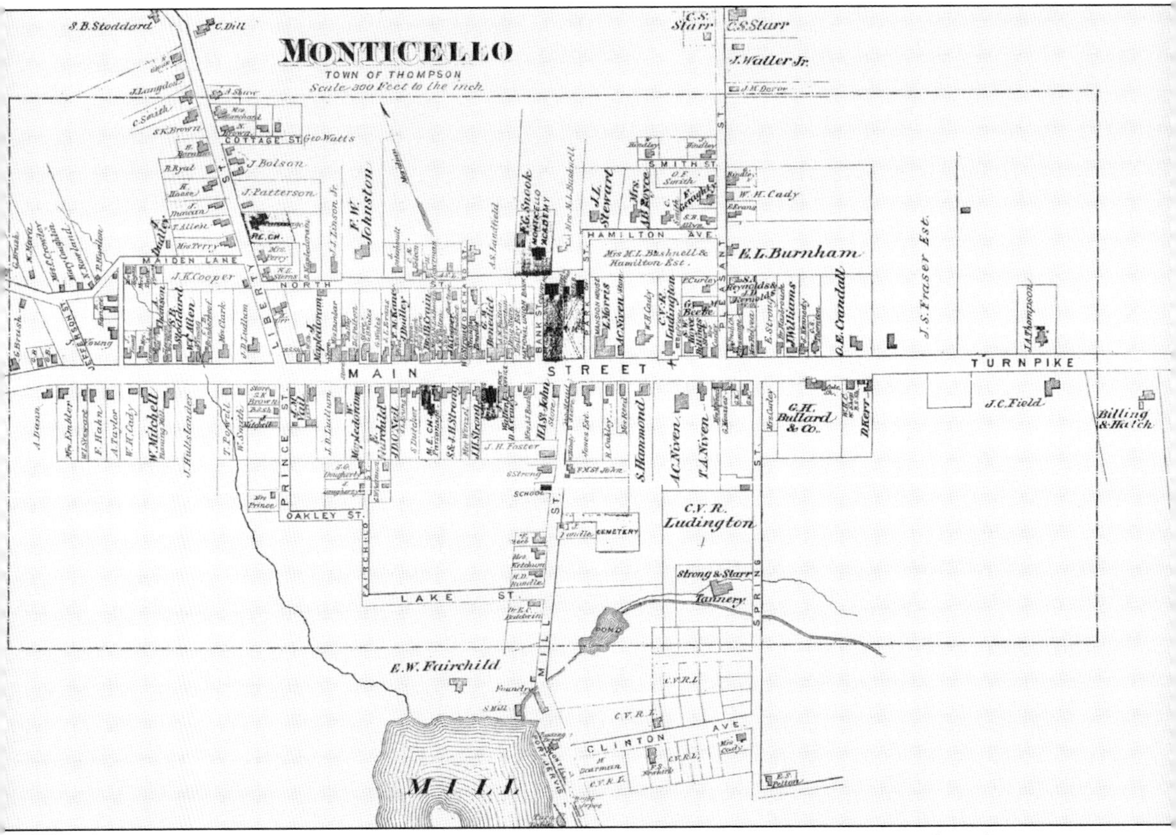

This map of the village of Monticello is from *Beers Atlas of New York State, 1875*. It also appears in *Old Monticello*, by Edward F. Curley, and the village of Monticello's sesquicentennial commemorative journal published in 1954.

BIBLIOGRAPHY

Benton, Alvin O. *Historical Journal: Monticello, N.Y. Sesquicentennial, 1804–1954*. Monticello, NY: Chic Press, 1954.

———. "Early Masonry in Monticello and Sullivan County: History of Monticello Lodge No. 532, F.&A.M." Monticello, NY: *Republican Watchman* 1942.

Best, Gerald M. *Minisink Valley Express: A History of the Port Jervis, Monticello and New York Railroad and its Predecessors*. Beverly Hills, CA: self-published, 1956.

Bulken, Fred, ed. *Historical Milestones in the Growth of the First Church of Monticello Presbyterian, 1810-1960*. Monticello, NY: Self-published, 1960.

Butts, Arthur C. *Monticello: A Picture of the Past*. New York: Knickerbocker Press, 1898.

Conway, John. *Retrospect: An Anecdotal History of Sullivan County, New York*. Fleischmanns, New York: Purple Mountain Press, 1996.

Curley, Edward F. "Old Monticello: A Series of Short Stories and Historical Sketches." Monticello, New York: *Republican Watchman*, 1930.

Kaufman, David. *16th Annual Souvenir Journal, 2004*. Monticello, NY: Congregation Tifereth Israel, Landfield Avenue Synagogue, 2004.

Ginel, Robert *125th Anniversary Journal*. Monticello, NY: St. Peter's Roman Catholic Church, 1999.

Hindley, Arthur L. *Something To Cherish: Service Record Book of Men and Women of Monticello, New York and Community*. Monticello, NY: Ruddick Trowbridge (American Legion) Post No. 73 and Monticello and Community Business Men, 1949.

Quinlan, James Eldridge. *History of Sullivan County*. Liberty, NY: G. M. Beebe and W. T. Morgans, 1873.

Reid, Walter White. *The History of St. John's Episcopal Church, Monticello, New York for One Hundred Years, 1816–1916*. Self-published, 1916.

Scriber, Adelbert Marvin. *Methodism in Monticello, 1844–1944*. Monticello, NY: First Methodist Church, 1944.

Wakefield, Manville. *To the Mountains by Rail*. Fleischmanns, NY: Purple Mountain Press, 1989.

Waugh, Arthur J, ed. *Centennial Celebration of the Presbyterian Church*. Monticello, NY: Self-published, 1910.